TEACHING
the
ELEPHANT
to
DANCE

TEACHING
the
ELEPHANT
to
DANCE

*Empowering
Change in Your
Organization*

JAMES A. BELASCO, Ph.D.

Crown Publishers, Inc. • New York

Published by Crown Publishers, Inc., 201 East 50th Street, New York, New
York 10022

CROWN is a trademark of Crown Publishers, Inc.

Manufactured in the United States of America

Library of Congress Cataloging-in-Publication Data
Belasco, James A.
Teaching the elephant to dance : empowering change in your
organization / James A. Belasco.
p. cm.
1. Organizational change. I. Title.
HD58.8.B455 1990
658.4′063—dc20 89-25122
ISBN 0-517-57478-0

10 9 8 7 6 5 4 3 2 1

First Edition

This book is dedicated to my teachers—the thousands of executives working to change their organizations. May your words and deeds—captured in the ink on these pages—help others learn faster and enjoy the journey more.

Contents

Acknowledgments

No one writes a book alone. This particular effort has been the product of thousands of special people's brains, eyes, hands, energy and time.

This is the fourth full version. Many individuals read, commented, and corrected previous editions. Each of their insights dramatically improved the manuscript. Their conviction that *Elephant* worked for them sustained me through the long hours at the computer.

Even more listened to presentations about the book. Their comments and reactions became part of the fodder for these pages. Yet more important, the fire of need burning in their eyes and their excitement about using *Elephant* to change their organizations encouraged me through the inevitable dark days of doubt and waiting.

I have been blessed with an extraordinary cast of teammates. Meredith Kunsa rightfully earns accolades from every one of our clients for her positive, helpful, competent manner. Her sharp administrative mind is without peer. Without her, *Elephant* would still be a sheaf of scattered papers. She is a gem.

Peggy Covert, who directs the Professional Development Program at San Diego State University, created numerous opportunities for me to test *Elephant*. Her entrepreneurial spirit is rare in university settings. SDSU, the San Diego business community, and I am fortunate she invests her considerable talent with us.

Chairs Penny Wright and Jim Beatty—and my colleagues in the Management Department at SDSU—were very helpful in supporting me during the writing of *Elephant*. Thanks to them we have an excellent department. I am grateful that they continue to find ways in which I can contribute to our growing educational and research competence.

Acknowledgments

Editor Jim Wade has been stellar. Book publishing can prematurely age authors and editors alike. Jim's belief in *Elephant*—and his competence in piloting it through the publishing shoals—converted potential traumas into gratifying experiences. Jim writes the best copy on short notice that I've ever seen (he's the fastest man in the East with a typewriter). Jim's excellent assistant Katie Towson handled the myriad details with aplomb.

I owe a debt to the thousands of practitioners from whose words and deeds *Elephant* draws life. Several of them are specifically cited in the text—including Sam, Paul, and Ralph. Many others live between the lines, embodied in the printer's ink on the page. This book is my effort to repay that obligation for the benefit of all those who follow.

This has been an incredible learning experience for me. As is typical, the credits for *Elephant* lie elsewhere. The faults rest with the author.

TEACHING
the
ELEPHANT
to
DANCE

1

Teaching the Elephant to Dance
Empowering Change
in Your Organization

We need to change. We're in trouble. Business as usual is out.
Here's why.

- **Lower real wages. A weekly paycheck buys less today than
  it did twenty-five years ago.**

- **U.S. and other Western countries' market shares have declined in every major market since 1980.**

- **Foreigners are buying national crown jewels for pennies.
  The papers are full of raiders crossing borders for asset
  grabs. Americans have seen such "native" jewels disap-
  pear into foreign ownership hands as Columbia Pictures,
  CBS Records, and Rockefeller Center (Rockettes and all).
  The British have seen Morgan Grenfell Group PLC—the
  sixth largest British merchant bank—bought by Deutsche
  Bank, important pieces of the defense firm Plessey wind
  up in Siemens' stable, and one of the last British luxury car
  medallions—Jaguar—bought by U.S. car maker Ford.
  And, the Belgians have seen their largest company—So-
  ciete Generale de Belgique SA—come under combined
  French and Italian control.**

- **In less than twenty years, if the trade deficit isn't improved, foreign companies will own enough dollars to buy
  every publicly traded company in the U.S. Today, one
  Japanese computer company has sufficient cash to buy all
  of Europe's computer companies—and still have $7 billion
  left.**

1

- **Both the United States and United Kingdom trail in significant productivity measures. The U.S. is behind Japan, Britain, France, and Italy in terms of productivity growth. We're way behind Japan in other measures of competitiveness.**[1]

In market after market the U.S. as well as European countries are being outsold, outhustled, and outproduced.

I know I'm not alone in feeling like Peter Finch, star of the movie *Network,* who urged his listeners to open up their windows and shout out, "I'm mad as hell, and I'm not gonna take it anymore!"

There are plenty of positive examples out there of people changing things around, bucking the trend. Big organizations. Small organizations. Government organizations. Manufacturing companies. Service organizations. There are examples we can learn from. This book is about how to do it in your organization.

ORGANIZATIONS ARE LIKE ELEPHANTS—SLOW TO CHANGE

Over the past decade I've consulted with, studied, and managed a wide range of organizations. My experience tells me that organizations are like elephants—they both learn through conditioning.

Trainers shackle young elephants with heavy chains to deeply embedded stakes. In that way the elephant learns to stay in its place. Older elephants never try to leave even though they have the strength to pull the stake and move beyond. Their conditioning limits their movements with only a small metal bracelet around their foot—attached to nothing.

Like powerful elephants, many companies are bound by earlier conditioned constraints. "We've always done it this way" is as limiting to an organization's progress as the unattached chain around the elephant's foot.

Success ties you to the past. The very factors that produced today's success often create tomorrow's failure. Consider Xerox, for example. Xerox had a close call with disaster—and it was mostly because of its own success. In the early and middle 1970s

Xerox could do no wrong—at least that's what they thought. They hired the best people, had the best marketing activities, and "owned" the market. Even to this day executives say, "Make me a Xerox," when they want a copy. But all the "right" activities led the company to the brink of disaster.

Believing they were invincible, Xerox executives refused to take the Japanese competition seriously. They didn't realize, for instance, that the Japanese had a 50 percent cost advantage until five years after they lost significant market share. CEO David Kearns saw the need for change.[2] He is busy now getting his elephants to leave their past constraints behind.

Talking about institutions trapped by their successful past, how about Sears? Sears was (and still is) the largest U.S. retailer. But it was—and still is—in serious trouble. Between 1978 and 1980 Sears's merchandise sales actually declined 2.4 percent—during a period of double-digit inflation. Sears's stock price fell from $62 a share in 1972 to $14.50 a share in 1980. Yet no one was willing to change the creaking bureaucracy that assured high overhead costs—forty executives in the drapery department alone—and slow response to changes in consumer tastes.

It took massive intervention to save the unwilling patient. Nothing less than all-out war—in the words of Sears CEO Ed Brennan—"to destroy a thing called Headquarters and a thing called Field and create a thing called Sears." Store closings and 21 percent reduction in employment, including the early retirement of 1,500 career executives, prodded the elephant to consider new ways. Slowly, the "Store of the Future" took shape—very slowly—too slowly for customers as Sears continued to lose market share. Even today the "revolution" is far from complete. Can Sears survive? There are hopeful signs. But the jury is still out.[3]

Or look at Courtaulds, the $3-plus billion U.K. textile manufacturer. When Sir Christopher Hogg arrived in 1980 it looked like curtains for Courtaulds and the rest of the U.K. textile business. Managers were trapped in the vicious cycle of poor results, more conservative management, which led to even poorer results. Hogg realized that he had to break the mold.

The elephant was caught in a death dance.

Hogg reorganized into six business sectors. He insisted on meeting or beating the standards set by the best world-class competitors. Those operations that did not meet the test were closed or sold—unheard of in the U.K. textile business.

The results. Since 1982 Courtaulds's pretax profit rose an average of 37 percent per year.[4]

Previous successes and past practices root American and European companies firmly to old ways of doing business. We can count on the fact that the old way of doing business will not succeed in the future.

In today's fast-paced world, elephants are an endangered species. Slow, ponderous, bulky pachyderms can't move fast enough to escape the competitive laser gun. Fleetness of foot is required. So gazelles survive, not slow-to-change elephants.

EMPOWERMENT CREATES CHANGE

Needing change doesn't make it happen. Too many organizations still have metal bracelets around their feet. You need to mobilize the support of your people behind *your* change.

There's no doubt that General Motors needs to change. Consider these facts. In 1986 GM had the highest labor cost of any U.S. or Japanese car company, $4,148 per vehicle compared with $2,379 at Ford and $630 for Toyota. And that's after GM invested $45 billion to improve its competitive position. Ford workers turn out 85 Tauruses per person per year, while the best GM workers turn out 68 Corsicas and Berettas per worker per year. Quality has been a big focus for GM over the past several years, stung by Ford's success with the "Quality Is Job 1" motto. Quality has improved. The number of defects for GM cars reported by new car owners after ninety days has dropped 8 percent over the past two years. But the Japanese imports report a similar 8 percent improvement, and they still show a stunning 37 percent fewer problems.[5] There are positive signs indicating that GM is changing—slowly. Can GM make it? No one knows. We do know, though, that the need for change doesn't necessarily produce change.

Jaguar, the U.K. luxury car maker, faces similar problems. Though it has doubled output per employee over the past four years, it still lags behind its principal competitors, Mercedes and BMW, by as much as 50 percent. The huge cash required for new models and equipment modernization pose additional challenges. Perhaps that's why Jaguar directors were willing to sell their British heritage for some American porridge from Ford Motor Company. All over the world organizations face the need to change—and mobilize the people to create it.[6]

How about strategies when you are in a volatile multinational market and try to dance with a gorilla? Ask Steffen Edberg. He's the Managing Director of the highly successful IBS, a Swedish-based IBM software and services business partner. Steffen's organization is the largest IBM mid-range system agent in Europe. He's grown by acquiring small, well-positioned firms in several European countries. Lychgate plc, for instance, is his 95 percent-owned U.K. subsidiary.

Steffen brings to the table cross-border contracts, bargaining clout with the gorilla of the industry (IBM), and a depth of experience in the software and systems industry. Each firm retains its present management and draws from the capital and accumulated experience base of its other multinational offices, strengthened by the group's synergy.

As Europe '92 approaches Steffen also brings a Pan European perspective and insight which helps national subsidiaries win local business. All of this with a low overhead mentality. When asked the location of his headquarters he replied, "Wherever I happen to be."

Listen to several experts on how to create change.

Jack Welch, CEO of General Electric, is one expert in producing change. He says, "We have found what we believe to be the distilled essence of competitiveness. It is the reservoir of talent and creativity and energy that can be found in each of our [302,000] people. That essence is liberated when we make people believe that what they think and do is important—and then get out of their way while they do it."[7]

Welch's message: Empower people to change. Help them focus their energies on the new ways.

Welch restates the words of Mr. Matsushita, founder of the successful Matsushita Electric company: "For us, the core of management is the art of mobilizing the intellectual resources of all employees in the service of the firm."[8]

"Get people to create the change," says Mr. Matsushita.

Peter Drucker, the greatest management mind in this century, wrote similar words in 1946. He said, "Any institution has to be organized so as to bring out the talent and capabilities within the organization; to encourage men to take initiative, give them a chance to show what they can do, and a scope within which to grow."[9]

This idea is not new. In the late 1700s Adam Smith similarly felt that the empowered actions of millions of people were much more likely to create economic progress than the intelligent decisions of a few royal appointees.

Empowerment creates change.

THE DISTILLED ESSENCE
OF HOW TO EMPOWER CHANGE

Several persistent themes haunt my experiences in changing organizations. In a world of seeming complexity, they are simple themes—themes that sound clarion-clear messages. These themes form the nexus for this book. I believe they are the way to empower people to change their organization. This is the way to *teach the elephant to dance.*

LEADERS CREATE NEW TOMORROWS

Markets continually change. Customers continually change. Technology continually changes. Competitors continually change. Each change triggers the need to create a new tomorrow.

The active leader—at any level in the organization—identifies this need and moves quickly to develop a new strategic approach. This new strategic approach contains three elements:

1. Reposition products/services to build a competitive advantage;

2. Talented people to execute the new strategies; and

3. Organizational resources that tightly focus on the new strategies.

First come *strategies* that meet the new conditions in the market-place, strategies that give you an advantage.

The need for a strategy based on product differentiation hasn't changed much in 2,500 years. In 431 B.C. Pericles recognized the need to identify those factors that made Athens superior and gave it the upper hand in its war with Sparta. He identified Athens's openness, optimism, and opinion leadership position. Pericles sounds very much like many Silicon Valley executives as they wage war against the Japanese imports. In fact, niche players are the survivors on today's *Fortune* 500 list.

In San Francisco, Fritz Maytag has crafted a similar competitive edge–producing strategy. He's president of Anchor Brewing Co., a microbrewery that sells less than forty thousand barrels of beer a year and employs fourteen full-timers and seven part-timers. He saw that quality in beer making was his competitive edge. He's organized his entire company around the competitive edge of a quality beer made in the pure, traditional way.[10]

In the same industry, Anheuser-Busch—which sells more beer in one day than Fritz sells in a year—uses target marketing as its way to gain a competitive edge. Anheuser-Busch sponsors events and advertising that tailors its message specifically to 210 different U.S. target markets. From the military beer drinkers ("This Bud's for all the men and women who proudly serve this great country") to the waiters and waitresses ("This Bud's for everyone who serves 'em up cold"), Anheuser-Busch seeks to be unique by being everybody's hometown beer.[11]

How about strategies when you face disaster? Ask Joseph Parkinson, CEO of the U.S. company Micron Technology. In the space of a year and a half his firm went from being one of the most profitable semiconductor businesses in the world—reporting profits of $29 million on sales of $87 million—to sustaining a fourth-quarter loss of $11.5 million on $5 million sales. The reason? Dumping on the part of Japanese firms.

What new strategy could a small producer put in place in the face of such traumatic market change? Circle the wagons, hunker down, and look to survive the crises, right? Wrong! "The only way to play the game is to *win*," Parkinson said. So, he attacked. Joe put on an extensive legal campaign charging the Japanese with illegal dumping—which he eventually won. He cut his staff in half. He boosted

R&D on the new generation of DRAM chips. He invested in plant maintenance and upgrading (yes, even continuing such cosmetic activities as janitorial services and landscaping) to demonstrate that Micron intended to survive the holocaust. Why? He said, "We continued to do the little things that say the company has a future. . . . It was a war . . . and we were sworn to prevail. . . . That was our war cry, and we took it everywhere."

It worked! For the February 1988 quarter, Micron reported sales of $58 million and profits of $16.9 million. All kinds of strategies work in response to changing marketplace demands.[12]

Second, get the "right" *people* to execute your new strategy. At Anheuser-Busch, August Busch III is the driving taskmaster. But he is not the outgoing personality required to lead the many glitzy events his company sponsors. He has Michael Roarty—showmaster extraordinaire and executive vice-president—cheerlead for him. Roarty leads the marketing events all over the country—from boat races to multimillion-dollar distributor meetings. Busch does what he does best—setting the tone and driving the business details—and he hires others, like Roarty, to do what he doesn't do well.[13]

When Fritz Maytag first started his brewery twenty years ago, he couldn't hire the "right" kinds of people to work full-time at the wages he could afford. He found he could hire very qualified people who wanted to do exciting things a few hours a week and earn good money for the hours that they worked. So Fritz hired a small group of part-timers, who turned out to be the "right" people.[14]

Pat McGovern, founder and chairman of $300-plus million U.S. company IDG Communications, knows the importance of finding the right people to run his operation. His company published over one hundred publications in thirty-six countries with over 2.8 million subscribers. His publications dominate information services for the information technology industry.

How do you run sixty-five semiautonomous business units? "With great people," Pat replies. Recognizing his own tendency to want to do everything himself, Pat has become an ardent delegator. He gives each manager complete autonomy to submit business plans and then run his/her business as long as the critical performance standards are met. Pat abhors central control and direction.

"If they want to do it—they can do it," he says. "No one in the central office—including me—ever says no."

Does it work? Compound growth rates of better than 30 percent and after-tax margins exceeding 10 percent—several times the industry average—speak for themselves.[15]

Third, focus the *resources* on your new strategies. Without resources your new strategies will be nothing more than pipe dreams. Jack Welch, CEO of General Electric, sold off more than $5.6 billion worth of industry "also-rans" and shifted resources into businesses where GE was either number one or two in the market. The result? GE's profit margin grew by two percentage points to 10.4 percent and earning grew at a compound annual rate of 10 percent.[16]

Together these three prerequisites—new strategies, key people, and focused resources—help you decide on the "right" new directions. It's essential to *move fast* to make it happen. August Busch III is a classic example of a change-managing executive who makes tough decisions—quickly. When his highly successful beer operation was rocked by scandal in 1987, Busch moved in aggressively. He fired the three executives involved and accepted the resignation of his longtime friend, Dennis Long, the president of the beer unit. Busch then committed to run the beer unit directly for the next two years to ensure that the roots of scandal were all stamped out.[17] It takes guts to change, but—if you don't—the economic end is no less certain, only more painfully time-consuming.

GE's Jack Welch built his organization to respond quickly to changing circumstances. He eliminated two executive organization levels and had the more than thirty business unit heads report directly to him. He also eliminated 40 percent of the headquarters staff to remove the nay sayers. The system works. Brian Rowe, senior vice-president and group executive of GE's aircraft engine business, reported that quick decision making enabled his division to develop a new midsize fan jet for the Airbus 340 that resulted in $1 billion of orders. "Under the old bureaucratic system, we'd still be just talking about it," Rowe says.[18]

Consider IBM, the most successful commercial company in the world during 1984 and 1985. In those two years IBM made more money than any other organization and was chosen as the "Most Admired" company by *Fortune* magazine. IBM rested on its laurels—a dangerous position—and got in trouble. CEO John Akers moved quickly to change. Akers designed the new strategy that focused more effort on the midrange product line (where IBM's offerings were particularly weak). He shifted the emphasis from selling "boxes" to selling "solutions." At the same time he transferred a number of people out of office jobs into direct marketing and selling jobs, thus getting more of his talented people out in front of customers. Akers also focused the organization's R&D efforts on fewer projects and made the R&D activity more responsive to marketing.

IBM's Akers knows—there is no rest. Change is a *continuous process* for large companies and small companies alike. Take the case of E.T.C. Carpet Mills, Ltd., a Californian carpet manufacturer. President Michael M. Berns saw that the way to grow his company was to put some fun into what was a dull and boring industry. So he gave wild theme parties for employees, suppliers, and customers (like the time he announced a new vice-president at a "coronation for the Prince of Sales," where employees wore sixteenth-century costumes and a carriage delivered the new vice-president to the podium). He gave crazy names (like Cold Hands and Closed Wednesday) to his carpet colors and issued comic books instead of sample books. It worked as sales went from $1 million in 1973 to $33 million in 1978.

But then in 1979–1981, Berns almost lost his business as interest rates soared and the economy (particularly for big-ticket items like carpets) fell through the floor. He saw clearly the need for a new strategy. Berns knew that if he couldn't become the low-cost producer, E.T.C. Carpet would be history. He set a new strategic direction of efficiency, redeployed his key people by returning managers to the working levels and adding a key financial controller, and redirected his resources from comic books to developing new efficient methods. He also worked hard to mobilize his people to support his new strategic direction. (I'll get to how he did that in a few pages.) Berns survived and prospered (his 1986 sales were back at $33 million with record earnings) because he saw the need to change and moved fast to do it.[19]

Unfortunately, seeing the right new tomorrow isn't enough. You need to mobilize the support of your people to create that new tomorrow.

10

A VISION FOCUSES AND
ENERGIZES THAT NEW TOMORROW

My experience tells me that an energizing, inspiring vision is the key to mobilizing support. This vision is the picture that drives all action. It includes both deeply felt values and a picture of the organization's strategic focus.

Father Theodore Hesburgh built Notre Dame into a major American university during his thirty-five years as president. He infused his vision of a revitalized Notre Dame in students, alumni, faculty, and the general public. Talking about his role in changing the university, he said, "The very essence of leadership is you have to have a vision. It's got to be a vision you articulate clearly and forcefully on every occasion. You can't blow an uncertain trumpet."[20] Father Hesburgh's trumpet was never uncertain.

A vision is a certain trumpet. It identifies clearly for all concerned—employees, customers, and suppliers—exactly what the organization stands for and precisely why they should support it. A vision both enhances an organization's marketplace competitive advantage, such as IBM's "Provide the best customer service," and provides deep personal identification with the organization's work, such as ServiceMaster's "To serve God in all we do."

Consider Rubbermaid, a U.S. company in a fiercely competitive no-growth marketplace where most of its competitors compete on price. It sounds like a prescription for disaster. Yet CEO and chairman Stanley Gault has doubled sales, tripled earnings, and earned a high place among *Fortune*'s "Most Admired Companies" list at the same time. He's accomplished this enviable record by empowering his people consistently to use his vision of 15 percent growth in sales and profits. With Gault's growth vision, managers work eleven-hour days to stay in constant touch with customers. Employees in one division submitted more than 12,600 suggestions for cost cutting.[21]

Fritz Maytag has a vision for his company—quality beer made in the pure, old-fashioned way. He works with his employees by making the best beer, gathering the best malt, learning the best ways to brew. He takes his employees to England to visit little breweries, to Germany to learn how to brew wheat beer, and to Oregon to ride the combine that gathers barley for their beer. He spends much of his time talking to people about his vision, making certain that everyone remembers what the brewery stands for.[22]

In the same industry, but on a much larger scale, August Busch III pushes his vision. Every evening Busch samples the beers produced by his eleven breweries that day. He examines each one for balance and taste to be certain that it meets his personal standard of quality. Then he tells his chief brewmaster whether or not they can ship that day's production. To ensure that his public image matches his vision, Busch personally supervises the details of his advertising program. (He once insisted that an entire commercial be reshot because the horses looked too thin.) He then makes certain that all the advertising is also posted throughout his organization. No one will forget the company's vision.[23]

Part of CEO Mike Berns's vision for E.T.C. Carpet calls for self-management in the improvement of efficiency. He spends a lot of his time talking to employees about self-management and teaching it at his "Carpet University." He works hard to get his supervisors, managers, and employees to use his vision.

Vision tightly directs attention to the critical factors that produce long-term success. It may be the customer service and employee respect at IBM, or the search for the unshakable fact at DEC, or the new product development at Ralston. Whatever, your vision becomes a decisional guide. At every juncture employees ask, "Is my action in keeping with the vision?" This focus—and inspiration—empowers people to change.

Vision is needed at all levels in an organization. The supervisor of the mailroom needs a vision for that mailroom. The manager of data processing needs a vision for the DP department. The accounts payable clerk needs a vision for his/her job. Vision—throughout the organization—focuses and inspires effort.

PARTICIPATION EMPOWERS CHANGE

The single thread that runs through all of my "success" stories—and correspondingly is absent in most of my "failures"—is the involvement of large numbers of individuals in drafting the vision. Cross-disciplinary-, multifunctional-, multiorganizational-level teams empower people to understand and support the vision.

Royal Insurance (U.K.) Ltd. is the second oldest non-life insurance company in Britain. Managing Director Peter Duerden saw the changing nature of the insurance business. After he had studied the winners and losers among his product lines—and discovered that the presumed winners were actually losers and the assumed also-rans actually the big winners—he launched Operation "Staying Ahead." He appointed sixteen managers to work with the Boston Consulting Group in planning and implementing the new strategic direction. Duerden kept the entire staff informed—including the unionized work force—asked for, and got, more than two hundred personal letters from staff members with suggestions. After study, the group recommended and installed a reorganization that shifted more than half of the jobs geographically or skillwise, dropped management levels between customers and service providers, and lowered the age of management by ten years. Participation in the program led to its swift adoption and payoff at the bottom line. In 1986 Royal's income grew 21.7 percent.[24]

ORGANIZATIONAL SYSTEMS
REINFORCE THE VISION

Organizational systems give people the tools to use the new vision. They give people permission to use those tools. Performance systems guide day-to-day activities. They must expect, measure, and reward using the new vision. Human resource/personnel policies give permission to use the new vision tools. Selection, orientation, training, promotion, and compensation policies encourage the use of the vision. Last, the cultural system—heroes and symbols—subconsciously reinforces the use of the new vision.

ServiceMaster, the $1-plus billion janitorial services U.S. firm, provides extensive training to its people to empower them to use the ServiceMaster vision. General partner William Pollard said, "Before asking someone to do something, you have to help them be something." Pollard's organization provides detailed instructions on the "something that needs to be done"—a three-inch manual that breaks the job of floor polishing down into detailed, five-minute cycles. And they provide a plethora of individual training programs designed to help employees "be something." The vision plays a prominent role in all of these training activities. It is discussed frequently during the meetings.[25]

Rubbermaid CEO Gault empowers the use of his growth vision by paying managers bonuses based on both profits and increases in book value.

Organizational systems empower using the vision.

ACTIONS TELL THE TALE

Your actions tell the tale. You are the point person toward whom everyone will look—and most people will follow. The bottom line in all change efforts is the dedication and commitment—as it is reflected in concrete, specific actions—of the individual driving the process.

Consider the following example of how Ray Kroc instilled his vision of cleanliness:

> On his way back to the office from an important lunch at the best place in town, Ray Kroc asks his driver to pass through several McDonald's parking lots. In one parking lot he spots papers caught up in the windscreen of shrubs along the outer fence. He goes to the nearest pay phone and calls the office, gets the name of the local manager, and calls the manager to offer to help him pick up the trash in the parking lot. Both Ray Kroc, the owner of the McDonald's chain (in his expensive business suit), and the young manager of the store meet in the parking lot and get on their hands and knees to pick up the paper.

This anecdote is told and retold thousands of times within McDonald's to emphasize the importance of the shared vision of cleanliness. In short, your actions in living your vision, much like Ray Kroc's action in living his, will motivate your employees to use the new vision.

To graphically symbolize this process—and provide you with a continual program of the book—the following graphic heads every chapter.

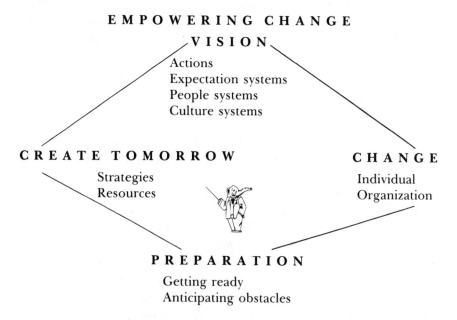

EMPOWERING CHANGE

VISION

Actions
Expectation systems
People systems
Culture systems

CREATE TOMORROW

Strategies
Resources

CHANGE

Individual
Organization

PREPARATION

Getting ready
Anticipating obstacles

This graphic symbolizes the book's overriding theme: when you create the right marketplace and personal value vision, you empower people to change. At each step I'll elaborate on the model by adding specifics.

GETTING STARTED—THE PLAN OF THE BOOK

In the following chapters you'll walk through the basics. I'll spice up your reading with examples from large organizations—IBM and British Air—as well as midsize organizations such as Mrs. Fields Chocolate Chippery and local government departments, and the small start-up companies such as Lychgate Ltd. I believe that *every* organization can change. My examples reflect my belief.

I intend to give you lots of examples to demonstrate that change can happen. The elephant can learn to break its chain to the past.

Change is not an event, it is an enjoyable and rewarding journey. I'll help you by pointing out the trails left by others.

At each of these phases you'll walk through the most important operational decisions that indelibly shape your effort. At each stage you'll be actively involved in the process. I intend this to be a hands-on book, one that will provide you with the opportunity to work along with me.

MY BIAS—JUST SO YOU KNOW

No first part is complete until the author lays out his biases for you, the reader. In that way you can evaluate whatever I say in terms of my prejudices.

I believe in *action*. In this world it is not what you know that matters. Rather, it's what you *do* with what you know that counts. Information is valuable—action is *in*valuable.

I want to encourage you to act *today* to begin the change process. I want you to talk *today* with your people about the vision you and they would like to see for your organization. I want to encourage you to meet *today* with your people and discuss how all of you can use your vision to accomplish your new strategies.

And so, on with the journey!

2

Getting Ready to Change

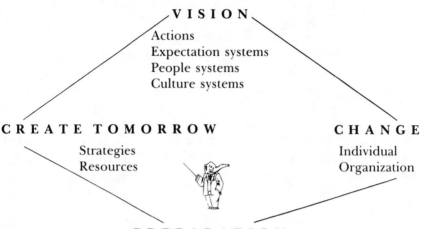

EMPOWERING CHANGE

VISION
Actions
Expectation systems
People systems
Culture systems

CREATE TOMORROW
Strategies
Resources

CHANGE
Individual
Organization

PREPARATION
Getting ready
Anticipating obstacles

Changing things can be fun—and successful—sometimes! More often, change efforts fail because people really don't sign up to change. It's tough. People hang on to old habits and old behaviors long past their usefulness.

Remember the elephant training parable. Trainers shackle young elephants with heavy chains to deeply embedded stakes. In that way the elephant learns to stay in its place. Older elephants never try to leave even though they have the strength to pull the stake and move beyond. Their conditioning limits their movements with only a small metal bracelet around their foot—attached to nothing.

Like powerful elephants, many companies are bound by earlier conditioned constraints. "We've always done it this way" is as limiting to an organization's progress as the unattached chain around the elephant's foot.

Yet when the circus tent catches on fire—and the elephant sees

17

the flames with its own eyes and smells the smoke with its own nostrils—it forgets its old conditioning and changes. Your task: set a fire so your people see the flames with their own eyes and smell the smoke with their own nostrils—without burning the tent down. And anyone can set the fire at any level in the organization.

Look at General Motors. That elephant clearly needs to see the fire and smell the smoke. GM executives worked hard to improve the quality of their products. CEO and chairman Roger Smith saw clearly that unless GM could also advertise that "At GM, Quality Is Job 1!" Ford would eat into his market share. Several years and $45 billion later, GM still brings up the rear in quality levels for American car manufacturers—and continues to lose market share.

What happened at GM? Why didn't the people change? It's obvious that there is no market for junk cars, particularly at sticker shock prices of $10,000 to $15,000. Is it the overpaid unionized American worker who can't do quality work? Hardly. Look at the high-quality work done by unionized American workers at the Freemont, California, Toyota/GM plant. No, you can't blame GM's problems on the workers.

The sad truth is—GM's people didn't feel empowered to change. No one saw the flames or smelled the smoke. So they stuck to the old ways. People change slowly when they don't feel the urgency—very slowly! Ask Roger Smith; he's struggled with how to establish the urgency. It seems to be working for him—finally.

Or look at David Kearns at Xerox. He watched his organization lose market share to the Japanese for five years before acting. He began his restructuring activities in 1982 and his quality program in 1984. The report card thus far is encouraging but hardly sparkling. Profits and returns are still well below 1980 levels, though revenues are up and margins are coming back. Kearns said, "When I look back, the most critical I can be of myself is for not moving fast enough." It takes time, David, and people—including yourself—are slow to change until they feel empowered to change.[1]

Yet some individuals empower their organizations to execute pirouette-type changes. Jack Welch moves General Electric into new and different areas—gobbling up and then straightening out such huge firms as RCA—with a nimbleness that leaves corporate presidents trembling and wondering whether Jack will land next in their boardroom. Once they got their act together, Xerox in three short years improved the quality levels of its products by 92 percent and shortened product development cycles by more than 60 percent. Kodak introduced one-hundred-plus new products in 1987—more than in any previous year in Kodak history.[2]

Percy Barnevik, CEO of the newly formed $18 billion Swiss-German-Swedish energy powerhouse ABB, took five months to focus his jigsaw puzzle of 180,000 worldwide employees in 140 countries. His five-person internal task force—composed of the top managers of each of the former companies—set up four main business segments with 40 separate business areas and designated new regional and geographical alignments. They recruited new top managers and orchestrated a meeting of the 250 top worldwide managers at Cannes to implement the new structure and strategy. Barely catching his breath, Barnevik purchased assets and forged alliances in Norway, Italy, and the United States.[3]

Yes, some individuals can get their people to change quickly—sometimes—when they feel empowered to change! Here's the success strategy to get people ready to change at any level in the organization—to light the fire without burning down the tent. Use the change process: build a sense of urgency, create a clear tomorrow, develop a migration path, and reinforce the new behavior. This process underlies all organizational change. I'll show you these steps and help you apply them.

THE CHANGE PROCESS

Change surrounds us. Consider these facts: Sony introduces over one hundred new products every six months. Apple makes a new product announcement every week. IBM announces an average of more than four new products every business day. Price Club turns its inventory once a day.[4] What a dizzying rate of change for the managers of these organizations, their competitors, and consumers! Alvin Toffler was right: the pace of change is picking up. And the watchword is—change or die.

All change relies upon the change process. Kurt Lewin[5] spelled it out in 1947, and it was expanded by Edgar Schein in 1961.[6] Lots of field and laboratory research validate their findings. This chapter is based on the Lewin/Schein process.

19

Build a sense of urgency. People don't change without pain—lots of it!—and anxiety—lots of it! Bad situations motivate change. *Very* bad situations. Pain and anxiety create the urgency to change, which creates the empowerment for change. Don't create this urgency, and people feel powerless to change.

We don't visit the dentist until the tooth hurts so badly that we can't stand it anymore. We don't change a light bulb until it burns out. We don't leave a "terrible" job until either we get fired or some awful triggering event occurs (such as a big fight with the boss). We don't end a personal relationship until it gets to be unbearable. (One of my psychiatrist friends tells me that most couples don't see her until they've been sweeping things "under the rug" so long that they can't live with their lumpy carpets anymore.)

Michael K. Berns, founder of E.T.C. Carpet Mills, Ltd., in Santa Ana, California, knows all about the pain and anxiety triggering the urgency to change. You read about him in chapter 1. He put fun into the boring carpet industry by having crazy theme parties and using far-out names for his carpets. It worked, until the bottom fell out of the carpet business in 1979–1981. One million dollars in losses, 27 percent interest rates, and 40 percent less sales made bankruptcy a frequent topic of conversation with bankers and suppliers. Berns saw the fire and smelled the smoke. He knew he had to change. So he completely redid his company. You read about it in chapter 1 and you'll see it again in a few pages.[7]

Venerable Rolls-Royce also saw the fire—and the need to change. In 1983 the directors forecast selling 3,400 cars. They actually sold 1,500. Panicked dealers discounted Rolls for the first time in history. To compound the problem, for the first time in twenty-three years workers walked off the job. The fire was raging—setting the stage for major revolutionary change. Rolls management created a clear new tomorrow that included shared decision making with their employees—unheard of in British management circles—and new team management focused production techniques. You'll read more about it in a few pages.[8]

Any change is uncomfortable. It won't occur until *after* the pain of realizing that current behavior must go. The head of nursing in a midsize hospital tried to improve her unit. She discovered—too late—that her people saw no reason to change. Her anecdote below shows how not to begin the change process.

Joan Wright's unit had a good reputation in the hospital, though she saw several areas that could be improved. She felt a strong need to improve the personal patient care offered in her area.

Joan thought of the theme "Improved personal care," tried it on a few trusted doctors, got reactions (mostly favorable) from a few employees, and announced it at a quarterly employee meeting. There was an immediate negative reaction from employees. During her rounds she asked employees about their reactions. One comment was typical: "We already provide personal care, why should we improve? What's wrong with us, anyway?"

Joan hastily revised her theme to "Continued personal care," but the damage to her credibility took months to overcome.

Joan left out an important step.

I worked with the president of a large company who didn't forget to create the need to change. Here's my experience helping him when he took over as CEO.

At the time of his appointment as president, his company had one of the worst on-time shipment records in his industry. Furthermore, it was a consistent money loser. Yet because of the "civil service" mentality in the organization, few people took the situation seriously.

He began a weekly employee letter in which he reproduced copies of customer complaints (blanking out the names of employees). He posted weekly information on bulletin boards comparing his company's shipment record with those of their competitors. In most cases his company came out second best. On each communication, he wrote in his own handwriting, "We can do better!"

After many months of this constant barrage of communication, employees were asking, *"How* can we do better?" His people were now ready to change.

Stop rewarding the current counterproductive behavior. The vice-president of a $4 million specialty chemical company learned this lesson the hard way.

21

Rod Cacey wanted to improve his company's innovative performance. He believed that technicians would be stimulated to come up with new product ideas if they were in closer contact with their customers. He urged them to visit at least two customers a month and find out how the company could help them.

Despite constant urging on Rod's part over several months, little changed. When he went to find out why, Rod discovered that his technicians valued their control over their time and didn't really know how to handle customers.

Rod realized that the rewards of not working with customers (continuing their present behavior) were greater than the potential rewards for changing. Reluctantly he abandoned his visitation program.

Establish the urgency to change—first. Create the need to change. Remove the rewards for present behavior. Empower people to want to change.

One word of caution, which you're probably feeling already: "Don't overdo it!" Don't burn the tent down! Establish the urgency to change without destroying your employees' self-confidence and perceived ability to win. The tag line "We can do better!" accomplished the dual purposes of creating the need to change and building belief that change is possible.

Personal Workshop

In reviewing your current situation, and thinking about how you might create the desire to change, ponder the following questions:

1. What are the behavioral "symptoms" of inadequate performance upon which I might capitalize?

Consider such "symptoms" as customer complaint letters, competitor comparisons, comparative evaluations from such independent sources as trade associations and consumer reports, field sales reports, and personal observations from talking with customers/users/employees.

2. What mechanisms can I use to mount a consistent campaign stressing these "symptoms" as a need to change?

Consider such mechanisms as frequent employee letters, frequent bulletin board announcements, competitor comparison displays in lobbies, cafeterias, production floors, and other high-visibility places, employee meetings, and public media (newspaper stories, television/radio interviews).

3. What words can I use to stress the need to change while also conveying the message that we can *change? What few words can I use to convey both messages?*

Remember the motto *"We can do better!"*

Create a clear tomorrow. People need a clear, simple-to-understand "promised land" to which they can travel. People need to see the end to the fire and the reconstruction of a better tent. This picture of the promised land becomes the pull for change. President Kennedy said it: "We will land a man on the moon in this decade."

Michael Berns at E.T.C. Carpet laid out that promised land—efficiency gained through self-management. Berns continually paints the picture of that new tomorrow. He talks about it with all new employees and regularly teaches it at his weekly Carpet University. "It's essential that people understand the company's goals," Berns says.[9] Right on!

The new managers at Rolls-Royce painted a clear picture of the new tomorrow. They meet monthly with all employees in free-wheeling discussions about company financial performance—an unheard-of event in tradition-bound English industry. Each employee knows what it costs to do his/her job—and he/she is urged constantly to improve. There's computers on the shop floor that link "real time" with dealers. Through the wizardry of electronics, shop floor workers learn directly from customers what they want and when they want it. Advertising is hung directly in the plant so everyone can see—every day—the picture of the new Rolls-Royce.[10]

It's an even bigger challenge when the new tomorrow is radically different from the golden yesterday. Consider the challenge faced by Colby Chandler and Kay Whitmore, leaders of Kodak. The

Great Yellow Father had taken very good care of its siblings. But by the middle 1980s the cupboard was growing bare, picked clean by competitors such as Polaroid and Fuji. The shock of losing the 1984 Olympics to Fuji Photo put fire in the eyes and smoke in the nostrils at Kodak.

Chandler and Whitmore published an eight-page document in November 1984. They praised the company's past great achievements and laid out the most dramatic overhaul in the company's eighty-year history. Functional departments were dissolved and independent business units were created. Centralization was curbed, and for the first time, Kodakers were laid off. The eight-page document was given to each employee. Meetings were held to assure that each person heard the message in both a group and an individual setting. Videotapes of Chandler and Whitmore were presented several times over the next year to assure that the picture of the new tomorrow remained clear.[11]

ADAC Laboratories had a problem—a real fire. They ran out of money. President Chuck Cantoni called in Q. T. Wiles, the "company doctor" partner for the big venture capital firm Hambrecht & Quist. Wiles immediately discovered that the problem lay in poor controls. "They were shipping money," he said, "and didn't know it." He created a new tomorrow. He put new people in charge of the business and installed an extensive set of cost controls so they knew when they were making or losing money.[12]

The new tomorrow: a set of good cost controls that are clear and easy to understand.

Light the fire to create the urgency to change. Then create the safe haven new tomorrow of a better tent.

Develop a migration path. We learn by copying. Little boys watch their fathers for the "correct" male behavior and imitate them. Little girls watch their mothers and shape their behavior accordingly. It works even beyond childhood. Successful executives model their behavior after a successful boss.

Present a clear picture of what you want. Empower employees by showing them precisely what you want them to do. Then encourage them—give them permission—to use the new behavior.

Furthermore, people learn best from someone they respect and admire. That's why little boys learn so much from their father, because they generally respect and admire "the old man." The same is true about little girls learning from their mother.

Model your new strategies—since generally you are the person whom your employees respect and admire. John Wolfsheimer is executive vice-president of a large aerospace company. He's one of the leading "change agents" commissioned by the CEO to radically transform the way his company does business. The following anecdote illustrates how John used modeling to get other employees to adopt his new vision.

> One of John's major activities was in trouble. Schedule shortfalls and cost overruns threatened to overwhelm positive cash flows. In olden days executives would sit in their offices studying reams of paper and then issue orders to correct the problems. John knew that traditional behavior needed to be changed.
>
> He decided to attack the problem in an unconventional manner. He traded his business suit, white shirt, and tie for jeans and sneakers. He went out on the shop floor directly to find out the problems firsthand. Even more radically, he assigned himself as an assistant foreman to one of the first line supervisors for a week.
>
> "I really saw the real problems for the first time. Incompatible scheduling systems, poorly trained foremen, and too much staff criticism combined with too little staff help."
>
> From that day forward the standard became "Get out of your office and find out firsthand what's going on."

John demonstrated his action-oriented vision. His employees felt empowered to follow suit. Be the credible role model. Demonstrate the new behavior. Show your employees precisely what you expect. Empower them to adopt the new behavior.

Michael Berns models his new self-management behavior. He works hard to delegate responsibility. He's constantly asking his people to make the decision without asking him first. Whenever someone brings him a decision he thinks they should make, he asks them, "What do you recommend?" When they tell him he says, "Go right ahead. That sounds good to me. And you didn't have to ask me. Please don't next time."[13] It takes lots of reminding.

Personal Workshop

As you consider how to demonstrate the new behavior, ponder the following questions:

1. What are the few (5-6-7) key behaviors required by my new vision?

Consider such behaviors as visiting customers several times a month, holding regular employee meetings, really listening to employees, actively encouraging employee development, and quickly handling customer complaints.

2. How and where can I demonstrate these behaviors to maximize their visibility?

Consider such possibilities as employee meetings, staff meetings, hallway conversations, company newspapers, and bulletin board announcements.

Reinforce the new behavior. Consistently reinforce people who use the new behavior. Empower your people through reinforcement.

Give your people the opportunity to practice the new behaviors they learned watching you. There are as many practice opportunities as there are interactions in a day—visiting customers, talking with employees, wandering on the shop floor. Encourage your people to take as many practice opportunities as possible. Begin in low-risk situations (with friends or those with whom they already have a good rapport), and graduate into the more unfamiliar and difficult.

Positively reinforce them when they do practice the new behaviors. People love applause and will work hard to win yours. Reinforcement empowers continued effort.

> Susan Redding, the manager of a fifteen-person drafting section in the engineering department for a local government, used public acknowledgment as the principal reward.
>
> Susan wanted to instill a new philosophy in her section, "Speedy accuracy to meet your needs." She wanted her employees to turn around drawings in twenty-four hours with no errors.
>
> She made certain that her own drawings got out on time and were accurate. She stayed late several times to meet the

deadline and made certain that her employees both saw her and knew what she was doing. In this way she demonstrated the new behavior.

At the daily "what's hot" meeting, Susan publicly commended each person who got his/her drawings out to the customer (without any errors) within twenty-four hours. Within two months every employee was doing the "twenty-four hour no-error" behavior.

Rewards needn't be big or expensive to be effective. People love little rewards, particularly if they are from you personally.

Personal Workshop

To help you think about how you can encourage practice and reward the correct new behavior, please ponder the following questions:

1. What are the opportunities to practice the new vision?

Consider such opportunities as meeting with customers, talking to employees, asking questions at staff meetings, and using formal means such as newsletters and bulletin boards.

2. How can I encourage my people to practice the new behavior more?

Consider such activities as personally accompanying them on their first visit, frequently asking for feedback on how the practice efforts are going, holding discussions with the staff about the pitfalls and difficulties in the new behaviors along with ways to overcome them, and bringing in a consultant to help people deal with the difficulties.

3. How can I reward my people for doing the "correct" new behavior?

Consider such rewards as personal acknowledgment from you, spending time with you, and formal actions such as promotions and pay raises.

In summary, use the change process to empower your employees to change. Move through each of the following steps:

Build a Sense of Urgency
Create a Clear Tomorrow
Develop a Migration Path
Reinforce the New Behavior

A CONTINUOUS PROCESS, NOT A DESTINATION

Change is a process and not a destination. It never ends. Regardless of how successful you are this year, there is always next year. In 1984 IBM made more money than any other company in the world. Could they afford to rest on their laurels and coast? Absolutely not! In 1985 the bottom dropped out of the computer business, and in 1986 mighty IBM's earnings dropped. Now Chairman Akers is busy rebuilding commitment to the IBM vision held by customers, suppliers, and employees. There is no rest. There is no ending.

Ask David Cook of a young start-up company about change—and change—and change. He's an expert, with the scars to prove it. It took a lot of work to raise the $8.4 million through an IPO (Initial Public Offering)—countless revisions of the prospectus and several changes in underwriters. But David had a good product—economic analysis software for oil companies—and a profitable company—sales of $6.1 million and profits of $901,000. The future looked bright.

Then another change occurred. The market fell out of the oil business. Sales dropped 41 percent. Profits evaporated like ice on the pavement in July. The stock price went through the floor. David said, "A child of seven could see that the industry was going to hell."

What do you do? Change again, obviously. From software to something else. But what else? David searched for a new product—and decided upon video rentals. He hired merchandising people and aimed to conquer the fragmented video rental business as Toys "Я" Us did in the toy business and Southland did in the convenience store business. He succeeded. By May 1987 he had thirty-five stores open, sales of $6 million, and profits of $397,000. Then he experienced the ultimate change—he sold his original

28

company. David knows about change being a continuous process. He's now starting up another company.[14]

Don Shula's words are apropos here (he's the coach of the Miami Dolphins National Football League team): "Success isn't final, and failure isn't fatal." Change is a lifetime endeavor.

Is your organization ready to change? Andrew Grove, president and CEO of Intel, urges you to complete the following mini-quiz to test your organization's readiness to change.[15]

1. An employee from three levels down calls your secretary and urgently requests to talk with you about a recently made decision. Is it practice in your organization to
   a. Take the call?
   b. Ask the employee to send a memo to his/her manager?
   c. Contact the employee's boss and let him/her handle the problem?

2. One of your junior marketing managers, while reviewing some manufacturing procedures, discovers several unnecessary steps. Is it practice in your organization for the individual to
   a. Write a memo to the manufacturing manager?
   b. Write a memo to his/her supervisor?
   c. Personally pursue the issue until it's resolved?

3. Your principal competitor unexpectedly launches a new product that takes market share. Is it practice in your organization to
   a. Get marketing managers to write weekly reports detailing steps to deal with the problem?
   b. Hire a consulting firm to help you deal with the problem?
   c. Create a multidisciplinary task force to solve the problem in thirty days?

4. Product release meets engineering schedules. The products are good. Competitors are just getting there first and gaining market share. In your organization do you
   a. Give marketing more control over engineering schedules?
   b. Replace the engineering manager?
   c. Figure out how to cut 50 percent off product development time?

Scoring

1	2	3	4	
a=2	a=1	a=1	a=0	
b=0	b=0	b=0	b=0	
c=0	c=2	c=2	c=2	☐

Total

Add your scores together. If you scored 0–2, you've got a lot of work to do to get ready to change. Your organization needs a big fire. If you scored 3–5, you need some work pointing out the smoke people already smell. Your organization is modestly ready for change. Now paint the clear picture of tomorrow and lay out the migration path. If you scored 6–8, your organization is already moving toward change. Keep clearing the migration path and reinforcing the changed behavior.

Now on with the journey!

3

Anticipate the Obstacles

EMPOWERING CHANGE
VISION
Actions
Expectation systems
People systems
Culture systems

CREATE TOMORROW
Strategies
Resources

CHANGE
Individual
Organization

PREPARATION
Getting ready
Anticipating obstacles

Watch out. It's not going to be as easy as it sounds. Empowering change is difficult. I'd be lying to you if I told you it was easy. You know it isn't. I know it isn't. But not only is it possible—it's absolutely essential.

Get ready to handle the inevitable obstacles. They always occur. So expect them, anticipate them, and be prepared mentally to deal with them.

Here are five potential problems that will pose significant mental anguish: it always takes longer, exaggerated expectations, carping critics, procrastination, and imperfections. None of these obstacles are fatal, if you stay fixed on your target: empowering your people to change.

OBSTACLE 1—IT ALWAYS TAKES LONGER

People learn slowly and forget easily. It takes a long time to change—usually a lot longer than you expected.

It's hard to change habits that have been established for years. The "don't think, just do" mentality dies hard. The larger your organization, the longer it will take. In large multinational firms it may take five to seven years. Be prepared to hang in there—and hang in there—and hang in there. Coach Vince Lombardi of the World Champion Green Bay Packers football team said, "Mental toughness wins more games than great skill and fancy game plans."

Take a long-term perspective—because it'll take that long. Be ready for your people's very short memory. They'll constantly ask, "What did you do lately about the vision?" And "lately" better not be too far away. Show the slightest diminishing of your dedication to empowering them to use your vision, and they see it as "the beginning of the end." Hans Schleimer, the managing director for a large consumer and industrial electronics multinational, discovered the longtime frame required to install his vision.

> Hans spent a year developing his "market-driven company" vision in accordance with many of the principles outlined in this book. He worked hard for the next two years personally visiting his company's more than fifty facilities worldwide to explain his vision and urge its acceptance.
>
> In some locations Hans's vision was greeted enthusiastically, but in many others Hans received polite attention but little overt support. Given the strongly decentralized nature of his company, which includes divisions concerned with VCRs and telephone switches and power plants, Hans relied upon persuasion to bring people around. After six years he felt that the vast majority of his senior management supported his vision, but support at the lower levels was spotty.
>
> Hans told me, "I'm retiring now. My successor is strongly committed to the vision, so I'm optimistic about the long-term future. But it's been frustrating. We've missed a number of market opportunities because we failed to be market-driven rather than product-driven—and we will con-

tinue to be an also-ran in products we developed for some time. My biggest disappointment in my time as managing director is the slow progress we've made in turning the company mentality around. I hope my successor is able to realize my dream in his lifetime."

Hans is not alone in his frustration. Many other executives share his feeling. Empowering change is not a short-term phenomenon. I wish it were, because that would make it easier. But it isn't.

Stick with it, though. Persistence pays off. Burt Yavonovich, the CEO for a large consumer products company, stuck with it and in three years succeeded.

> Burt initiated a vision that stressed being close to the customer and innovative in developing new products to meet changing customer needs. He put the vision together, using many of the procedures spelled out in this book.
>
> Along with his constant communication and personal visibility in living the vision, he reorganized the company into a number of small entrepreneurial product/market units. He wanted to empower his people to act for customers. Frequently he visited each unit to encourage the use of his vision.
>
> After three years company performance improved. He introduced a number of new products, margins increased, and market penetration rose. During a period of economic recession, many of his competitors cut back on their new product development activities. Burt didn't. In fact, he redoubled his efforts to push his vision. While earnings flattened out, his overall return of shareholder equity continued to climb.
>
> Burt told us, "I think we've got it [the vision] part of our culture now. People now talk about it as if it were their idea—that's how I know we've succeeded. But it took a lot longer than I thought it would. You just have to stick with it."

Stick with it over the long term. But your people need short-term validation that your vision works. They need to see a continuous stream of short-term progress produced by the use of your vision.

Dan Jiminez, the general manager for a small specialty chemical division of a large multinational, discovered this need for short-term results.

> Dan installed a new "quality for the customer" vision and used many of the suggestions we've already outlined. He was pleased with its initial success as quality levels improved, customer complaints dropped, and customer service evaluations rose. Profits per employee and sales per employee also rose to industry highs.
>
> After a year improvements leveled off. Quality was at a high level—the best in the American industry—but still below several Japanese competitors. Customer evaluations remained high—5.7 to 6.0 on a 7-point scale.
>
> Several steady no-improvement months went by and he began to sense a slackening off among his people. There were little signs such as fewer quality-improvement suggestions and less talk about customers. They're nothing serious, Dan thought. Just a normal leveling off before the next big push.
>
> The expected (hoped-for) big push never came. If anything, Dan noticed a downward trend in several of the indexes over the next six months. After nine months of steady performance, profits and sales per employee began to slip.
>
> Then Dan approached me with his situation. I sat through several of his staff meetings and spent several days in the cafeteria talking informally with employees.
>
> It was clear that Dan talked less about his vision. Employees in general didn't see much relationship between his vision and their jobs. "Oh, yeah," one chemical engineer told me, "we all believe in the 'quality for customers' idea—I think?"
>
> Dan told me, "I guess I moved on to other priorities—at least mentally—believing that I'd spent enough time to implant the vision. I guess I just have to increase the amount of time I spend talking about, reporting about, and encouraging the use of my vision. It sounds like a never-ending job."

Dan's right. It is a never-ending job. IBM talks about its vision in virtually every employee communication. ServiceMaster repeats its vision at every meeting. It is a never-ending job.

Overcome this inevitable obstacle. Continuously report short-term results achieved from using the vision. Keep empowering change to the new vision. Keep the drumbeat up for years—in fact, forever!

Personal Workshop

As you consider how to overcome the obstacle of time, please ponder the following questions.

1. Am I really prepared to spend the time necessary to empower people to use my new vision—even if it takes years?

2. How can I demonstrate a continuing series of short-term (monthly) results from using my vision?

3. How can I constantly report the positive results in many different media?

OBSTACLE 2—EXAGGERATED EXPECTATIONS. EVERYONE WANTS EVERYTHING, NOW.

Turn people on—and they get turned on! Deliver some progress, and people want lots of progress—immediately. And they look to you to deliver that progress—instantly. You can easily become the Messiah—able to walk on water, instantly cure the lame, and produce magical answers to all problems. Attaining gurulike status has its benefits. It's gratifying to sense the heads swivel as you walk by. But—and it's a very big "but"—lots of dangers come with "superhuman" status.

We look for heroes to believe in, to follow, to imitate. We expect our heroes to be perfect, to handle every situation with aplomb. We carefully examine our hero's every action to be certain that it meets our impossibly high standards. Unfortunately you are not perfect. You will make mistakes. It's bound to happen. It's easy to be perfect in the short run. But you'll likely slip up as the months wear into years. In fact, you will certainly drop the ball, at least a few times. And when the inevitable fumble occurs, there's another reason for your people to hesitate about using your vision. I can hear the whispers in the hallway now: "See, even he/she isn't doing it. So why should I?"

In addition, people believe that if they use your vision, they will instantly cure the organization's problems. When improvements don't appear instantly, a letdown comes, one that often drives performance down. Dorene Greene, head of the in-house graphic arts group in a large U.S. city government, discovered the negative consequences of unrealistic expectations.

> As part of the reproduction department, Dorene's nine people created artwork and copy for project proposals made by engineers. She put together a "creatively working together" vision using many of the techniques spelled out in this book. Initially she received acceptance and enthusiasm from her small staff.
>
> As part of this vision, she wanted closer contact between her staff and their customers. She urged frequent customer calls—both during and especially after the delivery of the material.
>
> Her staff had been frequently criticized by the engineering department for being out of touch with that department's needs. She concentrated her personal customer contacts on the engineering staff. "Love them to death," she urged them. After several months she saw some improvement in the relationship between her group and the engineering department.
>
> One day several of her people came to her and said, "Look, all these customer calls cost time, and we're falling behind in our work. We're not certain that it's worth it. We see some change, but it takes so much time. . . ."
>
> To prevent the collapse of her efforts, she admitted that maybe her idea wasn't the best one. She suggested that several members of the engineering department attend their staff meeting and talk about whether the personal customer contact program was worth it. At the meeting everyone agreed to substitute weekly brief stand-up meetings involving those people working on the project from both departments.

One and a half years later there's a close working relationship between the two departments. Dorene said, "It was a close call. Many of my folks would have gone back to the old ways when the new methods didn't show instant, dramatic improvement. I'm glad everyone decided to use the stand-up meetings as a communications mechanism. Interestingly, now that things are better between the groups, I've noticed more informal contacts—just the kind I wanted to get some time back."

Your vision won't instantly cure all the organization's problems. In fact, just the opposite may occur. Problems may appear that have bubbled below the surface for years. Don't let your expectations, and those of your people, outrun your ability to deliver. Visions are not a magic elixir.

Prepare yourself for this obstacle with the twin "H's" of humanness and honesty. It's fun to be a guru. But it's much more effective (and realistic) to be Human with a capital "H." Lionel Richie wrote and organized the production of the popular song "We Are the World." He invited the luminaries of the music world to cooperate in the record to raise money for the starving in Africa. He posted a sign next to the studio door that said, "Check your ego at the door." His message was clear. The success of the record depended upon the cooperation of everyone, not the brilliance of a few.

Heed Richie's message. It also applies to your empowerment of change. "Check your ego at the door," and let others take responsibility. Be less of a guru/hero and more of a facilitator/coach. Empower others:

1. Encourage others to take responsibility for executing the vision in their area. Get each person to set goals and action plans and then follow up with them.

2. Set up regular multiple communication channels where supervisors discuss the new vision with their people. Monthly employee gatherings in each department—chaired by the department supervisor—are one way. Keep direct contact, yourself, through informal channels and regular (quarterly, semiannual, or annual) employee meetings.

3. Refer questions and comments about the new vision to supervisors, rather than answering them directly. Build communica-

tion linkages that exclude you. However, be careful not to put employees off or look like you're evading responsibility. Personally follow up, to be certain that the question/problem gets answered.

4. Lionize others. Constantly communicate about the hero actions of others in multiple mediums. Keep up the drumbeat about what others are doing—and their successes using the new vision.

5. Talk about "the team" and "our vision" and "our results." Your language has a dramatic empowering impact.

6. Avoid having answers to all questions/problems/difficulties.

"I don't know" is a legitimate answer. Employees will respect you for not giving glib, and often incorrect, answers just for the sake of giving an answer.

Let people see you as a "real person," not some demigod. Highlight the expertise and efforts of others. Let your humanness show.

The second "H" is honesty. Honestly share your mistakes, rather than trying to hide them. It's often said that a good surgeon buries his/her mistakes—and most managers wish they could do the same. A large dose of reality is one of the best antidotes to inflated expectations.

A little known fact is that the Apollo moon missions were on course less than 1 percent of the time. The mission was composed of almost constant midcourse corrections. That's also true of most business situations. Yet few business people have the guts to own up to that reality. Be different and share your uncertainties—"A could happen, or B happen. I'm not certain. No one is. We think A will happen, and here's what we're planning if it does. If B happens, here's what we're planning. And don't forget, C, D, E, and F could also happen." At very least, let your people know how uncertain the future really is.

Then it's easier to share the things that didn't work out. I heard an executive tell his assembled 675 employees at a quarterly meeting, "Well, we really blew the forecast this time. Remember that we thought business would continue its 20-plus percent increase during the quarter? You probably noticed that we were a little off—like maybe 30 percent off. Rather than an increase, we had a slowdown and scrambled for orders. We didn't anticipate that X would get that new product to market quite so quickly. I really appreciate your pitching in to save money. We think we have a better handle on what's coming up this quarter—at least I hope so!"

Invincibility is great—but difficult to attain and maintain. Honesty about your own human limitations is more comfortable and permanent.

Personal Workshop

As you consider the obstacle of exaggerated expectations, please ponder the following questions.

1. What do my people expect from my vision? Have I promised great things, either directly or implicitly?

2. What are the biggest problems facing my organization right now? Can my vision help to solve these problems? In what way can I clarify the relationship between these big issues confronting my organization and my vision? Can I demonstrate the way my vision can—and can't—help to solve these pressing problems?

3. How can I empower others to take responsibility for implementing my vision?

4. What multiple communication channels can I establish that do not include me in the loop? Can I empower my direct reports to hold frequent employee meetings? How about their direct reports? Can I get even the front-line supervisors holding meetings? Can the employee newspaper be used as a mechanism to keep people up to date, and even generate a two-way flow of information?

5. By what methods can I accelerate the identification and discussion of heroes—individuals who use my vision? Can I talk more about these heroes?

6. How can I empower more people to spread the vision? What about putting the director of human resources in charge of redoing the personnel policies? Could I get the director of manufacturing and engineering together to work on the standards of performance? There must be dozens of people who would love to help. How can I get their help?

7. What strategies can I use to share more openly with my people the business uncertainties and miscalculations? How can I facilitate a more open organization by sharing my problems more with my people?

OBSTACLE 3—CARPING SKEPTICS

There are professional skeptics in every organization. You've met them many times. They're the folks who constantly say, "That's a great idea, but . . . We tried that before and it didn't work. . . . What makes you think you can do *that?*" These individuals find clouds on a summer's day and glory in pointing out all the pebbles on the beach at Monte Carlo.

Unfortunately, you can't ignore these skeptics. Who knows, they may be right! They may even point out significant obstacles that you've overlooked. Furthermore, a large number of employees hear them. They are often loud and persistent in their carping negative comments. By sheer repetition these critics can be believed. Steven Birowell, shift manager in a large textile machinery plant, discovered the consequences of ignoring the critics.

> Steven installed a "quality first for customers" vision by incorporating many of the processes discussed in this book. He got good cooperation from his people and was enthusiastic about initial improvements. Quality rates improved and customers seemed pleased.
>
> Pockets of resistance remained, though, particularly in the engineering and field service departments. There were a constant stream of complaints from these two departments about the impracticality of the vision. Although these groups didn't report directly to Steven, he relied upon them for assistance in executing his work. So their resistance, although not fatal to his vision, posed a serious threat. Steven ignored the comments, choosing instead to stress the positive benefits.
>
> Little by little Steven observed that the negative comments seemed to increase, and not only from these two departments but from all over the plant. He also noticed that the rate of improvements slowed, and he felt that his

words were having less and less impact on his people. Steven still chose to ignore the critics and continued to emphasize his vision.

Two years after launching his vision, Steven quietly stopped talking about it. He said, "It reached a point where I could tell that no one was listening to me. The bored looks, the yawns, the disbelief in the eyes, were all too strong to ignore. The slowly falling quality rates were another. I continued to hear the negative comments, even from my direct reports. And they grew more and more frequent. I just got tired of swimming upstream."

Critics don't give up easily. As was the case with Steven, they can drive you, like a gale wind, off your course and shipwreck your plans.

Don't give up. Steel yourself to deal with the carping critics. Ignore them. That works in the short run—most of the time. But test out how serious and widespread the critics are. Capitalize on the enthusiasm of other employees and on all the initial short-term progress you can report. This often either silences or converts these critics. Shawn Courtlander, production manager for a consumer products company, used her employees' initial enthusiasm to overcome carping critics. Shawn's company manufactured plastic consumer items such as bowls and wastebaskets.

Shawn put together a "quality first" vision by using many of the techniques spelled out in this book. She got lots of enthusiastic response, except for the undercurrent of disbelief from a small, vocal minority. She spent many hours in direct personal contact with employees talking up her vision and empowering employees to use it.

Despite her personal efforts, the critics kept carping. Shawn decided to silence the critics by running an employee meeting, where employees would demonstrate how their use of her vision was producing good results.

Shawn told me, "The meeting was a huge success. A group of employees organized it, planned it, and ran it. They were great! They got several customers to come in and tell us how much they appreciated the quality of the

41

products. They got employees to talk about how much they enjoyed making the quality products. And to cap it all off, they asked all those in favor of using the vision to stand up. I held my breath. Who knows, some of those critics might just be rooted to their chairs. But everyone stood up—and the cheering and whistling filled the room. The critics all but disappeared after that."

Cut the carping off early. Drown it in the enthusiasm of short-term progress. Confront the negative comments directly and diffuse them if they continue.

Talk directly to the critics. Personally find out the problems and what you can do to improve the situation. When you show personal interest you often can transform the critic into a supporter. Direct talks also can surface problems that may have been overlooked.

Another strategy in executing the vision is to enlist the aid and support of the critic. Give people a piece of the action. That often transforms even the harshest critic into an enthusiastic supporter. Dave Zeit, manager of the auto repair shop, successfully used that strategy to silence his biggest critic.

Dave installed the "quality for customers" vision using the approach outlined in this book. Jose, one of the oldest mechanics in the shop (in terms of seniority), strongly opposed several of Dave's suggested policies, particularly the "fix it free" policy. "You won't get me fixing something for nothing. The company will pay me, or it won't get done."

In the first days of the effort none of Jose's work came back, so Dave avoided a confrontation with him on the policy. Realizing that it was only a matter of time until it happened, Dave approached Jose and asked him to organize a "maintenance standards" policy for the shop. Dave told Jose, "If the work was done up to maintenance standards before it left the shop, then if it comes back, the company will pay to repair it. If the work was not up to standards and it comes back, however, then the mechanic will repair it free. Please set up the standards and a way to monitor them. You know the business better than anyone. You're the logical person to do this for us."

Jose went to work enthusiastically. He asked the other mechanics what they thought and then ran drafts of the standards by Dave and the other mechanics. Jose held a shop meeting to discuss how the mechanics would monitor each other's work. Within three weeks the system was operational.

With the new standards in place, very few cars came back. Eventually, though, it happened—one of Jose's cars came back, and it hadn't been checked before it left the shop. Dave held his breath when he saw the car come back and knew that Jose would be faced with repairing the car for free. Jose went to work and repaired the car without a word, and there was never a mention of payment. Jose was one of the most vocal supporters of the new vision and its policies.

Dave learned a valuable lesson. Convert an opponent by giving him/her responsibility for a piece of the action. Critics are everywhere. They spring forth spontaneously like weeds in a garden. Sometimes they signal deep stresses and problems in your organization that need to be addressed. Most often they are individuals executing their own private agenda. Ignore them in the early stages, and count on the initial enthusiasm to convert them. If that doesn't work, use either direct confrontation or power sharing. Remember, most people want to do the right thing. Get in touch with your own basic belief in people. This will help you get your mental toughness going so that you can handle the few carping critics.

Personal Workshop

As you consider the critics in your organization, you might ponder the following questions.

1. Where are the critics located? Are they in one or a few departments? Are they in certain job categories? Which types of employees? Certain geographic locations? What does the distribution of the critics tell me about what's bothering them?

2. How long can I ignore the critics? Just how long is enough "enough"?

3. When and how can I talk to the critics directly? When I do, what will my approach be? What do I want to accomplish?

4. How can I share power with the critic? What does the critic want that I can provide in return for his/her support for my vision?

5. How can I get back in touch with my own basic values that assert that most people want to do the right thing? Can I reaffirm my own thinking and not let the few critics spoil my attitude toward the vast majority of my people?

OBSTACLE 4—PROCRASTINATION

To empower a new vision consumes time—like a black hole consumes light. Most of your staff face an overflowing in basket. They already have full plates. It's easy to see using the new vision as "just one more task to do." "How can I put it off?" they'll likely ask themselves—if not you.

Visions involve the intangibilities of running a company—such as customer attitudes and employee motivations. They deal in uncomfortable and difficult areas, and they are all too easily postponed.

Generally, managers avoid intangible measurements. It's more difficult to defend subjective measure against challenge. It's just easier to deal with numerical values.

Here's an uncomfortable situation. Imagine the terror managers experience when they go on their first informal "How are things going?" customer visit. "What do I say?" the executive of one large chemical company asked me. "What happens if they ask for something we don't make, or a question I can't answer? It could be terribly embarrassing." No wonder that executive has been putting off making his first customer call for six months, using the excuse that he's "too busy."

Vision-supporting activities are all too easily postponed. They are difficult to do and often are viewed as not a part of the individual's "real job." Here's how to deal with this obstacle.

Break vision-supporting actions into small, "doable" steps. The tallest building is built one brick at a time. The longest journey is made one step at a time. Breaking the overall effort into small, easy-to-accomplish, short-term steps reduces the cost of taking action now. It also reduces the likelihood of putting off the action. Christine Damonweld, the manager for an order picking department in a large pharmaceutical distribution company, discovered the progress that could be made by insisting upon short-term actions to empower people to use her vision.

> Christine wanted to improve the delivery time for her customers. She put together a vision—"on-time delivery"—and received very enthusiastic support from her thirty-seven employees.
>
> Immediately she began to notice that although everyone was positive about the vision, very little change occurred in the day-to-day operations of the department. Everyone gave lip service to the vision, but little was actually happening. Checking around, she found that most people "intended" to do something to improve delivery times in the future, but they were too busy filling orders today to take any action.
>
> Christine met with her people and asked each to set one action step they could take the next day to improve deliveries. There were some people who pleaded overwork in an effort not to make such a commitment, but she was able to effectively point out that "anyone can do one thing."
>
> She asked each person to post his or her particular action on the bulletin board when it was done. Then she went around every day to ask each person if that action step had been completed and what step was going to be taken tomorrow. After several weeks of this daily one action per day, she was satisfied that the habit had been implanted. Even though she stopped following up daily, months later her people continued to post the daily action steps on the bulletin board.

Break large tasks into small pieces—or else it's likely to be postponed.

Keep up a steady drumbeat, pushing for short-term action. Use your reporting system to flood the organization with information about the vision's successes. Maintain a steady flow of informal communications that stress the vision. Identify and lionize heroes who use your vision. Hold frequent meetings—with employees, managers, suppliers, and customers—to dramatically demonstrate your vision. Keep up the public pressure for the use of your vision.

Success is the best antidote to the disease of procrastination. Nothing persuades individuals to "get with the program" more than to have "the program" look like a big winner. Everyone likes to back a winner. Make the act of using your vision look like a winner, and many people will rush to climb on the bandwagon.

Personal Workshop

As you think about how to overcome the problem of procrastination, you might consider the following questions.

1. How can I break the overall change into small, manageable steps for my people? Many of the items discussed previously apply here as well.

2. How can I maintain a high level of pressure to use my vision, without inflicting undue stress on my people?

3. How can I continue to emphasize successes—short term, immediate, and dramatic—in order to impress my people that it pays to "get on the bandwagon"?

OBSTACLE 5—IMPERFECTION

Prepare yourself for failure—at least some of the time. A vision does not guarantee perfection. Don't be disappointed when you achieve less than perfection. Aim for constant improvement rather than the attainment of some permanent nirvana.

Charles Lazarus, chairman and CEO of the very successful U.S. toy store chain Toys "Я" Us, constantly strives for improvement. He aims to make his toy chain the largest in the world. It's already reached over $2 billion in sales. He closely monitors product sales. This tells him which toys are selling and which aren't, so that he can order more of the former and get rid of the latter. He takes every opportunity—big and small—to add a few more dollars to his sales volumes. He's even installed a computer in his home to help him keep track of sales during his "off" hours. During the last twenty-two years, Lazarus has made lots of mistakes—bought the wrong toys, priced them incorrectly, or merchandised them poorly. But he continues to make midcourse corrections, to seek improvement in his performance, and to learn from his failures.[1]

You will make mistakes. Your people will make mistakes. There will be backsliding from time to time. Expect it, anticipate it, accept it, because it will happen. Here are some ways to handle this obstacle.

Attitude is the first way. Yours! It's difficult to admit that you're less than perfect and even more challenging to accept it in others. But realize that even the smartest people sometimes do dumb things—from which they usually recover. Mistakes are not the end of the world. You and your organization can recover. Keep your cool, and remember the good things you and/or your people previously did.

Turn the mistake/backsliding into a learning experience. Ask yourself and the others involved in the situation, "What can we learn from this experience? What can help us use the vision even more effectively in the future?" Make a list of the learnings, circulate it, post it on the bulletin board, and ask frequently, "Are we using the lessons we learned from our mistakes?"

Use the backsliding/mistakes as an opportunity to refocus on the vision. Reclarify the individual's part in making that vision live. Ask, "Are you clear on the vision and how to use it?" "What can I do to empower you to use the vision consistently?" Mistakes present you with a golden opportunity to gain recommitment to the vision. Use mistakes to your advantage.

Personal Workshop

As you ponder the problems of imperfections, consider the following questions.

1. How can I maximize the learnings from the imperfections? Are group meetings the answer, where I share my mistakes—sort of a "Mistake of the Month Club"—or are one-on-one meetings better? Both may work.

2. How can I use the imperfections as a way to refocus and recommit to the vision? In other words, how can I convert a potential negative into a significant positive?

3. How can I share that mistakes are like falling down while you're learning how to ski?

The path is not smooth. Rather, it is strewn with rocks. It'll take longer than you expected—it always does. You will probably encounter exaggerated expectations. There will always be carping skeptics who doubt you and your effort. It is all too easy to put off tackling the difficult new activities. And you will likely be less than perfect in empowering your people to use your vision.

These are real obstacles. Steel yourself mentally. You can confront the obstacles and win.

4

Create Tomorrow

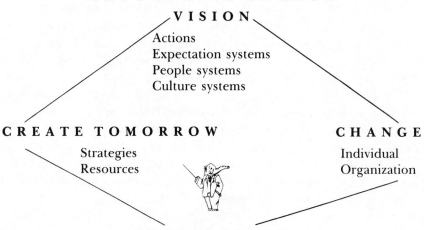

EMPOWERING CHANGE

VISION

Actions
Expectation systems
People systems
Culture systems

CREATE TOMORROW

Strategies
Resources

CHANGE

Individual
Organization

PREPARATION

Getting ready
Anticipating obstacles

You got the message. The slipping margins, the fading sales, the rising costs, tell you in unmistakable terms—you are in trouble. What's worse, you've just seen your competitor's new product and you shake your head, saying to yourself, "That's so simple. Why didn't we do that?" Finally one of your closest customers tells you, "Why don't you do something? You're falling behind."

Organizations get "old." Some organizations, like IBM in the middle 1980s, begin to believe their own press clippings. Belief in their own invincibility led salespeople to spend less than 30 percent of their time with customers.[1] Chairman John Akers saw the problem—and decided to change the strategy.

Other times a competitor emerges with a far better product. That happened to Canon camera. Canon dominated the single lens reflex market until Maxxum. Maxxum, with its automatic-focus system for the 35-mm SLR, swept the market. Canon's market share dropped precipitously. Canon knew they had to do something to regain the lead.[2]

49

Some other times customer tastes change and leave you with a great product but no customers. Ethyl Corporation made tetraethyl lead, the antiknock compound in gasoline. The Environmental Protection Agency banned the product, drying up the market for Ethyl's only product. Ethyl fought the ban at public hearings and in the courts—buying time to diversify into new areas.[3]

Overall strategy shifts produce the need for massive internal change. Consider IBM. It's estimated that more than 150,000 people changed job assignments as the result of the "Year of the Customer." Complete divisions were dissolved and reassembled in new forms. New procedures, new visions, new activities—new departmental tomorrows—were required to implement the new strategic direction. Three years later, many IBMers are still struggling to create the "right" departmental strategy to implement IBM's new tomorrow.[4]

Often internal changes produce the need for new internal strategies. New bosses, new technologies, new philosophies, all demand new strategies. Sometimes even attendance at a conference or workshop produces the urgency to design a new departmental strategy.

The reasons for change are legion—and largely academic. The question "Why change?" is the stuff for long winter night conversations around the fireplace. The question "How to change?" is a boardroom agenda item and high on the executive "to do" list. If you're really going to survive into the twenty-first century, you've got to change *today!*

Leaders create a new tomorrow. The "right" new tomorrow. One thing is certain: tomorrow will not be an extension of today. The common thread throughout all success stories is the action of leaders—at all levels in an organization—to create a right new tomorrow—and then empower people to achieve that tomorrow. Here's how.

THE TIMES THEY ARE A-CHANGIN'

Both Woody Guthrie and Alvin Toffler are correct. Guthrie sang, "The times they are a-changin' . . . " and Toffler warned us that the pace of change is picking up. The half-life of successful tomorrows is painfully short—and growing shorter all the time.

Consider Henry Ford. In the early days of this century he pioneered a low-cost automobile—and created the mass automobile market. His low-cost strategy gained him the lion's share of the market. Yet he held on too long to his one-model, high-volume car strategy. Soon General Motors, by offering product diversity (you could have a car in colors other than black) combined with consumer financing (to make their somewhat higher-priced cars affordable), overtook Ford and by the 1950s held three times Ford's market share.

But even GM got old. In recent years the pendulum swung back to Ford again. GM stuck with an obsolete 1970s plan well into the middle 1980s, giving them high-priced, poor-quality, look-alike cars. Ford's twin emphasis on "Quality Is Job 1!" and new car designs paid off when they were selected the best quality American car for four years in a row and the best car in the world twice in a row. In 1987 and 1988 Ford made more money than GM.

U.S. airline People Express also suffered from premature aging. Donald Burr blazed the path to low-cost air fares. In the early 1980s, using a strategy of low costs, he revolutionized the air transport business by providing air fares that effectively competed with bus fares. But within two years other airlines narrowed the cost gap, as GM did to Ford. The edge shifted to those airlines charging almost as little as People, but that provided such value-added amenities as free meals, baggage handling, computerized reservations, and on-time arrivals and departures.

There is a constant need to redefine your tomorrow and empower your people to create it. Consider Kodak, long the dominant force in photography. Spurred by the competition of Fuji and its own slow-footed responses, CEO Colby Chandler was forced to find a new strategy and focus his 121,500 people on creating a new tomorrow.

Chandler defined "new products for customers" as the key strategy. He reorganized the firm into smaller, market-oriented business units, focused on enhancing the feedback from customers, and encouraged the introduction of product modifications to meet customer needs. In 1986 Kodak introduced more than one hundred new product modifications—the most ever—ranging from minor improvements in the film container lids to make them easier to remove with one hand to more dramatic, sharper film colors.

Chandler is also moving the firm into other, related fields, such as batteries and pharmaceuticals, in an effort to capitalize on

Kodak's excellent consumer franchise. His marketing-oriented, entrepreneurial strategy is sharply different from that of his predecessors—and will likely change again as the market calls a different tune in the future.[5]

So every tomorrow has its day in the sun, then passes into eclipse. The only constant truth is that today's strategy will need to be replaced tomorrow.

You've got to get a new tomorrow. And it needs to be clear—to everyone. In the early 1960s the Martin Company built Pershing missiles for the U.S. Army. It took a massive inspection program, costing millions of dollars, to get the missiles right, and then it took ninety days after shipment to get all the equipment operational. The army insisted that Martin had to do better or lose the contract. Martin promised that it would deliver the next missile thirty days early and that it would be fully operational ten days after delivery. That clear tomorrow—delivery one month early and fully operational in ten days—created a blizzard of activity. They made the deadline. Revised operational procedures eliminated many inspections as employees focused on doing it right the first time. The clear tomorrow empowered the change.[6]

"The times they are a-changin' . . ." That's today's theme song. Nothing is safe. Better be working on new products and strategies now—even though you're still successful with your current activities. Knowing you have to change is the beginning. Everyone's got to change. But, knowing what to change, as Hamlet said, "Aye, there's the rub."

Which new tomorrow is right for you? Any new tomorrow won't do. It's got to be the "right" new tomorrow. What is the right new strategy for that new tomorrow? Simply put, the right new strategy is that which distinguishes you from all the other "look-alikes." How do you do that? I'll give you some guidelines in the next section.

STRATEGIC GUIDELINES

At the risk of sounding negative, here's what I'm not going to do. I'm not going to give you a new strategic planning model. There are lots of those out there already, and several are excellent. Choose whichever one you can work with best.

I'm also not going to provide you with a substitute for your strategic planning process. Use whichever process works for you—centralized or decentralized, short-term scenario planning or long-term budgeting.

I will give you guidelines for thinking about new strategies—and help in using those guidelines to build the strategy for your new tomorrow. My book is not about planning or strategizing. It's about empowering change to improve performance. So, onward.

The basic purpose of the new strategy is to develop a different—better—product/service. Follow these three general principles: 1) lead from strength, 2) follow customers, channels, or production processes; and 3) be a little bit—but not too far—ahead.

Lead from strength. "Lead from strength" is a well-established rule in the game of bridge. The same rule applies to the building of the right strategy.

Concentrate on cash flows and cash-based returns. That's the way to create value for shareholders and employees. The value of a business is the value of its future cash flow after it's discounted by its cost of capital. Walker Lewis, chairman of consulting firm Strategic Planning Associates, sees two roles for leaders in the coming years. "First is to be an aggressive investor, cleaning and pruning. Second is to be the keeper and builder of the company's core skills." In other words, lead from strength.[7]

William LaMothe must have been listening when Walker Lewis spoke. As chairman and CEO, he's successfully led Kellogg into the dominant and dominating position in the breakfast cereal business. During the 1970s Kellogg was severely criticized for being the only food business not to diversify. After all, the logic went, with the aging of the population the cereal business was "mature." That's Wall Streetese for "boring, washed up, over the hill, past its prime, no growth."

Using the charge that Kellogg was "past its prime," LaMothe rallied his troops. Instead of looking over the fence at the "greener" pastures elsewhere, Kellogg looked in its own backyard. "If people ate cereal when they were children, why can't we get them to eat it when they're older?" they asked. Why not? So they set out to entice the yuppie crowd into the cereal market. They boosted R&D to 1.1 percent of sales (competitors spend about half that amount) and cranked out more than forty new products in 1987, double what they had turned out five years ago. They targeted these new products at niche markets, such as health foods, designed specifically to appeal to the twenty-five to forty crowd. To move these new products off the grocer's shelves, they invested huge sums in marketing and advertising. They spent 20 percent of sales in advertising—an estimated $865 million in 1988—easily twice competitors' expenditures. And to assure themselves of the low-cost producer spot, Kellogg invested $1.2 billion in the Memphis factory, which will boost cereal capacity by 35 percent. The fully automated plant will improve quality and give added flexibility to product shifts.

The result of leading from its strength? Kellogg increased market share to 41 percent—double its nearest competitor. Return on shareholders' equity sparkles at 33 percent—also double the industry average. Lead from strength. Chairman LaMothe is an expert. He's taught his fellow industry executives a thing or two about creating value. As he said, "Not bad for a company that's past its prime."[8]

Size often creates a strength from which you can lead. Borden dominates the fractionated pasta business. As the largest player in an industry of small players, Borden's size gives it significantly lower operating costs. These lower costs translate into growing market share—from 6 percent in 1980 to 31 percent in 1987. Being able to tailor pastas to regional tastes and produce odd sizes and shapes quickly allows Borden to capitalize on rapidly changing customer tastes. Who says big is necessarily bad?[9]

Look at H. J. Heinz Company. It owns the ketchup business. Last year it produced 70 percent of the ketchup sold to institutions and 57 percent of the stuff sold to you and me in supermarkets. And it made a ton of money doing it. Its ketchup has one of the highest profit margins (21 percent) of any processed-food product sold in the world. How does Heinz do it? They lead from their strengths. Market size gives them strong buying power in the tomato marketplace. In fact, they're so big that they've developed their own tomato seeds. Then their huge volume enables them to use economies of scale at their three processing plants (two in California and one in Ohio). No wonder Heinz has the highest margins in the industry.

Chairman and president, CEO Anthony O'Reilly capitalizes on that volume and low cost to pump large advertising expenditures that enhance his market share still further. Heinz has doubled the amount spent on advertising in the last decade and bumped market share several points.

Heinz applies the same "lead from strength" formula to the mundane markets in frozen potatoes, tuna fish, and canned cat food. No wonder he's generated twenty-three years of consecutive earnings increases and an enviable competitive position.[10]

Siemens is the biggest electronics company in Germany, and one of the biggest in Europe, but, it has lagged behind in penetration into profitable segments beyond medical electronics in most countries. With the coming of Europe '92 and the arrival of cutthroat competition from Japan, Managing Director Dr. Karl Kaske saw the need to use Siemens' size to open up new markets. An abortive run at the U.K. computer market resulted in one disaster. Licensing and marketing problems in France accounted for another debacle. But, it's been in the U.S. that Siemens has faced its biggest challenge.

The U.S. accounts for between 25 percent and 35 percent of the world electronics and electrical-goods market. Siemens targeted motor vehicle electronics and telecommunications as the growth markets. A string of purchases and R&D and marketing investments pushed U.S. sales over $83 million. But Siemens lost Dm 449 in 1987, half that amount in 1988, and hopes to break even in 1989. Size gives you staying power, though. Dr. Kaske has patience. He expects it will eventually pay off.[11]

Sometimes small is successful in leading from strength. Ask Walter Forbes. His small size enabled him to *move fast* when his target market evaporated. Chairman Walter Forbes of Comp-U-Card International, Inc. knows all about leading from strength—and relying upon that strength to find a new strategy. Comp-U-Card goes back to the early 1970s. It was a brilliant idea put together by Harvard professors and investors to sell goods to the home through PCs using an electronic catalog. Great idea. But after building the catalog and arranging for dramatically low prices through promised mass buying, there weren't enough PCs around to make it profitable. Great strategy, but no customers.

Forbes's answer—switch from PCs to the more ubiquitous telephone. Have the public call in and let operators use the electronic catalog. Brilliant strategy, particularly after Citibank agreed to market his service under their name, Citi Shopper. Today almost three million Visa and MasterCard holders use Comp-U-Card services through various bank names. Comp-U-Card shows a 12 percent operating profit and has the market to itself. Leading from strength—its computerized catalog and low prices due to mass buying—Forbes led his company from the brink of disaster to the competitors' winner's circle.[12]

Growth isn't a necessary precondition, either. Even in a declining business, leading from strength produces success. Consider L. F. Deardorff and Sons, makers of handmade wood-framed studio cameras. Deardorff makes the finest cameras in the world. Guaranteed thirty years, four of the original ten Deardorffs made in 1921 are still in use today. Building on his strength of product quality, Deardorff sells three hundred cameras a year at $3,295, garnering 25 percent of the high end market. Leading from strength pays off in competitive advantage, even in a declining market.[13]

Every organization has one or more strengths on which to build, even if it's only *past reputation.* Ed Pott's experience, as reported in the following vignette, shows us how to build on the strength of past reputation.

Ed took over as the general manager of a faded private club. At one time the club was "the place to go." But as newer properties opened and the owners refused to change the "charming facilities," the club slipped into declining memberships and financial losses.

When Ed took over he saw that the club was in deteriorating physical as well as fiscal shape. There was a core of dedicated and competent employees who had been with the club from its former glory days. Ed developed a strategy that tapped the strengths of the club—"the traditional club elegance"—and spent considerable time preaching it to employees.

The owner was not about to invest heavily in new facilities until it was clear that the club could be made profitable. So Ed spent a lot of his energy translating his strategy into improved service elements for his people. Largely on the strength of the improvements in personal service, and the resultant increase in membership income, the loss was reduced by 75 percent and permanent capital improvements were begun.

Ed's strategy also works for broken-down companies. Ask Michael Cappy and Tommy Hewitt. They turned around struggling Servus Rubber. In 1972 Servus was a healthy $25 million supplier of high-quality boots. Ten years later the company was losing $1 million on $14 million sales. Why? Its then owners had tried to compete with cheaper Korean boots by cutting costs and prices. Cappy and Hewitt saw the company's salvation lay in just the opposite—stress the quality of boots and sell at a premium. So they bought the company at distress sale prices and set out to lead from its former strength—quality products.

Cappy put together a new motto: "Servus sets the standard." He met with union officials and employees every day to establish the "we don't produce junk" mentality in the plant. He and Hewitt visited previous customers in mid-1983 and reintroduced them to Servus. "We're back producing top-of-the-line boots," he told them. "Are you guys still in business?" many customers asked. "We haven't seen a Servus salesman for five years!"

Cappy gave his salespeople cross sections of boots to show customers the superiority of Servus's boots. He appealed to customers' patriotism, pointing out that his sixty-year-old company was struggling to survive with 350 people eking out a living on $6 an hour. And besides, Servus promised delivery within seventy-two hours rather than the nine months often required for Korean boots.

He pushed into specific market niches using superior quality as the flagship. In the fire boot market, for instance, Cappy relined the boot with Kevlar-Nomex—a superior fire retardant—and doubled his advertising in such trade magazines as *Fire Chief* and *Fire House.* He raised his prices 15 percent and sold 30 percent more. He used the same approach in the dielectrics market (boots for electric utility workers). Competitors were selling boots that withstood 14,000 volts. Servus developed boots that could withstand 20,000 volts. He's selling ten thousand more pairs a year now, all through direct mail.

Resurrecting a previous strength also works. In 1986 Servus sold $20 million with "substantial pretax earnings."[14]

Internal departments also have strengths upon which to base new strategies. Sia Amoala was the manager for a fiscal control office in a county government. She relied upon the strengths of her department in building a new strategy.

> Sia's eighteen accountants and clerks tracked the fiscal activities for a social services department in a local government. The department was known for accurate work.
>
> The local government installed a new computerized control system. It required the decentralization of much of the local government's accounting function to departmental fiscal groups like Sia's.
>
> This new system required considerable change for Sia's department. To plan that change, she built upon her department's strength of accuracy and the pride in that accuracy. She held several meetings with her people to review the new system. At these meetings she stressed the need to maintain their level of accuracy. She consistently asked, "How can we work with this system so we can maintain our high standards?"
>
> Sia also recruited several internal users/customers to work with her group in determining new procedures. She developed a customer-focused organization where individuals were assigned to work with specific end users. The flexibility in the new system permitted this new strategy.
>
> Several months after the system installation, Sia's group received a governmental "E" for excellence award. She said, "It was difficult making this change. Virtually everything everyone did changed to some extent. But as long as we kept our focus on doing it accurately, everyone cooperated to make it work."

Personal Workshop

As you ponder how to lead from your strengths, please consider the following questions.

1. What are your strengths?

Who are your principal competitors? (Even internal departments have competitors, such as other uses of resources.) How do you measure up to them?

2. What drives your users'/customers' purchasing decisions?

Why do people buy from you rather than your competitor? Why do people buy from your competitor rather than from you?

3. How can you match your strengths to what drives your customers' purchasing decisions?

Follow your customer, channel, or production process. "Do what's familiar" is the best way to summarize this guideline. Most people cannot manage just any business. The more familiar the activity, the more likely the successful execution.

Sell new products to old customers, for instance. Black & Decker is looking to do just that. CEO and chairman, president Nolan Archibald's flood of new products for the industrial professional tool market has competitors reeling. He's moving his company—long known for standard tools—into high-tech new applications, such as cordless power tools. Building on his consumer franchise, he's expanded into household appliances. He bought a losing GE small appliance division, spruced it up with new products, and turned it into a big money maker. His favorite saying is, "There are no mature markets; only mature managements"—and they don't work at Black & Decker.[15]

Paul Hube, CEO of a small ($35 million) U.S. computer graphics company, recognized the need to move closer to his customers. Here's how he did it.

> Paul saw the computer graphics business changing from the sale of specialized hardware boxes to software application on specialized chips. As this occurred he anticipated that prices would fall precipitously and foresaw the real value-added shift from hardware to systems solutions. When that happened Paul saw the end of his hardware-focused business.
>
> His first move was to explore linkages with several software and systems houses. He wanted his firm to supply the hardware and got his partner to supply the supporting software applications. He then bought the VLSI technology license and hired two custom chip designers to put the software on a chip. Although it's still too early to tell the final outcome, at least Paul's company is still around.

Jose Alvaradez managed a small highway maintenance group in a municipal government. He worked out a way to "sell" new products to old "customers" and give his people a big boost in the process.

> Jose's eighteen-person crew maintained the streets in the summertime and cleared the snow in the winter for a small city in northeast America. He was proud of his people. They were proud of their work. The department enjoyed considerable stature in the community.
>
> Jose felt that his group could do more for the city. There were a number of days when his people had little to do. So they spent that time maintaining their vehicles. That gave Jose an idea. Why not also maintain the other city vehicles?
>
> Jose asked his group how they felt about taking on this new assignment. They were enthusiastic, but they raised the question of additional compensation. Jose talked to the city manager, who was supportive. They talked informally to several city council members. They agreed.
>
> Jose and his people put together a proposal. Initially they would do all the preventative maintenance on city vehicles—because that could be scheduled in advance and did not have a time pressure factor. For that his people would receive an extra payment per vehicle serviced.
>
> The preventative maintenance program worked so well that within a year Jose set up a maintenance section to perform all maintenance activities for city vehicles. His people earned more money. They loved the challenge and variety of the new activity. And Jose earned a bonus—the first one ever awarded by the city.
>
> All this for "selling" new products to old "customers."

Sometimes you must sell new products to old customers if you want to keep them as customers at all. Ask United Parcel Service. One thing about "Big Brown," it has a lot of "old" customers. More than 47,000 trucks handle more than nine million packages a day for more than 850,000 customers—mostly businesses. Beginning as a messenger service eighty years ago in Seattle, United Parcel has grown to be the most profitable U.S. transportation company, earning more than $700 million on revenues of $10 billion. It also consistently finishes at the top of *Fortune*'s corporate reputation survey in its industry.

Five years ago UPS decided to challenge Federal Express in the air express market. Federal owns a dominant 57 percent of the market share. But UPS figured they couldn't afford to let their current ground transportation customers go elsewhere for their air parcel service without running the risk of losing the customers altogether. So "Big Brown" took on the leader. They entered the business and held air rates steady during the past six years, becoming the low-priced supplier in the market (thus validating their advertising claim that they "run the tightest ship in the shipping business"). They also purchased two software firms and are in the process of rolling out hand-held on-board computers to go one up on Federal's technology. They've already won a 15 percent market share—and they've only just begun to fight. UPS knows that you have to sell new products to current customers—particularly if you want to keep your current customers as future customers.[16]

Often you can use technology to sell new products to old customers. McKesson Corporation is doing that—very successfully. McKesson started life as a liquor distributor. When Prohibition hit, McKesson migrated into the wholesaling of nondrug items for independent pharmacies. As that business withered under pressure from the drug chains, McKesson knew they had to find something else. Using their information technology skill, they offered drugstores computerized ordering, pricing, financial management, and insurance claim processing. Since introduction in 1976, sales to drugstores rose from $900 million to $5-plus billion.

McKesson now sees another new field to enter with its information technology services—providing independent grocery stores with its unique computerized service merchandising. It's just a short walk down the strategy street from the independent drugstore to the independent supermarket. They carry much the same line of products—health and beauty aids. They face much the same competitive environment—big chains that can outbuy and outprice them. In 1988 McKesson generated $670 million in revenue in this new field—and it's even more profitable than its old drugstore business.[17] Which leads us to the next point.

Sell old products to new customers. Avery International, makers of pressure-sensitive labels, do just that. Chairman and CEO Charles Miller now sells gobs of self-sticking labels for computer printers and copy machines. They recently sold GM and Chrysler a labeling system to monitor auto parts. The new customers for Avery's old products are virtually limitless. Miller says, "We could be in any manufacturing operation that has inventory control or product identification problems." That's a lot of new customers for Avery's old product.[18]

Jose, mentioned in the previous example, wanted to offer vehicle maintenance services to private parties. That's old products for new customers. But the city council turned him down. That would be competing with private enterprise, they said. Someone's probably doing it, though.

U.K.'s Lucas Industries refocused its efforts on international customers in order to return to profitability. The $3.5 billion company sold off marginally profitable U.K.-focused divisions in auto starters, alternators, and lights. Instead, they took their long-established brakes and specialized aerospace components products into the international markets. The results: a $200 million profit in 1987.[19]

Many internal staff departments look to offer old products or services to new customers. The training and development department, for instance, often seeks new internal department clients for its professional services. Similarly, the management information systems department, accounting department, and human resources department all seek to provide services to an ever-expanding internal customer universe.

How about *new customers for new products?* The U.S. company Sun Microsystems thrives on this strategic guideline. They've gone from nothing to $1 billion plus in less than six years. Sun counts on a blizzard of new products for new customers to maintain its position as a leader in the workstation market. Building from the technical workstation base, using off-the-shelf hardware and software, Sun broadened up to minicomputers with multiworkstations, even farther up to minisupercomputers, and down to powerful PCs that approach workstation capability. These new products look to broaden Sun's customer list from its current technical and engineering base.[20]

Pall Corporation is another believer in finding new products for new customers. Pall is the world leader in fine filters. It designs and manufactures filters that perform some of the most critical tasks for customers. From aircraft jet filters to filters for semiconductor production, Pall is the expert in fluid purity. Following the trail left by technology, Pall engineers continually seek new customers for their filtering applications. An 18 percent compound growth rate in sales and a 37 percent growth in profits—over the past seventeen years—demonstrates the success of this strategy.[21]

Whatever you do, *stay close to your current distribution channels.* Borden has discovered how to boost earnings and returns by pushing new products through the same distribution channel. Borden's bought many regional brands in pasta and snack foods and built sales by adding other Borden products to the line. In Chicago one of their purchases held a leading position distributing potato chips but lagged in the cheese puff market. So Borden added its Wise's Cheez Doodles to the truck and boosted sales 22 percent and profit margins by 2.5 percent.

By sticking to its distribution channels, Borden can take advantage of economies of scale in its pasta business. To keep its fourteen U.S. plants running twenty-four hours a day, seven days a week, they buy 800 million pounds of durum wheat a year. That gives them the advantage of quantity discounts. In addition, its multiple plants enable Borden to avoid costly shutdowns to switch over to specialty pastas. They just dedicate several plants to make them full time. This specialization enables Borden to own 31 percent of the pasta market, the largest single share in a generally fractionated market.[22]

Mr. Richard Mohn understands about staying close to your distribution channel. That's how he's built the largest and least-known media empire, Bertelsmann. His company generates Dm 10.5 billion ($6.3 billion) in annual sales and has operations in 43 countries. But, because he doesn't operate newspapers or television stations he's not as well known as smaller Murdock, Maxwell, or Springer.

Mohn began in print media (books and magazines) distributed through retail bookstores. His companies distribute thirty-seven magazines in five countries including *Stern* and *Brigitte* in Germany, *Best* and *Puma* in the U.K., *Parents* in the U.S., and *Femme Actuelle* in France—all 1 million or more sellers. Following his channel, Mohn began distributing book and record club memberships through retail stores. Many operators sold these clubs, mostly through expensive and chancy direct mail. By going through retail stores Mohn limited his marketing costs and greatly improved his penetration. Today, these clubs generate more than half of the group's sales and the largest piece of the profits. Stick to who knows you to maximize your returns and limit your risks.[23]

Regardless, the right new tomorrow involves sticking to what's familiar—either current customers, current products, current production processes, or current distribution channels.

Personal Workshop

As you decide how to build on what's familiar, please ponder these questions.

1. What other products/services that I can produce will my customers/end users want?

2. What other customers/end users might want the products/services I currently produce?

3. What new customers/end users might there be for new products/services I can produce and distribute?

A little bit ahead. Woody Allen—that famous management philosopher—summed up how early you want to be. "Fifteen minutes," he said. "Take a movie, for instance. If you get there one hour ahead of time, no one knows where to put you—you're in the middle of the previous show. Come ten minutes late and they won't seat you. Be fifteen minutes early and you have time to get popcorn and your choice of seats."

It's also true for your new tomorrow. You want to be just ahead of the crowd. Not so far ahead that you're "far out"—or so behind that you look "me tooish." Xerox developed the computer mouse—fifteen years too soon. It sat on the shelf waiting for a market. Apple took it and made it immensely popular.

Sony masters the art of being just a little bit ahead. Take the Walkman product. After it was introduced in July 1979, Sony changed the product over one hundred times to stay ahead of the clones. They introduced smaller versions, solar-powered versions, water-resistant versions, attachable-to-sweatband versions, playback-only versions—models to fit every pocket, use, and taste. By staying a little bit ahead, Sony continues to dominate the personal tape player market with over 30 percent of the world market.[24]

Edwin Land, founder of Polaroid, knows the importance of being a little bit ahead and not a little bit behind. Land pushed Polavision to compete against videotape. By the time it came out in 1977, videotape was already well established. Though Polavision was technically superior, it couldn't make up the lost ground. Polaroid ate $68.5 million in loss in 1979 to fold the project. But the Spectra story is different. With Spectra Polaroid delivers 35-mm-quality pictures instantly. Spectra is just enough ahead of the market. Polaroid sold more than six hundred thousand in 1986, and it contributed to record earnings in that and subsequent years.[25]

Kennametal pulled a little bit ahead of its competitors in quality and doubled market share as a result. Kennametal produces carbide tools. CEO and chairman, president Quentin McKenna decided to guarantee all Kennametal tools to be perfect on delivery. Even though fewer than 2 percent of the delivered tools had difficulty, McKenna felt that the guarantee would give him a little edge in the market. It cost more to produce the tools, and the extra inspection added additional cost—all of which was recovered by the profits generated by increased sales within the first year.[26] It pays to be a little bit ahead of the competition.

Personal Workshop

As you contemplate how to be a little bit ahead, please consider these questions.

1. How can you gain a small advantage?

new product design?

new cost reductions?

new quality improvements?

new customer service improvements?

These are fundamental guidelines. Here's several specific strategies for you to consider in creating that new tomorrow.

SPECIFIC STRATEGIES

Nichemanship. "Hit 'em where they ain't," was Wee Willie Keeler's motto. He did that through a very successful baseball career. The motto of a successful niche player might be, "Hit 'em where the big boys aren't, and the big money is."

Find the crack—the crevice—that piece of unfulfilled demand. That's what successful niche players do. In the United States, president and CEO John Burns did that when he bought Conoco Oil's losing chemical division from new parent Du Pont for $507 million in a leveraged buyout.

Renaming it Vista Chemical, he set out to find profitable niches. He's shifted the emphasis from low-margin, high-volume products to higher-margin specialty products using the same compound. In the surfactant alcohol business (the basic ingredient in liquid cleaners), for instance, Vista continues to supply large-volume purchasers like Lever Brothers and Procter & Gamble. Vista sells a variant of the compound to a growing number of specialized users, like Helene Curtis, who are willing to pay higher prices for higher quality and more service. Burns has been successful in taking basic commodity products and finding upscale, higher-margin applications. Operating income increased five times since he's taken over in 1982.[27] Burns shows us one way to play the niche game—*find niche applications for commodity compounds.*

You can't find a more "commodity" product than food super-marketing. Yet Vons Supermarket has moved from number four to number one in southern California's tough food market by finding and servicing specific niches. Take the Fresno store in a poor Spanish-speaking neighborhood. It was built thirty years ago—and showed its age. To appeal to its new customers, Vons added new lighting, new displays, and a black-and-red color scheme. Out went 5,000 items, including egg noodles, Chinese foods, and Pepperidge Farm bread (all "yuppie" foods). In came 2,500 items, including inexpensive ice-cream novelties, sharper-seasoned soups, and Mexican cookies. Sales rose 25 percent and profits rose 52 percent. Vons surveys its neighborhoods and customers in the stores and uses computer-generated sales and inventory data to "understand the customer," according to chairman Roger

Strangeland. Using this customer information, Vons sells more than $700 per square foot per year, almost double the industry average of $440.[28] That's another way to be a successful niche player—*stay close and responsive to your customer.*

The metal bending and textile industries are two candidates for early burial. But several niche players survive, usually by following the "avoid the big guys and move fast" strategy. Take Phillips Industries, for instance, which produces a wide range of metal bending products like whirlpool tubs, recreational vehicle windows, and aluminum wheel covers. None of these products, in and of themselves, is large enough to attract big competitors. So Phillips has the small market all to itself. They've got enough of these small markets to sell $538 million last year and show 25-plus percent ROE (return on equity) over the past three years.[29] Not bad in a dull business. Whatever your niche, be certain that you *dominate it.*

Other firms in the metal bending industry show how to be successful niche players in the international market. Take Zero Corporation, for instance. They produce a wide range of products ranging from cooling equipment for supercomputers to frames for disk drives to housings for Stinger missiles. Zero is a specialist in customized products for more than seventeen thousand companies around the world. Woody Godbold, Zero's president and CEO, uses two principles to govern Zero's success. First, he stays away from large customers and large production runs. No single customer represents more than 3 percent of Zero's sales volume, so the company is immune to price pressure. Second, by supplying customized solutions to customers' problems, Zero earns 9–10 percent return, rather than the 3 percent most metal fabricators eke out.[30] Zero shows us another rule for success in the niche game—*minimize your dependence upon any one customer or product.*

If metal bending is a tough industry, textiles is an absolute disaster. Yet Guilford Mills survives and prospers in the lightweight nylon for lingerie business. How, in the face of awesome foreign competition? It's obvious! Pick a niche in which low-cost labor doesn't count and where you can move faster than your competition. CEO and chairman Charles Hayes focuses Guilford's efforts on the dyeing and finishing niche. He produces nylon knit fabrics that look like flannel, velvet, or suede for dressmakers and bathing suit manufacturers. As a niche player in a decimated industry, he survives by avoiding competition and being fast on his corporate feet.[31] Guilford's advice: *Stay away from the big boys.*

In the U.K., computer maker ICL has learned the same lesson. Bruised from battle with mainframe makers IBM and DEC, the company almost went bankrupt in the early 1980s. To survive, chairman Peter Bonfield shifted ICL's focus to systems integration software and services for niche markets where the big boys don't play, such as point-of-sale equipment for retailers. During the past three years profits rose to more than $200 million.[32]

Borden shows us how you can take a commodity product—milk—and *use advertising* to create a differentiated high-end niche. Milk is milk is milk, right? Wrong. Borden consistently charges a dollar a gallon premium to take home Elsie's shining face. How do they get it? Borden advertises heavily on radio, painting itself as the local dairy farmer delivering fresh "this morning milk" direct to you. The stress on quality—the "Borden difference"—reinforces hometown, old-fashioned values. Milk may be milk may be milk, but Borden's milk is significantly more profitable.[33]

Sleeping with a bear can be dangerous. But when the bear owns your end user market, what choice do you have? IBM's put more companies in business and then out of business again than any other company in the computer business. Through the ups and downs, and for a remarkably long time, Memorex Telex Corporation survived sleeping with the bear. President and CEO George Bragg's secret? Stick to his niche, supplying IBM-compatible 3270 terminals for airlines and travel agents, *introduce extra functions more quickly* than the big bear, and provide high-quality, customer-responsive service.[34]

Even in the highly competitive computer systems business—where even mighty IBM has taken its lumps—niche players can successfully carve out a profitable business. Point 4 Data Corporation manufactures multiprocessor systems—in the $50,000 to $100,000 range. It either sells them to high-tech middlemen, who add peripherals and resell them into such vertical markets as hospitals and hotels, or it builds individual systems to the specifications of individual customers. Both markets require a high degree of cooperation and communication between Point 4 and its customers. Their Los Angeles location gives them a time and closeness advantage that cheaper Asian competitors find impossible to match.[35] Being *fast on your feet and close to your customer* secures a competitive advantage.

In the United States, ADP is an expert at turning itself inside out to meet changing conditions in niche markets. In the early 1980s the growing network of PCs threatened its mainstream payroll processing business. ADP responded by making it possible for its clients to send payroll data over personal computers. This secured ADP's position as the payroll processor and raised margins in its payroll processing niche to its highest levels.

Now, its 40 percent market share in providing information services to Wall Street brokerage houses is being threatened. And ADP is responding with its usual speed and flexibility. They've built an entire sales and marketing system for retail brokers around IBM's new PS/2 machines. Their $15 million proprietary software system allows brokers to call for up-to-the-minute news and quotes and the current status of the client's account. ADP's deals with Merrill Lynch and Shearson Lehman Hutton assure them of a dominant position in this niche as well.

In addition, as their mainstream business has matured, ADP has pushed into other niche markets. For example, their service that estimates damage costs in auto collisions for insurance companies now generates $75 million in revenue at a 22 percent margin.[36]

ADP demonstrates that you can protect several different niches—all by being *fast and flexible on your corporate feet.*

Use technology to give you flexibility. Honda did in its famous H-Y war during the early 1980s. Yamaha initiated the war by building the largest motorcycle manufacturing plant in the world. Honda responded with *"Yamaha wo tsubusu!"* ("We will crush, squash, slaughter Yamaha!") In the next eighteen months Honda put 113 new models on the street, effectively turning over its product line twice. Yamaha managed only a quarter of that. Furthermore, Honda turned motorcycling into a fashion activity and introduced a blizzard of new technology that left Yamaha "eating its dust." Honda's manufacturing flexibility gave it the upper hand. Yamaha called off the war.[37]

Atlas Door also used flexibility to gain the number-one position in its industry—after only ten years in business. Historically it takes four months to deliver a custom door. Atlas cut that to two weeks.

They built just-in-time factories, automated order entry, and tightly controlled logistics. The result: growth at a compound annual rate of 15 percent—triple the industry average—and return on sales of 20 percent—five times the industry average.[38] *Flexibility* pays.

But you've got to *stay nimble.* Taking your eye off the ball can lead to disastrous results. Ask Leon Levine, chairman, CEO, and treasurer of Family Dollar Stores in the U.S.: he's an expert, unfortunately. Family Dollar had a good niche strategy. Convenient locations and weekly loss-leader specials on shirts and shoes, which offset higher margins on automotive supplies and health/beauty items, helped to create the discount image. Family Dollar owned the small-town retailing business and showed 6.9 percent net margins—double the industry average. But then management took its eye off the discounting ball. Prices began to creep up, until they were almost 10 percent higher than competitor Wal-Mart. Management was preoccupied with expansion, and no one was minding the store. Family Dollar finally woke up and has launched a new campaign—"We will not be undersold."[39] But customers once lost are hard to get back. One mistake in this niche business could be your last.

There you have it: the basic niche players' strategies—avoid the big boys, be flexible, dominate your niche, find upscale applications for commodity products, create niches through advertising, stay close to your customer, avoid dependence upon a few products and/or customers, and stay alert.

Personal Workshop

As you consider how to find and play the niches, please ponder these questions.

1. What upscale applications might there be for my products/services?

2. How can I meet customer/end user needs not now being met?

3. How can I set up my organization so that I can move faster?

Focus. It's an old saw—validated by modern corporate history—"Jack of all trades, master of none." In the fat 1960s and 1970s, U.S. companies grew—and grew—and grew. The management philosophy then was, "A good manager can manage anything"—and many tried to manage everything. As long as earnings per share grew, everyone—shareholders, employees, managers—were happy. But then, unfortunately, reality struck. Inflation cooled, and with it the "automatic" earnings per share increases. The returns from many of the diversifications proved disappointing. And all the while that management was so involved in diversifying their core business withered on the vine. The list of blurred focus companies reads like the *Fortune* 500 list.

No more. The T. Boone Pickens, Sir James Goldsmiths, Carl Icahns, and Sam Heymans of the world forced every CEO to look hard at their companies and restructure them—before someone else did it. Focus is the single biggest benefit of restructuring. Getting back to basics.

The tire industry looks like one of your casualties of change. During the past several years, tire companies closed down more than 40 percent of the industry capacity. No one's done well—except Cooper Tire. In an industry beset with competitive pressures, Cooper shows a 19-plus percent return (twice the industry average) and 40 percent capacity increases. How do they do it? Focus, focus, focus. While other tire companies diversified into broadcasting, car repairs, and blimps, Cooper just made tires. Cooper focuses still further on the secondary market and private labels such as Atlas, Hercules, and Dean. Not much pizzazz to the company, just money.[40]

Goodyear—the major player in the tire business—learned the focus lesson from Sir Jimmy Goldsmith. He forced Goodyear to get rid of the distractions such as aerospace and energy and focus back on its core tire business. James Bailey, president of North American tire operations, says, "The trick . . . is to try to decommoditize the product." Goodyear's Eagle tires are an excellent example of "decommoditizing." The company created a new product niche—tires built for speed and performance rather than long life. They sell for more, last less time, and have a 50 percent higher margin. And the good news is, they constitute 25 percent of Goodyear's sales. Results have never been better. Profit on operations is up 47 percent in 1987. Focus pays.[41]

Focus works because it forces you to ask the hard questions about your business. James Koch is an ex-strategic planner and Harvard graduate. He learned about the importance of focus when he started his business—the Boston Beer Company. In the beginning, Jim spent a lot of time searching for the "essentials" of a good business—computer systems, location, and office furniture. Then his uncle, a partner at Goldman, Sachs, urged him to focus on first things first. He said, "I've seen a lot more businesses go broke because they didn't have enough sales than I've seen go under from lack of computers. Go find a customer—and then another—and then another."[42] Focus forces you to do first things first—a very valuable discipline when you're inundated with myriad "important" details.

David Alliance understands the importance of focus. He came to the U.K. as a teenager with no money. He didn't even speak the language. Today, thirty-five years later, he runs the U.K.£ 1.75 billion Coats Viyella textile company with operations in over thirty countries. It's the largest textile group in Europe and the most profitable in the world. David's secret: focus on the customer. He began his odyssey by buying the agency network system of J. D. Williams Wonderworld. When he went to visit his new agents the doors were slammed in his face. So to find out what customers wanted he took a briefcase and airmail letter to show he was a foreigner and talked to customers directly. Armed with that knowledge he bought the main direct sales operations of J. D. Williams, invested in carefully targeted advertising, and built the business from a turnover of UK£ 2 million to UK£ 100 million in 1988. When he bought Carrington Viyella in 1982 he told his managers to forget about the banks and focus instead on the customers. Within two years turnover rose from UK£ 103 million to UK£ 385 million and rose further during the next two years to UK£ 675 million. Focusing on the customer really pays, even in the cutthroat textile business.[43]

But be careful. It's easy to lose your focus. That's what happened to Winn Dixie. Winn Dixie used to be the class act of the southern grocery chains in the U.S. They regularly showed margins of 1.6 percent of sales—the best in the industry. Dividends increased consistently for forty-four consecutive years and were so certain that they were paid monthly.

No more, though! Stiff competition from national chains like Kroger and Albertson and regionals like Bruno's and Food Lion caused Winn Dixie management to take their eye off their ball.

They chose to compete on price—not service and merchandising—and saw margins fall to 1.3 percent (about the industry average). They've recently reorganized—put new management in place—and set out to buff up their image. In the tough supermarket business—or any business, for that matter—losing one's focus is dangerous to one's continued survival,[44] no matter how big you are!

Efficiency. Cut! Cut! Cut! Relentless cost pressure exists in all industries, at all levels. No one is immune. There's no place for a high-cost producer to hide. Cut people, cut management layers, close marginal plants, close low-producing offices, cut "nice but not essential" services. All these and more have been used to gain efficiency. But these are short-term Band-Aids. Anyone can bump the bottom line by reducing costs. The secret to long-term success is improving long-term efficiency—and short-term bloodletting only weakens the organization. Here's some long-term ways to improve efficiency.

President Charles Russell of Visa USA, Inc. (the large credit card processor) is waging war—on costs. His strategy in the U.S. to beat out rival MasterCard, American Express, and Sears? Become the low-cost provider of electronic transactions. How? He's invested more than $20 million to improved computer facilities and is dealing to get a piece of large transaction businesses (such as point of sale networks), which reduce his costs per transaction even further. With U.S. retailers—Sears and Penney—and large U.S. banks—Citibank—along with a prosperous and aggressive American Express, challenging for the business, only the most efficient will survive. Russell wants to be sure Visa is a survivor when the war is over, and he's using *automation/computerization* as his principal weapon.[45]

Caterpillar follows the same trail. In 1982 Caterpillar fell into a pit of red ink. Before it was over the venerable producer of world-class earth-moving equipment had spilled $953 million and lost 11 percent in market share to the Japanese. But Cat is back—with a vengeance—powered by massive investment in "peewaf"—the plant with a future. The plan was begun in 1985, and $1.2 billion later Cat reported $623 million profit on $10.0 billion in sales and a market share gain of 9 percent.[46]

Sam Walton and his Wal-Mart stores are the success story of the 1980s. The richest man in America, "down home" Sam is an American folk hero. Sam mixes old-fashioned customer service values with newfangled electronics to keep the goods moving quickly within his empire. He's got a satellite system that links each store with headquarters and ten giant regional warehouses. Sam knows every day what's sold, where, and for how much. He keeps his shelves stocked with fast-moving items that can be replenished in less than a day. His electronic state-of-the-art distribution network enables Sam to move fast and efficiently. Sam likes that— service with frugality. He preaches frugality on a par with customer service. He sets the tone with his executive office—which is decorated in "latter-day bus station," right down to the plastic seats. Wal-Mart earned the best return of any retailer in America over this past decade. Service at a low cost—can't beat the combination. Sam's using *advanced distribution technology* to gain his edge.[47]

The American appliance industry is the model of low-cost efficiency. How did they win the low-cost battle? By investing in *product redesign, automated equipment, training, and quality.* Take GE's dishwasher plant at Lexington, Kentucky. GE first redesigned its product incorporating a hard plastic tub with a ten-year warranty. GE then invested over $150 million in automated equipment. Then they restrained all workers in new teamwork activities and in quality control. The result? Reject rates fell 80 percent, reducing costs by 35 percent, allowing GE to offer longer warranty periods and more features at the same (or lower) costs to the consumer. That's an integrated way to wage war on costs and win the competitive battle.[48]

The *boss needs to lead the efficiency crusade.* Take H. J. Heinz chairman Anthony J. F. O'Reilly, for instance. He's constantly urging his people to cut costs. Sometimes it's in little things, like not putting the back label on ketchup bottles, which saved $4 million. He's actively improving efficiency, closing sixteen plants and spending more than $1 billion to upgrade those remaining. His aim is to be the low-cost supplier in the many niches he serves. He also sets the efficiency tone by keeping a lean corporate staff of sixty persons to run his $4.8 billion empire.[49] When the boss leads, the troops inevitably follow.

Several British firms are using *organizational mechanisms* to gain efficiency. Chris Lewinton, chief executive of TI Group PLC, a metal manufacturer from Birmingham in the U.K., broke up his company into several independent minibusinesses, each with its own profit responsibility. As a result, TI's corporate staff all but disappeared. Each of the minibusinesses also runs with lean staffs. One £160,000,000 engineering group runs with five corporate staff members, including the president of the group.

Lucas Industries, another Birmingham resident, similarly decentralizes its operations into small, market-oriented groups with profit responsibility. Several of these groups are in the United States, as Lucas along with many other U.K. firms have been taking advantage of the low dollar. Keeping staffs slim and organizationally focused on a specific group of customers often works to stimulate efficiency.[50]

Efficiency is the key to survival. There's no room for high-cost producers in the global competitive economy. Invest in automated equipment, install state-of-the-art distribution systems, redesign products to make them simpler to produce, reduce management layers, organizationally focus smaller groups of dedicated people with profit responsibility, and train workers in improving quality. These are positive ways to create the "right" new tomorrow, rather than short-term hits to the balance sheet.

Personal Workshop

As you consider how to improve long-term efficiency, please consider the following questions.

1. How can I redesign my products/services to reduce costs?

2. How can I use automated equipment to reduce costs in manufacturing, distribution, service?

3. How can I improve the quality of my products/services? Training employees? Redesigning production processes?

Customer service. In its February 2, 1987, issue, *Time* magazine's headline story was entitled, "Pul-eeze! Will Somebody Help Me? Frustrated American Consumers Wonder Where the Service Went." *Fortune* magazine's headline story in its March 13, 1989, edition was entitled, "Getting Customers to Love You." Had there been a change of heart in American business during that twenty-two-month stretch? Hardly. Had service levels improved? A little. But not enough to make a difference.

The message from the Profit Impact of Market Strategy (PIMS) data base is very clear: Customer service is a big factor in long-term market success for most products. Most Western firms have yet to get the message. Regardless of your business, improving customer service needs to be one of your key strategies for your new tomorrow.

Begin by *recruiting meticulously.* "Garbage in—garbage out" applies to the people in your organization as well as data. You're a ten. If you hire nines, and the nines hire eights, and the eights hire sevens, you soon wind up with an organization filled with ones. And ones do not generate consistent high performance. Singapore Airlines hires fewer than 3 percent of those who apply for its flight attendant positions. They "hire smiles." They've discovered that they can teach people to serve meals on planes, but they can't teach people to really like to serve people. So they hire smiles. By the way, Singapore Airlines was chosen "Airline of the Year" by *Executive Traveller* magazine in both 1987 and 1988 by its passengers.[51] Hiring smiles pays.

Next, *train extensively.* Merck, the powerhouse pharmaceutical firm with the amazing 30-plus percent return on shareholder equity, spends more than thirteen weeks training its detail people—before they send them out to talk to doctors. British Airways—which used to be known by its initials (BA) as "bloody awful"—sent all of its staff to a training program called "Putting People First." In that program employees took the place of customers. They were asked to experience having meals dumped in front of them, as happens on most planes; asking for service and being ignored, which also happens on most planes; and being told repeatedly, "It's not my fault. It's just company policy," which also happens a lot everywhere. Afterward, participants were asked what they could change. They made an action list of things to change—and then went to work on changing those things. Did it work? Passenger satisfaction rating rose dramatically—as did the bottom line. In fact, British Airways today has one of the highest revenue-per-passenger factors—$266—of any international airline.[52]

Next, *measure it continuously*. American Express is an expert in measuring service levels. American Express publishes a service tracking report each month that tracks over two hundred measures of customer service, including the following:

1. Time for new card processing (less than fifteen days is the standard);

2. Time to replace lost card (less than one day is the standard);

3. Completely accurate statements (currently run at 98-plus percent);

4. Statement out by due date (currently 99-plus percent);

5. Number of bad credits approved.[53]

Another very successful software and services organization establishes customer service standards in conjunction with its customers. Specific groups meet with their customers—both internal and external—every six months and establish standards. Depending upon the group, these measures are reported no less frequently than weekly and in some cases daily.

1. Time for new order processing (less than twenty-four hours is the standard);

2. Number of on-time installs/shipments (100 percent is the standard—currently at 98.9 percent);

3. Accurate maintenance and time charge statements (100 percent is the standard—currently at 98-plus percent);

4. Statement out by due date (100 percent is the standard—currently 99-plus percent);

5. Number of telephone rings before answer (less than four is the standard);

6. Time to handle customer call at help desk (less than four minutes is the standard);

7. Waiting or blank time during call (less than thirty seconds is the standard);

8. Number of callbacks after install (zero is the standard—currently less than one/install);

9. Number of customer complaints (zero is the standard—currently less than six/month);

10. Customer evaluation of service (8 on a scale of 1–10 is the standard—every customer surveyed every month—currently company average is 9.1).

Don't measure it, and your people know that you're not serious about delivering it.

Next, *use technology* to build it in. Genuine Parts Company in the U.S. makes a good living out of knowing such obscure facts as how many four-year-old Buicks there are in Topeka, Kansas, or eight-year-old Fords in Culver City, California. Genuine provides this information through its computerized data base so dealers know how many replacement parts to order. That knowledge, along with myriad other business facts, helps Genuine dealers do a better job of managing their businesses. Since Genuine's success varies directly with that of their dealers, it's not hard to see why Genuine has increased sales and earnings during the past six years of 33 percent and 36 percent respectively.[54]

Lastly, *reward it richly*. One specialty chemical company I know works hard to recognize its top-service performers. Whenever the company receives a letter praising an employee, a copy of that letter along with the employee's picture is sent to all customers. In a recent typical month 278 employees had their pictures published in the newsletter—out of 396 total employment. Rewards needn't be expensive—just visible.

Customer service is the undeniable competitive edge. Include it as a central feature of any new tomorrow you create.

You need to change. There's no doubt about it. Current products, services, and strategies get "old" very soon. You need a new strategy to create the "right" new tomorrow. But any old strategy won't do. It's got to be the "right" new strategy. The "right" strategy is one that distinguishes you from your competition. Your customers need to see your product/service as better than the others.

The first step in that new tomorrow: Create a new strategy—a general direction to your efforts. Build your strategy by leading from strength, doing what's familiar, and being a little bit ahead. Find a niche and dominate it. Be willing to find new niches quickly, as conditions change. Focus on a few niches. Stay away from dangerous diversification. Build long-term efficiency. Generate high levels of customer service.

Learn from the Benetton family—Luciano, Guiliana, Gilberto, and Carlo. They run one of the success stories of the 1980s, the Benetton Textile Company—one of the world's largest clothing manufacturers and the world's largest consumer of virgin wool. Their numbers are impressive. They supply the more than 4,500 Benetton stores from plants in Spain, Italy, Scotland, and the United States. The business generates $2 billion in revenue with an incredible 10.5 percent margin.

The family focuses on the brightly colored sweater and knitwear niche. Early in their development they learned to produce sweaters in unbleached off white and then dye them to meet customer demand. This enabled them to deliver the precise colors that were selling in each store within forty-eight hours, thus assuring that no store lost sales due to missing inventory.

Early on, the family also learned to tap the entrepreneurial spirits of others. Laborious hand work was contracted out to more than 450 entrepreneurs, thus saving the family investment money. Stores were set up by special franchising agents—more than seventy-five in number—who find new locations and retailer-franchisees. Benetton sets up several stores in contiguous geographic areas—seeking to dominate their niche in that area.

Benetton uses computerization to get rapid feedback on what's selling, so they can rapidly supply the shifting market demands. They also use computer-aided design and cutting to gain efficiency in the production process. Their CAD facility can design in 256 colors—and cut pieces at the rate of fifteen thousand every eight hours. Their automated warehouse handles up to twenty thousand pieces a day with a handful of technicians.

Benetton has recently expanded its line to include jackets, blazers, and coats—and the fabrics have expanded to include cotton and denim. Selling more to the same customer. The Benetton family demonstrates how to weave these many strategies together to make a successful competitive enterprise.[55]

These are simple, straightforward strategies. What I've said here is not intended to replace strategic planning processes or strategic planning models. Rather, think about these strategies and strategic principles when you plan the new tomorrow for your organization. Make certain it's the "right" new tomorrow.

Strategies are essential—but not enough to create that new tomorrow. You need people and resources to make the strategies work. Let's look at these next.

5

Focus Resources

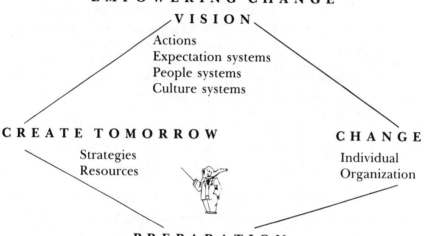

EMPOWERING CHANGE
VISION
Actions
Expectation systems
People systems
Culture systems

CREATE TOMORROW
Strategies
Resources

CHANGE
Individual
Organization

PREPARATION
Getting ready
Anticipating obstacles

"Plans are nice . . . but money talks," a consultant friend of mine once said. How right she is. Talk is cheap. Lots of organizations are long on talk. But show me your budget—how you spend your discretionary money—and I'll show you your real priorities. Who are your "hot shot" people, and where are they working? That's also your real priority. Regardless of the intentions expressed in the strategic plan, where you put your key people and money is the direction in which your organization is going to move. Back your new tomorrow with money and people—or else it will be consigned to the shredder.

Invest your resources in your new tomorrow. Get the best people. Get them in your key areas—marketing, operations, personnel, engineering. Free them up from other "pressing" responsibilities and focus them on creating the new tomorrow. Get them the resources they need: budget, facilities, staff. Free up these resources by downsizing, refocusing, and improved productivity.

It's a big job, one not to be taken lightly. Knowing what to do (the strategy) and having the resources to do it are different. How can you do it—get the people and resources? Read on.

I'll show you in the following pages how to identify the key leverage positions; fill those key positions with the best people—both internally and externally; get the budgetary resources you need by refocusing, downsizing, and boosting productivity. You won't get a financial treatise or detailed financial analysis techniques. There are many excellent books from which you can get these analyses. You won't get detailed productivity or quality improvement tools, either. There are many excellent books from which you can glean these techniques. I intend to show you what to do to get the right people and resources and give you some guidelines on how to do it.

GET THE BEST PEOPLE

Individuals are not created equal. There are talented people and there are not-so-talented people. Too many executives "settle" for less than the best people. Don't you. Get the best people. That's a prerequisite for the success of your new tomorrow.

It's difficult to find the right people and get them functioning quickly in executing your new tomorrow. It takes time to build relationships in an organization. The chemistry—rather than the competency—may turn sour, and the change effort fail as a result. It takes time—and patience—and more time. But it can be done. Here's how.

Identify leverage positions. George Orwell, in his classic, *Animal Farm,* wrote the right words. When the animals took over the farm they wrote a law that said, "All animals are created equal." Later on, when the pigs took over, they amended that law to read, "All animals are created equal, but some animals are more equal than others." Orwell's pigs were right. In change, all jobs in an organization are important. But some are more important than others.

Begin by asking, "What strategic directions/attitudes/orientations are required by my new tomorrow?" And, "What positions give me the maximum leverage to inculcate this new attitude/ orientation/strategic direction?" Campbell soup needed a new tomorrow. The red-and-white soup cans called up memories of "M'm! M'm! Good!" for fewer and fewer folks. CEO and president McGovern saw the need to change—the smell of smoke was in his nostrils, he saw the fire with his own eyes. He identified regional and ethnic marketing as the key attitudes he needed in his organization. So he divided Campbell into fifty quasi-independent business units, each responsible for its own profit and loss. His key leverage positions were the top spots in these independent units. He placed marketing-oriented leaders in those spots and gave them autonomy. They produced a blizzard of new products—more than four hundred in the years 1981–1985—with lots of regional and ethnic variations. There's now spicy nacho soup in Texas and California, Creole soup in the South, and red-bean soup in Hispanic areas. McGovern identified the required attitudes and orientations, the key leverage positions, and then filled those positions with people with the right skills.[1]

James Swiggert is a management pioneer. In 1983 *Inc.* magazine trumpeted his decentralized management style at Kollmorgen Corporation as the new wave of management philosophy. Tom Peters echoed the praise in both *In Search of Excellence* and *Passion for Excellence.* A funny thing happened to Kollmorgen and Jim Swiggert on their way to immortality—they tripped over reality. Several consecutive money-losing years forced a reevaluation of their management philosophy. A chastened Jim says, "To succeed, it [decentralization and an emphasis on culture] requires something else . . . it requires the right people in the right slots. . . . In the past we've known—especially at the level of the division president, which is the key role in our organization— what some of our deficiencies were. But we tried to carry them through. . . . We learned . . . never compromise with regard to the type of people you have in leadership roles, because if you do, you're going to compromise the company."[2] Jim, you're singing my song!

Rhonda Benvosti is department manager in the tax collection division for a large municipal government. She felt the need to improve both customer service and internal efficiency. Budget revenues were shrinking, and she knew it was only a matter of time until her department would "face the knife." Here's how she identified her key leverage positions.

Rhonda needed two new orientations—efficiency and service. She saw two key positions. The section head was the informal leader of the clericals in the department. They looked to her for both work guidance and personal support. The second key position was her secretary, who monitored all departmental expenditures. She knew what was being spent for what by whom. Rhonda figured that she needed the active support of these two key leverage positions.

The section head had been there for a long time—and was thoroughly imbued with the "civil service" mentality. It would take a bomb blast to move her. Rhonda's secretary was leaving shortly, so that gave Rhonda a chance to replace her with someone who was more efficiency-oriented.

Rhonda began a campaign to win over the section head. Initially Rhonda brought her along to division meetings, where the budget future was discussed. She then enrolled the two of them in a customer service management training program. As part of the program they submitted a plan to improve service levels in the department. Rhonda met with her section head frequently both during and after the training to discuss the plan and how it could be implemented.

After fourteen months Rhonda was pleased with the progress. She told me, "It took lots of doing. My new secretary keeps good track of the expenditures and gives us a report on where we can save. While she may not be the most liked person in the department, she does an excellent job. And I've been very pleasantly surprised with my section head. She's really gotten into the service thing and works hard on getting her people to deliver good service. Getting those two people behind me was the key to my success."

Identify the key leverage positions—those jobs that exert maximum influence. Most often it's the head of major operating units. The responsible people who deliver your product or service are the best leaders of your new tomorrow.

Sometimes it's a staff department that's the critical position. If internal efficiency is your strategic direction, then accounting and industrial engineering staffs are leverage positions. If new product development is your strategy, then R&D and product engineering are critical.

Other times it's lower- and middle-level operating management positions that become the leverage points. If quality is your new strategic direction, then first- and middle-level supervisors are your best bet. Whatever—first identify the leverage positions.

Define the requirements. Figure out what it takes to do the job you want done. Determine what a good employee looks like—not in physical appearance, but in terms of skills, attitudes, and what the person needs to do. No dull job descriptions here.

Begin with what you want that person to contribute. If you want a new entrepreneurial thrust in your organization—as with Kodak and Campbell Soup—then include that as one of your requirements. If you want an efficiency-oriented person, then include that. Include the basic requirement—and state it in action/behavioral terms. Write what the person must do—the specific, concrete, tangible results you want this job to create.

Then define the few critical skills that will produce that behavior. Royce Kanger determined what he was looking for in his key leverage positions—and got it. Here's how.

> Royce was branch manager for a large consumer finance organization. His new strategy was excellent customer service and rapid turnaround of new loan applications. The key leverage positions in his eleven-person organization were the lead clerical and the office manager. The lead clerical was responsible for the scheduling and training of all the back office people. The office manager supervised the telephone operator and all the front office personnel.
>
> Royce sat down with both key people. To both he asked the same question: "If you were opening a new branch, how would you describe the ideal person to fill your job?" He asked the same question of the entire staff. Then he summarized the answers, adding his own ideas, and held a two-hour employee meeting to discuss the results.
>
> The profile for the back office manager was:
>
> 1.   Experienced in loan processing;
>
> 2.   Meets deadlines;

3. People-oriented;

4. Able to work under pressure and not transmit that pressure;

5. Achievement-oriented—wants to accomplish goals.

The profile for the front office manager was:

1. People-oriented—strong people skills;

2. Achievement-oriented—wants to accomplish goals;

3. Understands loan processing, doesn't make unrealistic promises;

4. Handles conflict well.

Based on these profiles, Royce sat down with both people and asked them how they could do a better job of meeting these profiles and providing superior customer service and accelerating loan processing deadlines. Within weeks he noticed substantial improvement.

Determine what it takes to produce what you want—skills, attitudes, knowledge. Be simple, though. You may come up with twelve important dimensions—only three of which are critical. Look for the critical dimensions first, then the "it would be nice if . . ." ones.

Mitch Kapor, founder of Lotus, decided what Lotus needed to survive and prosper. He said, "The two chief priorities are building long-term corporate relationships and diversifying products and services around core offerings." These were the two principal behavioral outcomes for the CEO. He identified the ability to coordinate, delegate, and communicate indirectly (through memos and procedures rather than personally) and patience as the critical skills necessary for success. "My skills are not evenly distributed across that spectrum," he said. "It's a separate question whether Mitch Kapor is the best person to lead that effort. . . ." As Mitch says, selection is the next key step. As a preview of coming attractions, Mitch Kapor decided that he was not the best qualified to execute those priorities, so he resigned.[3] Identifying the right priorities and right skills only works when you put the right person in the slot. That's what I'll talk about next.

Search and select the best candidate. Find the person who best fits the profile. Look inside first. There are diamonds in the rough buried in your organization. Put out "feelers" with your trusted lieutenants. Ask if they know someone who meets the new profile. Tap your internal network. Internal recommendations reduce selection costs and turnover. Then expand into your industry. Call your industry contacts. Find out if there's someone available they'd recommend. Or call a trusted recruiter. Recruiters often have excellent contacts and can call people you can't. By whatever mechanism—pony express, smoke signals, whatever—send out the message that you're looking for a specific kind of individual. Choice is the key to good selection. The wider the pool from which you choose, the better the choice will be. So maximize the selection pool. Choose carefully from your pool. Here's some tips:

- **Be prepared for the interview. Review your profile and keep it handy to refer to during the interview.**

- **Ask open-ended questions—such as**
  "What would you redesign about your last job, and why?"
  "What did you do, your boss do, and your people do?"
  "How would your references answer the following question? . . ."

- **Listen and take good notes. (Trust your memory to fail when it comes to remembering who said what after you've interviewed several people!) Ask follow-up questions when there are contradictions or hazy answers.**

- **Ask tough questions—such as**
  "What are your weaknesses, and how do they show up in performance?"
  "What were your bosses' weaknesses, and how did that hinder/help you?"
  "What would you do differently now, in light of developments?"

- **Look for specifics, accomplishments (not just participation), and honesty.**

- **Hold multiple interviews, and get independent judgments from each interviewer. Trust your own judgment to be prejudiced, sometimes. Get a second opinion.**

- **Involve peers, subordinates, and even administrative/secretarial personnel. Managerial candidates at the large U.S. real estate and property developer Trammel Crow interview with secretaries and young leasing agents. Candidates who ignore lower-level people get dropped regardless of how much they've impressed the brass. Multiple interviews prevent myopic selection.**

- **Use a simulation to check the candidate's motivation. Use a "slice of organizational life" experience to see how the candidate reacts. Toyota asks its assembly-line candidates to spend 4.5 hours running a simulated business. Afterward they spend upward of six hours assembling and disassembling equipment, similar to the work they'll do on the line. Candidates who survive this simulation of organizational life do very well in the real world of the factory. One executive I know takes candidates out on his boat to measure their reaction to various situations. However you do it, find out how the person responds to real-life situations. Get beyond the talk and discover the person's actual behavior.**

When you are all done, you'll discover there are no perfect candidates. No one fits the profile perfectly. Selection is a process of trade-offs. Ask yourself, "Can I live with the person's deficiency?" "How serious is the deficiency?" "Can I correct the deficiency in some way—hire a complementary person or organize around it?" Choose the least flawed person—or at least the person whose flaws you can most easily live with.

Select the best candidates for the critical leverage jobs. Get the best people in the key positions. But even the best people can't do the job without resources. That's next.

Personal Workshop

As you ponder how to get the best people, consider the following questions.

1. What are the key leverage positions in my organization?
a. What are the strategic directions/attitudes/and orientations required by my new tomorrow?
b. What position gives me the maximum leverage over these attitudes/directions/orientations?

2. What is the profile of the ideal person?
a. What specific, concrete behaviors do I want from each leverage job?
b. What will it take—in terms of skills, knowledge, attitudes—to produce the results I want?

3. How can I maximize my search and selection probabilities?
a. How can I get my internal contact to search out good candidates?
b. Who in the industry can I contact who might know of successful candidates?
c. What executive recruiters do I know who can help find good candidates?
d. How can I prepare for the interview? What questions will I ask? How will I follow up the candidate's answers?
e. Who else can I get to also interview the candidate and give me an independent evaluation?
f. How can I organize a simulation of real organizational life to check the candidate's actual behavior?
g. How can I choose the least imperfect person for the leverage job?

GET THE RESOURCES

An executive without resources is like a ship without a sail—destined to go nowhere. Restructure? The question is not whether—but how? Cut costs? The question is not whether—but how? and where?

Anyone can bump the bottom line by cutting costs. Just shut down maintenance, or training, or advertising. Lay off half the staff. Close a plant. One turnaround specialist told me, "It's easy! Just draw a red line through every third name on the personnel roster. Then you've got the resources you need to do what you want." Unfortunately it's a lot more complex than that.

Get the resources you need to create your new tomorrow by 1) reducing expenditures in "nonessential" activities; 2) lowering the costs of "essential" activities; 3) refocusing activities on the most "essential" activities.

Reduce "nonessential" expenditures. "Get back to profitable basics" is the theme of this section. Identify what's crucial and not crucial to your new tomorrow. Organizations pick up a lot of excess baggage along the way. The more successful you are, the more excess baggage you pick up. Success breeds "wouldn't it be nice" extras. I've seen it happen all too many times. Lean-and-mean street fighters acquire plush offices, private jets, hordes of secretaries— and lose what got them there in the first place. Your first task? Get rid of the "fat"!

Begin by identifying essential and nonessential activities. Ask, "Does this activity contribute to the new tomorrow?" or, "What will happen if I eliminate this activity?" or, "If I started from scratch, and had no history, what minimum activities would I require?" or, "If this were my money, and I was paying interest on it, what is the minimum level of activity I would fund?"

Jack Good was the CEO of a recent leveraged buy-out in the retail business. He needed to cut expenses to meet the heavy debt service. Here's how he did it.

> Jack got his senior managers together at a two-day retreat. He asked each of them to prepare two lists before coming to the meeting—one of the absolutely essential activities required to meet the company's fiscal targets (along with funding levels) and a second of the way each of them (independently) would set up the business if they were starting from scratch.
>
> Jack integrated the lists with his own. He kept comparing the activities of each department with the 20 percent return-

on-equity hurdle rate. If the department didn't show a 20 percent return, he insisted that either the department show how it could meet the hurdle rate or be closed.

Jack said, "It was a tough two days. We worked into the night both days, but we came up with a 'hit list' of things we could stop doing or do less of. There were some sacred cows on that list—but we needed to face up to it. We covered our debt service—and then some."

At the macro level, think like a raider. Give up the emotional attachments to "old businesses" or "old ideas." Either the business builds current value for the organization (15–20 percent ROE), or it is growing at a fast enough rate that it promises to build the required value in a short time, or it must be ditched. Department stores are getting rid of "white goods," on which they've never made money but which they felt they had to carry. Chemical manufacturers are dropping products on which they have never made money, but which they felt they had to carry in order to "fill out the line." Monsanto sold off its commodity petrochemical businesses—reducing them from 25 percent of total assets to 4 percent—and invested in higher value-added, higher margin specialty petrochemicals.[4]

Focus and slim down. Your strategies will help you identify the essential macro activities to keep and the nonessential activities to eliminate. Identifying the micro activities to eliminate is more challenging. Most current cost accounting systems are little help in sorting essential from nonessential micro activities. In their book, *Relevance Lost,* Johnson and Kaplan provide one analytical approach. They argue that each product needs to identify cost drivers—those factors that cause cost variations. Report these drivers in a cycle that matches the time period needed to accomplish measurable units of output. In the case of some production products, that may be hourly, daily, weekly, or monthly. It may even be semiannually in the case of certain research and development activities.

In addition, to get a better handle on overhead costs—which constitute more than 75 percent of most product costs—they urge you examine the cost drivers for overhead expenditures, assigning the costs of overhead transactions as direct product expenses.

Their system gives you a clear picture of the true costs of various products.[5]

Jan Levy was the plant manager for a U.S. specialty chemical company. He applied the Johnson and Kaplan approach with startling results. Here's his story.

> I used their approach in my $15 million plant. Boy, was I surprised. Several products I thought were big margin items actually consumed huge overhead costs that significantly reduced their profitability. Of the ten products I analyzed using their approach, seven showed significantly different results from that of the traditional costing system. I changed prices on more than 60 percent of my product line after we completed the analysis. Profitability more than tripled, as I cut the line by 35 percent and eliminated more than 200 percent of the earnings drag. I only wish I'd learned about them sooner.

Use the Johnson-Kaplan approach to identify the "right" costs of various activities—so you can decide which to keep and which to eliminate.

If you don't like the Johnson-Kaplan approach, McKinsey and Company, the big consultant firm, has another system, "activity value analysis." This system looks at every task within an organization in terms of its bottom-line contribution. People keep detailed records of how they actually spend their time, then analyze the records to see if the time is well spent. It takes lots of time to keep the records and then meet together to analyze the results. At least this system helps you gather the data to answer the question, "Does this activity contribute?"

Get focused on those activities—both macro and micro—that contribute to the new tomorrow. Think like a raider, particularly about your sacred cows. Critically ask of every activity, "Does this contribute?" "What would happen if we didn't do that anymore?" Remember, sacred cows make great steaks.

Lower the cost of "essential" activities. Getting rid of the "hangers-on" helps. But it's not enough to free up the resources you need to create that new tomorrow. You've also got to get a lot more efficient at the "essential" activities. Squeeze out the water in what gets done in your organization to free up needed resources.

Begin in your own backyard and *improve your quality.* Most firms add 25–40 percent to their direct costs because of poor quality. In fact, the high cost of poor quality is one of the best kept secrets. It costs tons of money for rework; time lost due to product line start-up, shutdown, and switch-over; lost material; time spent sorting good from bad parts prior to next-stage production; additional inspections; and customer warranty and field service. Motorola found that by improving quality they saved more than 40 percent in production costs. Brunswick, British Steel, Corning Glass, IBM, Rolls-Royce, and AT&T all found similar savings. Improve the quality of your product, and you will save a lot of money. Sharon Ross, the manager for the order entry department for a fiberglass parts fabrication plant, improved her quality—and saved a bunch. Here's how.

> Sharon suspected that the quality in her department was slipping. She studied the nine separate operations and discovered that first-time quality ranged from 98 percent at one workstation to 18 percent at another. She also estimated that 60 percent of her direct labor costs were tied up in correcting errors.
>
> She talked to the operators at the eighteen percent quality station and solicited their ideas. They suggested several minor changes, including the purchase of an inexpensive error correction mechanism. Sharon gladly made the changes they suggested. Within weeks the quality level zoomed to 98 percent and the costs of that operation fell more than 75 percent. Suddenly the work backlog disappeared and there was time to do the file maintenance work that hadn't been done for years.
>
> Sharon applied the same quality improvement procedure to the other eight workstations. Quality levels improved to 99 percent or better. She was able to handle a doubling of the work load without adding any new personnel.

Quality pays!

Include *subcontractor and vendor partners* in your quality improvement and development activities. Treat your suppliers as partners, not competitors. Share schedules and design changes with them. Tap their creative juices. Involve them in reducing your inventories, shortening product design cycles, and upgrading quality. In the U.S. AT&T works only with "vendor partners," those suppliers whose quality, delivery, and price qualify as the best in the field. AT&T shared their schedules with Corning Glass, one of their vendor partners supplying electronic components like power resistors. Using this information, Corning reduced its lead time from six weeks to two and showed a one-time savings of $150,000 in work-in-progress inventory and $400,000 in finished-goods inventory.

Through vendor partnering, Levi Strauss and Co. eliminated incoming inspection on denim cloth. Levi and the supplier worked together to improve denim-quality levels. By sharing production schedules with the supplier, Levi uses a just-in-time inventory system, where the denim is delivered two hours before it's needed. Levi saves more than $6 million in inventory costs.[6]

Simplify operations by eliminating managerial levels and headquarters staff. Give people at the operating level—who are closer to the action—the responsibility and the authority to act. One general manager told me, "It takes me six weeks of committee meetings, and seven separate reports, to get a price change approved. By the time I get approval, we've lost the sale. So I've just given up. If those smart guys in headquarters think they can run this division better than I can . . . I just might let them try." Brunswick, a U.S. company, eliminated one whole layer of management at Mercury Marine, their highly profitable boat business. Not only did they save $6 million in direct costs, but with fast decision making on the scene, they added millions in revenues, getting jobs they previously missed because of slow response time.

Tap employee creativity in reducing costs. Employees know a lot about how to improve operations. Most managers don't ask. I know—because I learned the hard way. In one personal business situation we needed to save $17,000 a month in overhead expenses to bring the operation to break-even. My managers couldn't find the money, so we asked the employees. Within seventy-two hours there were $22,000 of savings suggestions from the employees. When I asked later why they'd never shared those ideas before, one of the production workers said, "You never asked!" Corning Glass forms short-term "corrective action teams" to solve specific situations. They also encourage employees to make "method improvement requests" to upgrade manufacturing procedures.

Corning's saved millions of dollars as a result. Suggestion systems also work to generate employee ideas.

Cooperate with unions in improving productivity. If the union isn't on your side in your cost-saving efforts—forget it. It takes patience to negotiate with the union. Unions are willing to cooperate when you clearly demonstrate the need. Even the militant United Steelworkers of America are working to improve productivity. Seven steel companies—Inland, LTV, Bethlehem, Acme, Wheeling-Pittsburgh, Armco, and Cleveland-Cliffs—joined with the USW to institutionalize joint "labor management participation teams" (LMPT). National Steel credits a LMPT with saving more than half a million dollars at one location. A. O. Smith, a component auto producer and consumer of steel organized by the USW, credits their LMPT with helping to save the company.[7]

Free up the money you need from current operations. Do whatever you need to do—improve quality and tap the talents of vendor, employee, and union partners. Get the bucks!

Refocus activities on the new tomorrow. You got the money! Now what? Spend it wisely. Get everyone to contribute. Here's how.

Begin by *making your strategic focus clear.* Make certain everyone knows the new tomorrow. Don't sound an uncertain or muffled trumpet. In the following chapter I'll talk at great length how to sound the clarion call. So let's save it for then.

Next, *mobilize support for your new tomorrow.* Chapters 7, 8, 9, and 10 are about how to do this. Use a vision to mobilize support. How to do it is coming up.

Personal Workshop

As you ponder how to get the resources, please consider the following questions.

1. How can I think like a raider about my business?
   a. Does every business contribute to the business (at least 15–20 percent ROE)?
   b. What would happen if I eliminated the activity?
   c. If I started from scratch, how would I start this business?

d. What are the cost drivers for each of my products?

e. What are the overhead transaction costs for each of my products?

Taking questions 1d. and 1e. together, what are the real costs for each of my product lines? Do I make money on the product lines, or should I discontinue them?

2. *How can I squeeze more money out of essential operations?*
   a. How can I improve quality?

   b. How can I develop productive relationships with vendors and suppliers to improve the quality of incoming material, reduce inventory, and shorten product development cycles?

   c. How can I simplify my operations—reducing manufacturing steps, eliminating decision-making and management layers, decentralizing operations?

   d. How can I tap employee creativity?

   e. How can I secure union cooperation in my cost-saving efforts?

Create the new tomorrow. But just any new tomorrow won't do. You need the right new tomorrow—one that distinguishes you from all the others out there. To create that "right" new tomorrow, you need the right people in the right spots with the right resources.

Put your best people in the leverage positions—those few jobs that move the organization the fastest in the direction you want to go. Identify those leverage positions, define their requirements, and search for and select the best candidate. There aren't any perfect candidates. So choose the least imperfect candidate.

Get the resources. Reduce nonessential activities by thinking like a raider about your own organizations. Sacred cows may not be so sacred after all, particularly when the organization's life is on the line. Identify the real costs of each product and eliminate those that don't contribute their 15–20 percent ROI. Squeeze money out of essential operations by partnering with vendors, employees, and unions, improving quality, and simplifying operations.

The combination of good strategies and adequate resources is hard to beat. But it alone won't produce the change you need. You need the active support of your people in using the resources wisely to execute the strategies. The balance of the book will show you how to mobilize your people to execute your change.

6

Vision Makes the Difference

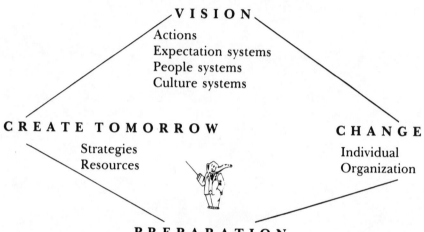

E M P O W E R I N G   C H A N G E

V I S I O N

Actions
Expectation systems
People systems
Culture systems

C R E A T E   T O M O R R O W

Strategies
Resources

C H A N G E

Individual
Organization

P R E P A R A T I O N

Getting ready
Anticipating obstacles

After one of my speeches, the president of a corporation challenged me. "Just what is vision, anyway? Isn't it just a new name for a mission statement? We did that exercise several years ago, and look what it got us—nothing but more paper on the wall. Why is this vision so important in achieving change?"

Vision is the difference between short-term "hits," like asset sales and cutting R&D budgets, and long-term change. Vision translates paper strategies into a way of life. Vision empowers people to change.

The editors of *Fortune* magazine said, "The new paragon of an executive is a person who can *envision* a future for his organization and then *inspire* his colleagues to join him in building that future."[1] (Emphasis added.) Vision must exist at all levels of the organization. The mailroom supervisor needs a vision. The swing shift supervisor needs a vision. The DP manager needs a vision. Vision is the difference between the long-term success of any organization and a certain second-rate position.

Vision plays a central role in many activities, ranging from family trips to changing organizations. Every family journey begins with a picture of a destination shared by everyone. Included is a picture of the major activities along the way. You don't necessarily have all the stops planned out or all the sights you'll be seeing. You don't even have all the various roles of the family members spelled out. What you do have is a general picture of where you're going and how you'll get there. That shared picture of a mutual destination becomes your vision for the trip.

Similarly, vision paints a picture of where you want your organization to go and what you want it to be. You don't have every policy, every strategy, every specific product, worked out in detail. Rather, what you have is a general picture. For instance, Philip Caldwell, CEO of Ford Motor Corporation, saw that Ford needed to improve its quality. From that strategy of quality improvement he produced a vision statement: "Quality Is Job 1." Only then did the specifics emerge, such as quality circles for employees, product redesign to reduce the number of working parts, closer working relationships with suppliers, and massive advertising programs both internally and externally. Before you can empower your people and mobilize them behind your new strategy, you need to put it into a simple-to-understand, inspirational, focusing statement like "Quality Is Job 1."

To plan a family trip or change an organization requires a vision. What exactly is a vision? An empowering vision spells out clearly what you want and inspires people to produce it. A vision specifies a mutual destination—the place everyone agrees to go—and the major activities that get you there.

Having a vision isn't enough, though. Hanging it on the walls isn't enough. You have to empower your people to use your vision. An empowering vision meets the following three criteria: a *focus* on your strategic advantages, the *inspiration* to deliver those advantages consistently, and *clarity to be used as a decision-making criterion*.

CRITERIA: WHAT A VISION NEEDS TO BE

The focus on strategic advantages. Begin by identifying your unique strategic advantage. Untold numbers of products and services compete in the marketplace. How can you distinguish yours from all the others? Every successful organization—whether selling soap or entertainment—whether selling accounting services or training and development activities to internal end users—develops a unique-unto-itself strategic advantage. Consider the computer industry. IBM's unique strategic advantage is its customer service and product compatibility. Apple relies upon user friendliness and superior graphics. DEC's strength is in its superior computing power as it is applied to the engineering and technical arenas. Compaq relies upon cheaper prices and greater computing power for IBM compatibles. The rest of the "bunch"—Honeywell, Unisys, and NCR—all work to create their own niches. Develop a unique strategic advantage.

Tom Golisano, CEO of Paychex, Inc., built his successful business—the second-largest payroll processing company in the United States—by identifying a unique strategic advantage. Rather than competing directly with Automatic Data Processing, Inc., the $1.2 billion leader in the field, Golisano went after the uncrowded small business market. To that market Paychex offers unparalleled service. Paychex has many more locations than its rivals, each with its own computer. Each location serves a small area. Paychex people emphasize their geographic proximity to their customers. "We're just around the corner—and you're one of our biggest accounts." He backs the "local" image by retaining local personnel and not transferring them from location to location as is typical in ADP. All of these strategies are designed to convince the small business owner that at Paychex he or she is "big." With that marketplace distinction, Paychex added sixty thousand new clients last year and showed a 25 percent return on equity versus 17 percent for ADP.[2] Paychex is successful because of its unique strategic advantage vision.

Vision focuses attention on your critical strategic advantages. Attention empowers your people to change in these key strategic areas. Paul Burke, the president of a real estate brokerage firm, identified the critical strategic advantage for his business. He incorporated it into a simple-to-understand vision with great success.

Paul's $50 million real estate firm had three offices throughout a large midwestern city. Over the past few years he'd watched his average sales per agent decline, costs per transaction rise, and profits fall.

He also saw the continued growth of investment syndications in his town. His firm was not involved in any of these activities. Paul tried many times to interest his agents in learning about this market, but his people expressed little interest in the "new stuff."

Paul asked himself the question, "Why would a potential seller or buyer come to my firm rather than go to my competitor?" Then he answered his own question: "Trust and credibility. People will use my firm because they'd trust in our capability to do a good job for them. That's true in both our current business and in the syndication market."

In an effort to get his eighty brokers and agents to provide better customer service (which he sensed would build better trust and credibility), he put together a vision statement.

He printed the vision statement—"We know, we care, we perform"—on every piece of paper in the office—business cards, stationery, and advertising. He even put it on his "For Sale" and "For Rent" signs.

Incessantly he talked about his vision—knowing, caring, and delivering—to all employees. He changed his hiring procedures to select caring people and increased his training to provide more knowledge, particularly in the syndication business. He also invited experts about syndication to many of his weekly staff meetings to excite the agents about the field. He wanted to be certain that his people heard over and over again about the new vision.

Within a year Paul's transaction per agent increased dramatically, his profits surged, and his firm participated in several syndications. He told me, "I knew that if I could get my agents to provide superior competent service to my clients, and really focus on the opportunities in the syndication market, I could sweep the market. Though the overall real estate market was down last year, my firm did very well."

Paul saw clearly his strategic advantages. He incorporated these into his simple, easy-to-understand vision statement. This statement empowered his people to change.

Defining strategic advantage, while important, isn't enough. All too many executives believe that their work is finished once they've got their advantage identified. In reality, their work has only just begun. Consistently deliver that advantage—or lose it.

People are the key. Ask International Harvester (now Navistar). Their people stopped delivering their marketplace advantage—and almost lost the company. IH was the dominant farm implement manufacturer. Their success had been built on product quality, availability, and reliability. But through a series of bitter labor disputes that alienated much of the work force, product quality and reliability slipped badly. Sales lost to competitors soared; IH almost went bankrupt. When the people who produce your strategic advantage aren't with you—your economic days are numbered.

The inspiration of adding value to others. When asked the question, "What kind of a company do I want?" most executives respond with either a product or market definition of their business or with a financial ratio measure of success.

But long-term successful companies stand for more than just profit and market share. They also stand for people—people who contribute net value to society. In 1915 Henry Ford put it well: "Wealth, like happiness, is never attained when sought after directly. It always comes as a by-product of providing a useful service." Bring Ford's words into the present. Inspiring visions create value for others—employees, customers, and the community at large. Inspiring visions empower people.

The answer to the question, "What kind of a company do I want?" must both *inspire* and *empower* people. History's great leaders have rallied people with the power of their value-creating visions. Gandhi led 450 million Indians to sacrifice for the vision of independence. Martin Luther King, Jr., persuaded 20 million black Americans to sacrifice for his vision of equality. President John F. Kennedy convinced 210 million Americans to sacrifice to land a man on the moon in the decade of the 1970s. In this decade Lee Iacocca of the Chrysler Corporation convinced six hundred congressional leaders and two hundred thousand workers to sacrifice in order to save Chrysler. John Ashcroft inspired many managers in newly acquired divisions to measure and reduce costs to live his vision for Coloroll, Ltd. People need to see using the vision as a way to accomplish some greater good.

ServiceMaster's vision—"Honoring God in all we do" and "Grow people"—is a classic example of a vision that inspires and empowers by adding value to others. They live that vision through opening and closing every meeting with a prayer and offering a wide range of educational programs. This vision inspires and empowers ServiceMaster's employees. ServiceMaster has the lowest absence rate in their industry and the highest return of any commercial company in the world.[3]

Inspire and empower all levels of an organization with a vision. Inspire government as well in private-for-profit organizations with an uplifting vision. The following situation illustrates an inspiring vision in a governmental organization.

> When Susan Larson took over as the department head of a 134-person general services department for a large state in the U.S., she saw the need to dramatically improve the department's performance. Her boss told her, "That place is a shambles. If you can't straighten it out in the next twelve months, I'll reorganize and give the administrative services back to the operating departments. The governor needs the money for education."
>
> Susan recognized the need to sharpen and clarify the department's vision. Historically, the general services department emphasized efficiency as its primary focus. Now Susan felt the need to broaden the department's charter.
>
> To clarify her new vision, Susan invited other departments who were users/customers to her staff meetings to discuss how general services could better serve their needs.
>
> After a period of time Susan announced a new vision for her department: "Helping people accomplish their purposes." Her vision, she explained, included assisting users more effectively in their work, and also helping department members to realize their desires for individual career growth.
>
> Susan met several times with her people and with important users to explain her vision. Almost immediately productivity in the department rose and her people started to go out of their way to help users. A clerk-typist in the department told me, "It [the vision] helped me to see how I was doing important work. Before all I did was type

forms. Now I see how I'm helping build the roads people need."

Her boss commended her on the "good feelings in the group."

Clear enough to be used as a decision-making criterion. Clarity is power. Clarity empowers people to use the vision as a decisional criterion to evaluate their actions. People ask, "Does my action support the vision?" The answer must be clear. Brevity helps. Use a short, simple, easy-to-understand statement of your vision to gain clarity, and empower its use as a decisional criterion.

In short, a focusing and empowering vision includes strategic advantages, the creation of value for others, and clarity for use as a decisional criterion. Check the following statements to see if they meet these criteria.

SPELLING OUT THE VISION STATEMENT

People use a vision to evaluate behaviors. But what is a vision, anyway? What does it look like? We're back to the president's quote at the beginning of this chapter.

Vision is a statement of what you want your organization to be. It conveys a picture of where you want to go and how you want to get there. It is a simple-to-understand, inspirational, focusing statement.

Vision statements focus attention on lofty aims with which everyone can identify. The vision statement becomes a deep, abiding belief, a rallying point that touches deeply the hearts and souls of everyone. Vision statements incorporate components that both add value to others and focus on strategic advantages. The first part of ServiceMaster's vision, the company with the highest ROI during the past ten years, is the ultimate "adding value to others" statement: "To serve God in all we do"—including cleaning toilets. Another—"To pursue excellence"—is the strategic advantage.

Gain commitment by including components that add value to others while focusing on strategic advantages. Help employees identify with a "cause" greater than themselves. Working at your company becomes a "calling"—like the "bringing of computer power to the people" that drives Apple Computer, Inc. Vision focuses employee attention and empowers consistent choice of the new changed behavior. Here are several examples.

DATA PROCESSING DIVISION

1. Our goal is to provide the best computing solutions to meet our customer's needs.

2. Your success is our genuine concern.

3. Together we can make a difference.

Statement one is a clear strategic advantage statement. Statements two and three are both strategic and value-adding. Statement two relates to customers, in that success as a customer is the division's genuine concern (because the more the customer succeeds, the more the supplier data processing division succeeds). Nevertheless, the success of the employee is also the genuine concern of the division. Statement three has a similar dual meaning. Together, customers and suppliers can make a difference. Together, employees and managers can make a difference.

MID-SIZE GRAPHICS TERMINAL SUPPLIER

1. Leader in high-performance graphics solutions.

2. Dedicated to the success of our partners.

3. Entrepreneurial work environment.

Statements one and three are strategic advantage components. Statement two has a dual meaning. It is a value-adding statement in that it applies to employee partners and is a strategic statement when it applies to customer partners.

TECHNICAL SUPPORT DEPARTMENT

1. Recognized as creative and innovative leader.

2. Maximize value, quality, dependability, and operability of products and services.

3. React quickly and accurately to market trends.

4. Provide timely and effective technical support.

All statements are strategic components. The group tells me that technical excellence is career opportunity for them. In that sense, all statements are then also value-adding statements.

DELIVERY DEPARTMENT FOR LOCAL NEWSPAPER

1. Neat and accurate product preparation.

2. On time, excellent-condition delivery.

3. Develop selves into professional team members.

Statements one and two are strategic components. Statement three is the value-adding component.

Here are some other vision statements.

LARGE EUROPEAN COMPUTER SOFTWARE AND SYSTEMS ORGANIZATION

Climb the next taller mountain together with suppliers, customers, and employees.

U.K. ENGINEERING SERVICES FIRM

Provide top-flight engineering services which maximize clients' results.

SPANISH SPECIALTY CHEMICAL FIRM

The chemistry of color: The Best Getting Better.

U.K. SOFTWARE FIRM

1. Grow partners, employees, customers, and suppliers.

2. Best quality and service.

3. Market leader in design productivity.

4. Constant improvement.

MUNICH CLEANING COMPANY

1. Keep good customers.

2. Keep good employees.

3. Do what we say.

4. Be the best in our field.

ROLM'S GOALS

1. To make a profit.

2. To grow.

3. To offer quality products and customer support.

4. To create a great place to work.

"Great place to work" means:

  1. Work should be a challenging, stimulating, and enjoyable experience.

  2. The work place should be pleasant.

  3. ROLM should have an environment where every employee can enhance self-image through achievement, creativity, and constructive feedback.

Therefore every employee should have:

  1. Equal opportunity to grow and be promoted.

  2. Treatment as an individual.

  3. Personal privacy respected.

  4. Encouragement and assistance to succeed.

  5. Opportunity to be creative.

  6. Evaluations based on job performance only.

Employees' responsibilities include:

1. Being honest.

2. Being helpful toward others to enhance teamwork.

3. Performing to the best of his or her abilities.

4. Helping to make ROLM a great place to work.

5. Understanding and supporting ROLM's goals.

THE H-P WAY

1. Belief in people: freedom.

2. Respect and dignity: individual self-esteem.

3. Recognition: sense of achievement; participation.

4. Security: permanence; development of people.

5. Insurance: personal worry protection.

6. Share benefits and responsibilities: help each other.

7. Management by objectives (rather than by directive): decentralization.

8. Informality: first names; open communication.

9. A chance to learn by making mistakes.

10. Training and education: counseling.

11. Performance and enthusiasm.

DANA'S FORTY THOUGHTS

1. Remember our purpose—to earn money for our shareholders and increase the value of their investment.

2. Recognize people as our most important asset.

3. Promote from within.

4. Remember—people respond to recognition.

5. Share the rewards.

6. Provide stability of income and employment.

7. Decentralize.

8. Provide autonomy.

9. Encourage entrepreneurship.

10. Use corporate committees, task forces.

11. Push responsibility down.

12. Involve everyone.

13. Make every employee a manager.

14. Control only what's important.

15. Promote identity with Dana.

16. Make all Dana people shareholders.

17. Simplify.

18. Use little paper.

19. Keep no files.

20. Communicate fully.

21. Let people set goals and judge their performance.

22. Let people decide, where possible.

23. Discourage conformity.

24. Be professional.

25. Break organizational barriers.

26. Develop pride.

27. Insist on high ethical standards.

28. Focus on markets.

29. Utilize assets fully.

30. Contain investments—buy, don't make.

31. Balance plants, products, markets.

32. Keep facilities under five hundred people.

33. Stabilize production.

34. Develop propriety products.

35. Anticipate market needs.

36. Control cash.

37. Deliver reliably.

38. Help people grow.

39. Let Dana people know first.

40. Do what's best for Dana.

TANDEM COMPUTERS' PRESIDENT AND CEO JAMES TREYBIG'S PHILOSOPHY

1. All people are good.

2. People, workers, management, and company are all the same.

3. Every single person in the company must understand the essence of the business.

4. Every employee must benefit from the company's success.

5. You must create an environment where all the above can happen.

HERSHEY CHOCOLATE

1. Protect and enhance the corporation's high level of ethics and conduct.

2. Maintain a strong "people" orientation and demonstrate care for every employee.

3. Attract and hold customers and consumers with products and services of consistent superior quality and value.

4. Sustain a strong results orientation coupled with a prudent approach to business.

THE LIMITED, INC.

1. To offer the absolutely best customer shopping experience anywhere—the best store—the best merchandise—the best merchandising presentation—the best customer service—the best "everything" that a customer sees and experiences.

2. To become the world's foremost retailer of life-style fashions.

3. To be known as a high-quality business with an unquestioned reputation for integrity and respect for all people.

4. To maintain a revolutionary and restless, bold and daring business spirit noted for innovation and cutting-edge style.

5. To maintain a management culture that is action-oriented, always flexible, and never bureaucratic.

6. To be tough-minded, disciplined, demanding, self-critical, and yet supportive of each other and our team.

7. To never be satisfied or content—to advance a leading, aggressive, and creative vision of the future.

J. C. PENNEY

1. To serve the public, as nearly as we can, to its complete satisfaction.

2. To expect for the service we render a fair remuneration and not all the profit the traffic will bear.

3. To do all in our power to pack the customer's dollar full of value, quality, and satisfaction.

4. To continue to train ourselves and our associates so that the service we give will be more and more intelligently performed.

5. To improve constantly the human factor in our business.

6. To reward men and women in our organization through participation in what the business produces.

7. To test our every policy, method, and act in this way: "Does it square with what is right and just?"

HONDA

1. Quality in all jobs—learn, think, analyze, evaluate, and improve.

2. Reliable products—on time, with excellence and consistency.

3. Better communication—listen, ask, and speak up.

Show people—in clear and understandable language—the "organizationally correct" decision, particularly about those few factors that produce long-term success.

Visions empower behavior. An American football team shares a vision—score touchdowns and win games. The quarterback, the fullback, and the linemen all know the location of the goal line they need to cross. All their actions are directed toward crossing that goal line. Most organizations are confused about their goal line. By focusing on the vision you *really* want, it becomes the compelling goal line that inexorably draws attention, effort, and accomplishments. Similarly, your vision becomes the decision-making criterion that empowers employees to change.

Employee actions reveal their understanding of your vision. IBM executives stay in touch with a broad range of customers to find out their needs and how IBM can meet them. IBM executives build campuses like serene buildings (to attract the new programmers they are busy hiring) rather than the noisy factories that they built in the late 1970s. IBM executives invest billions in factory automation projects. And so on . . . all of which reflects the following strategic advantage vision of IBM (in 1985):

1. To match or beat the growth in all segments of the information processing industry during the coming decade;

2. To exhibit product leadership across our entire product line;

3. To be the most efficient in everything we do;

4. To sustain our profitability, which funds our growth.

It's not just your staff who needs to understand your vision and be empowered by it. Your customers also need to understand your vision. Your customers judge your vision (whether you want them to or not) based upon their view of your people's activities. All Guests (with a capital "G") at Disneyland know how welcome they are by the way the staff welcomes them. Behavior is the best indicator of *real* vision.

To summarize, your vision is . . .

- **a short, simple statement . . .**

- **of some value-adding and marketplace-advantage factors . . .**

- **which positively distinguishes your organization . . .**

- **in the minds of everyone with whom your organization interacts (customers, employees, suppliers) . . .**

- **and provides clear, inspiring decision-making criteria.**

Personal Workshop

Let's think about your vision statement now. Ponder these questions.

1. How can your organization add value to others?

2. How does this vision help your employees identify with a "calling"?

3. What are your marketplace advantages?

4. How can your vision positively distinguish your organization in the minds of your customers?

5. Can you state your vision in a few words that are easily understood by everyone?

SUPPORTIVE ACTIONS

Throughout this book I've emphasized the importance of your *actions* that achieve the value-adding and strategic-advantage *vision*. Individuals at the Marriott Company, for instance, know that CEO Bill Marriott cares about customers. He travels more than two hundred thousand miles a year visiting locations, living his vision, checking on meal preparations at six A.M. and room cleanliness at eleven P.M.[4] People at Notre Dame, for example, knew that Father Hesburgh was committed to his vision of the university through his traveling more than 150,000 miles per year to drum up interest and support for Notre Dame.[5]

George Patterson knows all about the need to "live the vision." When he didn't it almost cost him his company. George's company, City Gardens, started life as a wholesaler of plants to offices. He was so successful that he decided to expand into selling to the general public. The retail outlets failed, so George pulled back into his original market. But in the process, George and his people lost something. "I fell out of love, that's all. I'd begun to hate plants."

To rededicate himself—and his people—George wrote to each of his 135 people about his vision. "I want City Gardens to be the best interior landscape company in the world. Second best is not worth the effort. Fairness, communication, and pride will get us there. Be fair to yourself, our customers, and the company. Communicate with your fellow workers, and our clients. Do work you can be proud of."

George funded his words with action. He redrew the sales commission plan, redoubled employee training, restructured orientation programs. He talked incessantly about living his vision. One of his managers became his hero, and he talked about him—Mr. Millikin—everywhere he went. Mr. Millikin loved his plants. He'd walk through the greenhouse getting his hands dirty. He loved his plants and showed it in everything he did. As George Patterson put it, "Mr. Millikin wasn't talking mission, he was living it. We use our mission at City Gardens."[6]

In the following vignette about George Tollison, owner of a fine restaurant in San Diego, we see the actions necessary to breathe life into a vision.

George knew that the vision of his restaurant was "to serve only the best." When he sat down every day to make up his purchase list, he only looked for top-quality products.

"But it's tough sometimes," he told me, "to really follow through. I remember one time when the last weeks had not been good and I was awash in red ink. As I sat there one Thursday making up my daily buy list, I spied a very cheap special on frozen salmon. I buy only fresh fish, because it tastes the best. Many customers wouldn't know the difference between fresh and fresh frozen, but it's part of my vision to serve only the best—and fresh is the best.

" 'Can I afford to buy the best today?' I asked myself. 'Besides, who will know, anyway? Maybe just this once?' And then I realized, either I was serious about living my vision or I wasn't—and if I wasn't, I should change it. You've got to live with yourself. So I bought the fresh fish and passed over the lower-priced frozen fish."

George's actions empowered his people to make similar choices. That's why George's restaurant is consistently voted one of the top restaurants in San Diego. You've read over and over again in these pages about the importance of action. Actions reflect genuine visions. Your actions lend credence and credibility to your words—and make them live in your organization.

RESOLVING DOUBTS: HAVE I CHOSEN THE RIGHT VISION?

It's not popular or chic. But it's very real. Most executives worry whether they've chosen the "right" vision. I've discovered that very successful executives, those who head good companies, pass through periods of sharp doubts about their vision. Sam's doubts are typical.

Sam Benes, president of a high-performance electronic supply company, told me, "It's one thing to think about what a vision might be. It's quite something else to write it down and stand in front of two thousand people and ask them to march to that tune. I spent lots of sleepless nights worrying about whether the vision was right and would work. It's easy for you consultants. You suggest something and then leave. I have to live with the consequences."

If you're typical, you are probably asking yourself such questions as "Is the vision correct?" "Will it be successful?" "Can I pull it off?" "Should I even try?"

Move through the doubts by taking these steps: Make certain that your vision will lead to improved performance; get in touch with the deep personal values upon which your vision rests; and see clearly how your vision relates to your personal development.

Make certain that it will work. The words are pretty, but . . . will it work? There are several ways you can check to be sure that you have the "right" new vision. You could be like Sam in the vignette below and use your kitchen cabinet.

> Sam Benes used several of his direct reports to try out his vision. He particularly valued the input of one senior executive who had the reputation for being the "conscience and soul" of the company. Sam talked to these few people individually, telling them what he planned to do, and asked for their advice. He made it clear he was going to go ahead and was only asking for advice, not approval.
>
> "Their input helped me allay some of the doubts," Sam said.

Use your "keeper of the corporate conscience," if you have one, to answer the questions, "Will it work?" and, "Will the people use it?"

Or contact other high-performing organizations to find out what they're doing. Paul's anecdote reports how one manager used the strategy of personal research to allay his concerns.

> Paul Casey was a manufacturing manager for a small computer peripherals supplier. He wanted to move his organization closer to the end-user customer and encourage more internal teamwork and entrepreneurial spirit.
>
> Paul wrote several tentative vision statements and then put them aside. When he picked them up again he would usually see all kinds of hidden meanings in his written words.

Paul wrote to several of the companies mentioned in *In Search of Excellence* and was surprised both with the speed and the informative nature of their response. He received copies of both their vision statements and their policy manuals.

Paul was both confused and comforted by his research results. "There are no standard words, no fixed policies," he told me, "and that's the typical good news/bad news finding. The bad news is I can't copy anyone else's statement knowing that it will succeed. The good news is that I have lots of room to develop my own individualistic statement. Knowing that there's no 'right' answer helps me sleep better at night."

Paul discovered that there are no "right" visions. There are only "right" processes, like those outlined in this book. Sometimes it takes personal research, like Paul's, to assure yourself that you have an effective vision. Do whatever it takes to prove to yourself that your vision will work. You'll need all the belief you can muster during the difficult launch period.

Get in touch with personal values. Do you really believe in your vision? Quell your doubts by returning to the fundamentals of your own beliefs. Sheri Owens-Ford, deputy director of a state social services agency, struggled for a long time with her vision. As the following vignette relates, she was able to resolve her doubts only when she finally got in touch with her own values.

Sheri wanted to encourage her people to be more innovative in developing new services to offer clients and new, more efficient internal procedures.

She thought long and hard about a vision statement that could summarize her own feelings and spark innovation. Finally she settled on a statement: "Creatively meet new (and old) needs."

She was uncertain about her vision statement. To help herself resolve these doubts, she spent a weekend at the seashore reviewing her own feelings.

She remembered her strong belief in people and how that had sometimes in the past led her to be disappointed. She wondered, "Am I really willing to trust people to be inde-

117

pendent?" She knew the need for independence as a pre-condition for creativity, but she wasn't certain she had the faith necessary to sustain her through the inevitable disappointments.

Finally, by the end of the weekend Sheri got in touch with her overriding beliefs. She recalled a number of situations in which people had faith in her and gave her the freedom to create. "It worked with me, and in the vast majority of the cases in which I've tried it. Now I need to keep the faith."

Only after these exercises did she feel comfortable in announcing her vision to other employees. "I needed to be certain that the words reflected my real values, since I know I'll have to live with these words for a long time to come."

Remember your own values. It'll be easier to resolve your doubts about your vision.

Link with personal development. Does using the vision pay off for you? Most behavior is based upon WIIFM (What's In It For Me). Getting your people to use your vision is no different. I've seen many examples where the WIIFM in vision implementation is tied to personal development. Mario's anecdote below is typical.

Mario Tamist was the manager of a seven-person fitness center for a large aerospace company. He wanted to improve the performance of his crew. He thought for a long time about his vision and talked to many people about it, including the personnel manager, the training director, and members of his management club.

At a seminar Mario attended a leader asked him, "Why do you want to do this? It will take lots of extra work and could be very risky. If it backfires, you could be fired. Why take the risk?"

The seminar leader's questions triggered a lot of soul searching. After many hours of thought, Mario arranged to see the seminar leader and told him, "I want to do this vision effort primarily to see if I can do it. Yes, I'd like to improve performance, and I think this will. But as you point out, there are lots of less risky ways to accomplish that purpose.

"I know how to help people get fit—I know I know! I know how to get people to do good work—I know I know! But I don't know if I can implement my vision and move the group to an even higher level of consistent performance. I need to find out if I'm capable of doing that. It's a part of me that needs testing. That's why I intend to implement this vision activity."

Are you like Mario, looking to test the boundaries of your own personal capabilities?

Organizations are uncertain places, particularly when you are blazing new paths. Doubt is your inevitable traveling companion. Remember that your vision will lead to high performance. Remain in touch with your own values. See the linkage between the vision and your personal growth. Move through the doubts.

CRAFTING THE VISION

Words are important—very important—but not enough. *How* the words get written is just as important as *what* gets written. Remember Chapter 1? Widespread participation empowers people. Empowering visions do not come down from the mountaintop—engraved in stone. Rather they are shaped—crafted—developed in cooperation with those who will live it. Empowering visions are developed much in the way a painter paints a picture or a potter crafts pottery. Each—the painting, the pottery, and the vision—is developed through an interactive process.

People can only be empowered by a vision they understand. Understanding is enhanced by participation. Participation produces empowerment. So before you begin, check to be certain that your vision can be understood.

Jeff Hamer knows the importance of this step. He put together the Computer-Aided Design Group (CADG) to help companies select software for managing real estate and other fixed assets. For several years his firm was wildly successful. Then, as frequently happens, he lost his way. CADG began offering software in other markets. They began to offer other services. Soon they were a collection of people in search of a focus. Jeff wrote out his version

119

of the company's vision—"The mission of CADG is to provide quality facility-management software, products, and services, which meet customer needs."

When he asked the five members of the management team to a lunch meeting to discuss the vision, he discovered that none shared his vision. Several meetings later the group came to a consensus. Now Jeff and his managers refer to the vision at every meeting, using it as a decision-making criteria. But had he not gone through the crafting process, he would never have known about the wide diversity in feelings about the company's direction.[7]

Test out this understanding in any of the following three ways.

Bounce it off a small brain trust. Do you have a small group of people whose opinion you value, with whom you feel comfortable when sharing ideas? Use this group as a sounding board to test your vision.

Privacy and confidentiality is the primary advantage of this approach. In the comfort of this trusting relationship you can voice ill-formed thoughts, test far-out ideas, and generally not worry about judgments that discourage creativity. In the following example, a general manager successfully used a brain trust in checking his vision.

> Paul Cofino was the general manager of the data processing division of a large company. He wanted to improve his department's productivity. He felt his division was not sufficiently customer- or people-oriented—and he wanted to change both of those attitudes.
>
> He formed a brain trust, composed of his vice-president of operations and a former boss who was now the division manager of a larger division for the same company in the same geographic area. The three met on several weekends to discuss several alternative scenarios he proposed.
>
> There were a number of heated discussions as the men had differing perspectives. Paul said, "These guys were helpful in my thinking through what I really wanted and what I could realistically do. We are a division of a much larger company, and I may not be around forever, so I need

to be careful that I don't overreach my bounds. Also, these guys helped me think through the possible consequences of various statements. I'm glad they were around to keep me on the straight and narrow."

Brain trusts provide additional confidential and trusted heads. Your brain trust can help you make certain that the words in your vision statement convey your meaning. You can also gain insight into your vision's possible acceptance.

This advantage of confidentiality is also a principal disadvantage. Sometimes the group can suffer from "group think." The use of a small brain trust as the only way to test your vision may give you a bad case of tunnel vision. One middle manager in a company where the vision had been imposed from the top as the result of a brain trust approach told me, "It's almost as if he didn't trust us enough to ask our opinion. What was he afraid of? Now I think his ideas are good, but we could have helped him be a little sharper and a little more focused and prevented some of the problems he encountered. I think it [the vision] will eventually work, but it'll be hard. He should have asked for our input."

Talk to the people informally. Ask people directly what they think. That's one of the best ways to get a reaction to your vision. You'll be amazed at how willing people are to talk with you. Generally people love to be asked their opinions—witness the immense popularity of the "man in the street" interviews and the radio/TV call-in talk shows.

You can talk informally with your people about your vision in several different ways. Try showing up at the coffee machines at break times or at the lunchroom at lunchtime. These are excellent opportunities to catch people at a relaxed time. You could also stop people in the hallways and ask their opinions.

Begin these informal contacts with an open-ended statement like "I've been thinking . . ." or "I'd really like your reaction to . . ." By asking the open-ended question, you stimulate the broadest-possible response. People may be reluctant to talk to you initially, particularly if you do not have a history of soliciting employee ideas.

You can encourage the other person to talk by making such

leading and supportive statements as "That's interesting, tell me more. . . ." or "I'd like to hear more of what that statement means to you." Asking open-ended questions and making leading and supportive statements will increase the depth of your responses.

Ask a representative sample of the organization so you get a good cross section of answers. Include important customers/end users and suppliers. They're important members of the team as well. The following vignette reports how one executive used a wide range of informal contacts to test out his vision.

> Paul Cofino was the general manager of a data processing center for a major U.S. firm. He put together a vision. With a preliminary statement in hand, he devoted a month to informal contacts to verify and refine his vision.
>
> He committed to talk with at least two employees every day in the course of his normal visitations about the center. He deliberately sought out programmers, data input clerks, and systems analysts along with project managers and department heads.
>
> He found that as he talked to people they became enthused about the vision and the new direction for the center. "I got lots of validation for my direction and good input on wording changes to clarify the ideas. I was amazed."

Use informal contacts to test out the impact of the words you've used, and build acceptance for the new vision.

Be aware, though, that there are thorns among the roses. You may receive more "advice" than you want. Many individuals may interpret your ideas through the prism of their own narrow, departmental interests. As a result you may receive conflicting opinions.

You may also uncover a sewer full of problems. Probably you'll find many "That's a great idea, but . . ." or "How does what you say you want now square with what one of your managers just did? . . ." or "We can't do that because . . ." Listen without promising that you will act on any specific response. Maintain that you're on a fishing expedition. After you've spoken to someone, follow up with a brief personal note to thank him/her. Use the note not only as a visible sign of your interest, but also as another opportunity to reinforce the "fishing trip" message.

Get formal input. Use any one of several formal ways to secure input when there are too many people to contact informally.

The first and most popular way is to use print media, such as employee newsletters, memos, and bulletin board announcements. You get high visibility for your vision (that's a plus). You get lots of information (that's another plus). You begin to build a broad base of acceptance (that's an even bigger plus). However, you gain little insight into the *real* meaning of what employees tell you (that's a huge minus).

Employee meetings can give you insight into what people really think. Get everyone together—either at one time or in several groups—depending upon the size of your organization. You enhance the personal exposure to your vision at the meeting (that's a plus) and get good insight into what employees *really* think (that's an even bigger plus). The principal disadvantages are the time it takes and its potential for surfacing deep-seated hostilities. You'll also need a capability in platform presenting and group leadership skills. In general, if you have the time and the skill, the general employee meeting is an excellent way to develop understanding and acceptance of your vision.

If you don't take the time to craft your vision, you run the risk of winding up like Charles Parry, former CEO for Alcoa. He got fired when the board rejected his vision. Parry trumpeted his vision of a "new" Alcoa. He bought companies making exotic materials. He invested heavily in his 2,300-acre research park. He drastically cut headquarters staff and decentralized. He boasted that 50 percent of Alcoa's revenue would come from nonaluminum activities by 1995 (up from 5 percent in 1987). And he created considerable confusion and consternation in the century-old Alcoa organization.

Finally, the board could stand it no longer. Parry was asked to leave. His vision of a "new" Alcoa was buried by a single statement in the annual report by the new president, Paul O'Neill, who said, "Alcoa's future lies in the core aluminum business." Period. Parry's vision was gone, a victim of noncrafting.[8] Don't join him in the corporate graveyard.

Stay flexible. As you go through this checking process, you'll discover that you need to be flexible. Developing a vision is similar to developing a winning game plan in football. Both require advanced planning and rapid real-time flexible responses to developing situations.

You are like a quarterback coming to the line of scrimmage. You've got a game plan and specific play in mind (that's like a preliminary view of your vision). In carrying out that play (let's say it's a pass play), you need to simultaneously monitor several different activities. You need to be aware of the progress of several receivers down field, the pass defense being played against those receivers, the pass rush tactics employed by the defensive line, how your offensive pass blockers are coping with these tactics, and the risks and opportunities of such other developing possibilities as scrambling.

This whole mental process takes four to seven seconds (it took you longer to read about it than it takes the average quarterback to do it!), during which the quarterback needs to simultaneously monitor these different processes. An executive crafting a vision needs to be like a good quarterback making a "quick study" of the situation, rapidly monitoring several different activities and capitalizing on the corridors of opportunity.

Lennie Price, the president of a small publishing company, learned the hard way about the necessity of being flexible while crafting his vision.

> Lennie decided that excellent customer service was the key to survival for his self-publishing service. When he shared his thoughts and intentions to put together a corporate vision based on this principle, it was greeted with strong enthusiasm.
>
> Lennie immediately got lots of advice from his employees about what his vision should say. He was also inundated with ideas for service improvements, ranging from dramatically upgrading the mailing equipment to establishing customer-based project teams to bring manuscripts to press. Many of the ideas cost more than Lennie thought his company could afford. Lennie intended to raise employee awareness of the need for good personal service. He never intended to make major capital investments.
>
> Lennie soon realized that he had a tiger by the tail. He hadn't sufficiently thought through the consequences of his vision. Faced with the staggering (for his small firm) costs,

he went back to the employees and announced that he was putting his ideas on hold for a while until he could get a clearer picture of the future of the business.

"It was tough doing it," Lennie said. "I was embarrassed as heck, and I think the employees were disappointed and demotivated as well. Next time—if there is a next time—I'll think through the consequences of my words before I share them."

Lennie learned the lesson the hard way—think through your vision before you announce it, and be prepared to be flexible about it while you're checking its acceptability.

Empowerment comes from understanding. Understanding comes from participation. Get widespread participation in crafting your vision. That will empower its use.

Personal Workshop

In thinking about crafting your vision, consider the following questions.

1. With whom do I feel comfortable in sharing sometimes crazy and off-the-wall ideas? These people could be either inside or outside your organization.

2. How can I use a brain trust for a preliminary look at my vision, to be supplemented by other, more participatory approaches?

3. How much time am I willing to devote to informal contacts checking out my vision?

4. How can I arrange to meet people (employees, bosses, colleagues, customers/end users/suppliers) at informal relaxed times?

5. How can I plan my schedule so that I informally get a cross section of functions and organizational levels?

6. Do I have the time to spend with individual departmental employee groups to discuss the vision? If the size of the employee group makes for too many meetings, are there ways to enlarge the groups by combining departments and reduce the numbers of meetings?

7. Do I have the platform and group leadership skills necessary to successfully run a meeting?

Vision makes the difference. A commonly held focusing and inspirational statement becomes the principal decision-making criterion to ensure that the 1,001 daily, mundane, often dirty details are all done well.

We've just looked at crafting your vision. Now we're ready to move on to empowering people to use the vision. Having a simple-to-understand vision is not enough. Too many executives believe that their job is done once the vision statement is published and widely disseminated. Nothing is farther from the truth. In fact, the "hard" work comes after the vision statement is published. In the next chapters we will turn our attention to the crucial process of empowering the use of the new vision.

7

Actions Set the Pace

EMPOWERING CHANGE

VISION

Actions
Expectation systems
People systems
Culture systems

CREATE TOMORROW

Strategies
Resources

CHANGE

Individual
Organization

PREPARATION

Getting ready
Anticipating obstacles

Act—and get others to act—to empower your vision.

An empowering vision focuses on strategic advantages, inspires by adding value to others, and can clearly be used as a decision-making criterion. But having the vision isn't enough. The walls of most organizations are littered with the graffiti of too many visions.

People must use your vision to make it real—to make it more than one more sign in the hall to ignore. Empower people to use your vision. Action is the rocket fuel that launches your vision. Here are four ways to get actions that empower people to use your vision.

PERSONALLY DEMONSTRATE THE VISION IN ACTION

Use your vision in doing things differently. That's the best way to empower others to use it. The injunction is clear—set the personal example!

First, *get clear on the actions that reflect your vision and demonstrate them personally.* J. W. Marriott, Jr., knows that guests in his hotels and restaurants look at the little things that spell the difference between so-so service and great service. So he spends his time visiting his properties, personally checking the little things that spell the difference for guests. During his visits he makes certain that employees see him personally using the vision. His managing by example (following the example of his father) produced many years of annual earnings growth.

John Catley was the state printer for a large U.S. state. Here's how he empowered his people by personally demonstrating the key actions that supported his vision.

> John saw the need to become more efficient in order to operate within the governor's reduced budget. In an effort to improve efficiency, he created a client service vision.
>
> John began by "adopting" several major clients. He visited them personally and asked, "What can we do to improve our service?" He then passed the information back to the printers involved and acted as liaison between the printer and the client.
>
> Seeing John visiting clients and getting a warm welcome, several printers asked, "Why can't I go directly to the client?" John quickly agreed, with the proviso that he be kept informed. Soon many printers were dealing directly with clients. Efficiency also improved.

John empowered others to use his vision because he demonstrated the "right" behaviors that supported his vision.

Japanese managers are experts in demonstrating the "right" behavior. During the early 1970s Canon became concerned about camera distribution in the United States. They sent a team of senior managers to personally investigate the problem and recommend solutions. By talking with dealers personally, the senior managers demonstrated Canon's vision of quality. They also demonstrated Canon's sincere desire to support dealers in their quality efforts. Empowered to use the vision, the American distributors contributed to the success of Canon's AE-1 camera.[1]

Do you want to empower decentralized decision making? Then look for ways to delegate high-visibility decisions you now make.

And make certain that people know you've delegated them. Do you want to empower people to produce high-quality products? Immerse yourself in reject reports and stay personally informed when poor quality occurs. Personally using the vision empowers others to do the same.

While you're at it, mix in a little *drama*. Don't shoot off fireworks. And don't worry about not being an extrovert, either. You needn't be a Lee Iacocca or a Bob Hope to use drama effectively. Drama underscores important events—and your vision is an important event.

Fritz Maytag uses drama to empower his people to use his vision—produce quality beer in the pure old-fashioned way. His uses travel to dramatize his vision. When his brewery set out to produce wheat beer, Fritz took several employees to Germany to visit small breweries that produced wheat beer. The employees could see firsthand how to brew the wheat beer just right. To demonstrate the importance of quality in ingredients, Fritz took his employees—all fourteen of them—to ride the combine as the farmer in Tule Lake gathered the crop of barley he'd specially grown for Fritz.[2]

You needn't travel to Germany or Tule Lake (or anywhere else, for that matter) in order to introduce drama into your effort. The manager of a data processing division personally hands out ten-dollar gift certificates as a real-time reward for using his vision. When he catches the person at his/her desk in front of other co-workers, it is a dramatic moment. Drama comes in all kinds of unexpected events, such as personal phone calls and visits. A little drama draws a lot of attention. And you need a lot of consistent attention to convince people that they are empowered to use the new vision.

Above all, *live your vision consistently*. Your people study your every move. If they catch you using the vision today and then not using it tomorrow, they'll resist using it. The following story about John Crisp, a restaurant general manager, illustrates the negative consequences of inconsistency.

> John's restaurant made a significant commitment to using the vision of "caring customer service." His entire staff attended training program, and John spoke glowingly of ex-

cellent customer service in his restaurant. After the training program, levels of customer service, as measured by secret shopper scores, hit record highs.

After several months, secret shopper scores began to slip. I noticed several contradictions in John's behavior. Verbally John continued to support the customer service vision. Yet one night John told one of the waiters, "That dirtbag customer on number five will drive us all crazy."

Also, John was visibly absent from the floor for long periods of time. He seemed preoccupied with "paperwork."

Furthermore, most of his comments at the monthly employee meetings concerned food cost controls and turning off the lights to save utility expenses. The last three secret shopper scores were neither posted nor shared with employees.

Inconsistent messages confuse people. Confused people are poor adopters of change.

Not only must the messages be consistent, they must be omnipresent. *Communicate your vision compulsively.* Take every opportunity to drive home the message. Each of the thirty to forty daily interactions is an opportunity for you to communicate your vision. Dave Zeit, who manages an auto repair shop, compulsively communicated his vision and empowered his people to use it.

Dave wanted to upgrade the quality of the workmanship done in his seventeen-person auto repair shop. He developed a "Quality is first" vision.

Dave made it a practice to ask each employee how he/she could improve the quality of the job. Suggestions were implemented as soon as possible.

Dave also asked every customer to evaluate critically the job when he/she got home and immediately report any difficulty directly to Dave. Rework was done free of charge to the customer.

Dave told me, "I must ask a question about quality a dozen times a day. I bet that my employees are sick and tired of hearing about it by now. But we haven't had a customer complaint for over two months. And the employees now come to me with ideas for improving quality work. All that emphasis on quality paid off."

General Bill Creech took over the U.S. Tactical Air Command and engineered one of the greatest turnarounds in history. He taught a very large organization—the United States Air Force—an entirely new vision. His vision was one of decentralization to the squadron level and integration of maintenance with flying at that level. His vision flew directly in the face of sixteen years of prior practice and official air force policy. To get his message out to the troops, Creech held frequent three-day meetings at headquarters on maintenance and squadron issues. The general himself came and spent a day sharing his philosophy. When the "old man" himself shows up to spend the time and talk about integrating maintenance—and this is the sixth time he's done it—the message gets across that using the vision is the thing to do.[3]

Get clear on the actions that reflect your vision. Dramatically demonstrate these actions in high-visibility situations. Consistently live and compulsively communicate your vision. Convince your people that you're serious about it. Then they'll be empowered to use the vision.

Personal Workshop

As you consider how to empower your vision through personal demonstration, ponder the following questions.

1. Is my vision clear?

2. What are a few high-leverage, high-visibility situations in which I can demonstrate my vision?

Consider such high-visibility situations as personally doing a safety audit, holding an employee meeting, spending an afternoon talking with employees to find out what they really think, personally handling the next five customer complaints that come in and disposing of them within forty-eight hours.

3. How can I add a touch of drama to a few of these situations to capture additional attention?

Consider personal visits or phone calls to highlight unique contributions, or do something unusual or unexpected (like showing up at shift start time at six A.M. to talk to people).

4. How can I consistently/compulsively communicate and live my message?

Consider how you spend your day and how you could use your normal, regular interactions to send your vision message. Review whom you see, what you talk about, whom you call, the questions you ask, the comments you make. Consider how you could live your vision message during these normal interactions.

PERSONALLY REPORT PROGRESS ON USING THE VISION—AND GET OTHERS TO DO SO ALSO

Personally demonstrating using your vision is important—but not enough to empower people. In addition, continuously remind people that the vision is working.

People listen for messages about what to do. What gets measured gets done. So be sensitive to the signals sent out by your information system. Does your information system send signals that empower using your vision? Or does it send powerful signals that say, "Don't change"?

Unfortunately, the information system usually reinforces current behavior. So to change behavior, you must change the information system. Fortunately there are several ways you can do this.

Chart a few key behaviors. Chart a few key behaviors that indicate progress in using the vision. Post these charts in work areas, lobbies, cafeterias, or other high-visibility locations. People are particularly sensitive to graphic, visual information messages. Capitalize on this sensitivity.

In the U.S., the executives who bought a losing Springfield Remanufacturing Center Company (SRC) from International Harvester know how to graphically report progress on their vision. Under IH management SRC lost $2 million on sales of $26 million. When CEO Jack Stack and his group of executives bought the company, they immediately involved the employees in their new vision—a company where there were no barriers between management and labor and everyone worked for the common good and shared in the benefits. The group set goals that would produce profits and create a pot for all to share.

In the lunchroom, shared by all employees including the president, there's a large red, electronic message board that flashes the latest hourly results of the activities (such as labor utilization) that have been agreed upon as leading to profitability. The people hear over and over again how the vision is working and how valuable it is to "get on the bandwagon." The overall results: sales are up 40 percent, operating income up to 11 percent, and the appraised value of the stock up from $.10 to $8.45.[4] Electronic message boards, anyone?

Charts send powerful informational messages. Ask Jack Stack at SRC. Concrete, tangible evidence that the vision produces positive results empowers people to use the vision.

Employee meetings. Get people together and tell them, "The vision is working." You needn't be a stage personality to run an effective meeting. Your sincerity and interest will show through. At SRC every supervisor meets with his/her people every Tuesday afternoon to discuss departmental issues—costs, quality, schedule. The meeting covers everything from the need to wear safety gloves to calls for suggestions for specific operations. At these meetings employees get the chance to hear firsthand how the vision is doing and what each of them needs to do to keep the numbers going in the right direction.[5] And none of the supervisors running these meetings is a "Golden Mike" winner. Empower people with information.

Review progress at staff meetings. Talk about vision implementation actions at staff meetings. That sends the empowering "this is serious stuff" message. Paul Cofino's experience shows us how to use staff meetings.

> Paul Cofino was the general manager of a data processing department. His vision was endorsed by most people in the division.
>
> He asked each of his direct reports to take three action steps in the next three months that reflected the vision. He then asked his direct reports to cascade the same three action-step assignments down throughout all management levels.

He scheduled thirty minutes at each weekly staff meeting for three direct reports (each with ten minutes) to summarize the results of these actions steps. The discussions were spirited and supportive and served as a motivator for all those present to work hard to make the vision efforts a success.

Paul told me, "Those weekly staff meetings helped everyone see the importance of using the vision as a guide to their actions. They also gave individuals a chance to learn from each other and avoid some of the more obvious mistakes.

"The principal advantage of the staff meetings, however, was the motivation it generated. People could see that the vision was working to help everyone be more effective. By sharing results, we generated more push to do more."

Harvey Mackay, best-selling author *(How to Swim with the Sharks and Not Get Eaten)* and owner of Mackay Envelope Company, regularly reviews his "Mackay 66" reports with his sales staff. Sales people gather sixty-six pieces of information about every customer. This includes hobbies, birthdays, likes, and dislikes, as well as such traditional facts as ordering cycles, buying criteria, and quantities. This data base is the basis for establishing an effective business relationship. Sales staff meetings are consumed with discussions about specific customers and how they can be sold using the "66" data base. Harvey's convinced that these discussions reinforce his vision for his company.[6]

People listen carefully for clues about what you *really* want. Use your information system to empower your people to use the vision.

Personal Workshop

As you consider how you can empower people by reporting those actions that reflect using your vision, ponder these questions.

1. Which information systems can I use to report progress in using my vision? Which are most likely to yield me the greatest return for my investment of time and effort?

Consider using charts, employee meetings, setting specific goals, and using your staff meetings to follow up.

2. How can I get my people to identify a few (1-2-3) key vision-supporting behaviors that can be charted and posted in a highly visible place? What behaviors of mine am I willing to chart and post as an example?

3. How and when can I hold employee meetings to discuss the results of employees using my vision? Is it better to have small groups (20–40), or can I effectively handle large groups (150–200)?

4. How can I use my staff meetings more effectively to report that the vision is working?

5. How else can I use information reporting activities to empower my people to use the vision?

Empowerment also flows from the *actions of others.* Managers at all levels need to use your vision. Unless your managers use your vision, it is doomed to an early funeral. I'll go over several ways to get the active support of managers in using your vision.

Similarly, employees must be empowered to use your vision. In the hundreds of decisions every employee makes daily, your vision must be foremost in his/her mind. You'll get several ways to empower your employees to use your vision.

EMPOWERING MANAGEMENT ACTIONS

You are the chief communication source. Your people want to hear it from you. But if the daily actions of your managers don't reflect and reinforce your vision, your empowerment efforts are doomed.

It's tough to get managers to act in support of your new vision. Ask Ron Shaich and Len Schlesinger. They are experts.

Ron and Len own the Au Bon Pain U.S. bakery chain. They were very clear on their vision—a specialty food and bake shop that had food you'd want to eat, served by employees who really wanted you to be there and who really wanted to be there themselves. They demonstrated their vision, talked about it at frequent management meetings, and reported progress in using it. But no matter what they tried, they couldn't get their managers to use their customer-sensitive, employee-supportive vision.

Finally, in desperation, they visited Pete Harmon's Kentucky Fried Chicken stores. Harmon was the first KFC franchisee. His stores earned 20 percent more than the best company owned locations and were often cited as the model of fast-food franchising. There they learned that Harmon's secrets were 1) make his managers owners (profit sharing and stock options); and 2) give them full authority to run the store within the guidelines of the customer service and employee respect policies. "The secret," Harmon said, "is to get managers to act and think like owners."

The pair took the advice home and immediately pilot-tested it in two stores. They were amazed at the quick turnaround and startling results.

Empowering managers to act in support of the vision really works. Ron and Len are believers—along with their thirty-one store managers.[7]

Gain this management action support in three ways: work through the hierarchy, use management group meetings, and be prepared to handle objections and obstacles.

Work through the hierarchy. Use your authority to get management action. Begin with your direct reports. Insist that your managers take specific concrete actions that embody your vision. That's precisely what Sam Benes did to develop management support for his vision.

> Sam was the CEO of a highly successful division of an electronic supply company. After getting his vision clear, he enlisted the support of his direct reports in getting the other people to use the vision.
>
> To set the tone for their units, Sam urged them to get out more with customers and employees, reorganize by simplifying organizational levels and assignments, and build in more direct ties between themselves and customers/employees.
>
> Sam's request was greeted with both enthusiasm and hesitation. Several people were uncomfortable, particularly with direct employee feedback, for instance, since they had rarely done anything like it before.
>
> The vice-president of engineering chose to visit the ship-

ping room as his first employee contact point. When he asked one of the employees, "What's going on?" the employee initially responded with puzzlement. When the vice-president followed up with, "How are things going?" the employee countered with the anxious question, "Why do you want to know? Am I doing something wrong?" The vice-president beat a hasty retreat and vowed to Sam that he'd stay within the friendly confines of engineering from now on.

To handle these and other similar problems, Sam put together a list of "do's and don'ts" when wandering and talked about the process extensively both one on one with individuals and at his regular staff meetings.

Sam told me, "Some of my direct reports were enthusiastic right from the beginning, and others were more hesitant. It takes time for some people to see how this extra visibility will help them be more effective."

Get your direct reports personally involved. They must enthusiastically support the vision both in words and actions. When they do, you're on the way to empowering everyone to use the vision.

Ed Finklestein, CEO and chairman of the R. H. Macy department store in the U.S., also gets his direct reports out there, living his vision of a customer-driven–cost-efficient retail store. Finklestein urges his store managers to spend some time each day personally selling, demonstrating using the vision. It must be working. Since being taken private through a leveraged buyout, Macy's increased sales 16.4 percent, quadrupling the industry average increase in the same period.[8]

Dave Packard, one of the legendary founders and chairman of Hewlett-Packard, also used his managers' actions to get widespread use of his vision. After returning from his assignment at the U.S. Department of Defense, he discovered that H-P was short $100 million in cash and had issued long-term debt. That violated Packard's basic vision of financing growth through equity and earnings. Packard got his key managers together and reminded them of his debt-free vision. He pointed out that the cash shortage could be solved by better managing receivables and inventories. He urged them to solve the problem. Within six months the company paid off the debt and had a surplus of $40 million. The secret? The managers left the meeting imbued with the "save cash" vision and acted aggressively to make the vision real. Led by the example set by the managers' actions, all employees were empowered to use the "save cash to be independent" vision.[9]

Your direct reports are important. But there are more managers who must adopt your vision. Work your way down the hierarchy. Get the entire management staff using the vision.

You may have to insist upon specific implementation objectives from your managers. That's what Gary Liebl did at Cipher Data Products. When he arrived, Cipher had a quality problem. Liebl appointed a task force of employees to investigate causes and cures. They recommended a new vision, training, designated communications channels, shared responsibilities, and real commitment from top management. Liebl then established schedules, budgets, and objectives, along with a regular review to assure that the new vision was carried out. "Sometimes," Gary Liebl said, "participative management can't be implemented participatively. Someone's got to take charge."[10]

One small note. It would be ideal if you could meet individually with each of your managers—but not very likely in a large organization. Empowering your direct reports to use your vision is the first step. Then you are ready to involve a wider range of managers in a less personal—but equally as powerful—manner.

Group management meetings. When you can't meet eyeball to eyeball, use group meetings to get action support. Aim to accomplish five things at these meetings.

First, *tell that your vision represents what you think and feel.* Your managers want to know that your vision comes from your own heart, not the pen of some clever public relations person. Relate several personal stories to show the roots of your vision. Share current personal actions that reflect your vision. Personalize your vision to make it more credible and powerful.

Second, *get understanding of your vision.* Managers need to say to themselves, "I understand the vision." Use extensive sports illustrations or other examples with which your audience can identify. People learn best from examples they understand. Or ask the managers to restate the meaning of the vision in their own words. This clarifies meanings and gets everyone on a similar wavelength.

Third, *keep building the need to change.* That's one of the underlying purposes of these management meetings. Sam Benes used several mechanisms to create the urgency to change (the first step in the change process). His charts showed dramatically some of the organization's faults, such as high personnel turnover and higher-than-expected reject rates. He stressed his personal commitment to his new vision. He pointed out the action steps he personally planned to take to live his vision. He emphasized that he would personally recognize individuals who practiced his new vision.

Fourth, *generate specific, concrete actions that support the vision.* Visions are ethereal. They are hard to translate into concrete actions. Therefore they are easy to avoid using. To avoid this problem, have your people set specific goals and action steps that use the vision. Then report progress on their specific goals and actions.

Sam Benes learned the hard way that you need to reduce the glittering generalities and "motherhood" statements to specific management actions. That's why he ended his management meeting asking each manager to commit to three action steps to reflect the vision, as reported below.

> Sam met with all 250 of his managers to announce his vision. He kept his presentation short (fifteen minutes) and snappy (he used several graphs and charts to spice up his talk).
>
> During the presentation he related several personal stories about how he came to his vision, why it was important to him, and what he was doing to live it. He also used extensive sports examples.
>
> At the end of his presentation he asked each person to write on a large sheet of paper three action steps that he/she was willing to take over the next three months to implement the vision in his/her area.
>
> Sam hung these sheets all around the room and asked everyone to read what their fellow managers were planning to do. He then collected these sheets and published the collection of action steps for all participants.

It's all too easy to point out what "they" ought to do to make the vision live. In my seminars managers are quick to point the finger of responsibility elsewhere. There's a long list of what the company needs to do, the top management needs to do, the immediate supervisor needs to do, the personnel department needs to do, and so on. All of those suggestions need to be listened to and acted upon. But the rubber meets the road when a manager says, "I will do *this* in order to make the vision happen in my area."

At the Springfield Remanufacturing Center Company (SRC) individual managers commit every week to action items that support the vision. Every Tuesday morning all managers meet with CEO Jack Stack to review how they are doing in living the vision. They review specific results and set specific targets that are then shared with all employees in departmental meetings in the afternoon. The concrete actions taken by all managers help everyone use the vision.[11]

General Bill Creech set out the general goal areas that related to his vision for TAC—number of sorties flown and number of aircraft ready to fly. Each squadron set their own goals within these two areas. Creech then reported each squadron's progress on these two goals. In just a twinkling squadrons were working to beat out the others—and the sortie rate climbed 11 percent per year and the number of aircraft ready for flight doubled.[12] When the people set goals and saw the results of their actions, they were empowered to use the vision.

Empower your managers to use the vision by announcing your own action steps. Also, circulate the managers' proposed action steps. This builds peer pressure both to write down and then accomplish actions. Publish periodic updates. Keep up the pressure for performance. Sam Benes used these methods effectively.

> Sam found that many managers wrote down very general actions, such as "improve customer relations" or "increase communications." Wanting to make the actions more specific, he gave everyone the opportunity to sharpen/revise his/her statements. Sam also published his action steps as examples.
>
> Sam told me, "It was frustrating at first dealing with the nonspecific action steps. But I realize now that it was a phase through which my people had to pass. In the course of my wanderings I talked to a number of managers about their actions, and found that from our interaction they learned a lot about how to make them more specific."

Specificity doesn't come easy. It takes time to think in specific terms. And don't expect perfection.

Paul Cofino successfully used this specific goal- and action-setting technique to empower his managers to use his vision.

> Paul is the general manager for the data processing division of a large company. Since his unit provides data processing development and support to the other activities of the company, Paul developed a vision: "Together we can make a difference."
>
> To convince his people to use the vision, Paul held departmental meetings with all 150 managers in his division. At these meetings he asked each manager to set three goals to carry out the vision. He then asked each manager to set up a timetable to achieve these goals with measurable milestones along the way.
>
> Paul collected these goals and timetables, distributed them to all managers, and included them in the formal monthly performance review.
>
> "In this way," Paul told me, "I can be certain that we are making progress in using our vision. Each month at our formal review session I report progress on my goals and action steps. I'm not bashful in pointing out when I fall short of my intended progress and in sharing what I intend to do to make up the shortfall. That helps everyone else to up-front as well."

Fifth, *emphasize short-term actions.* Management action takes place within a short time frame perspective. Most managers think and plan thirty to ninety days in advance. Therefore your vision actions should fall within the same time perspective.

Forty-eight hours is the magic time frame. If action isn't taken within forty-eight hours of attendance at a meeting, it will likely never take place. Therefore you want actions that use your vision within forty-eight hours and within thirty to ninety days. Paul Cofino used the short stroke action drill to get manager support for his vision.

> Paul got his managers together to set action steps to use his vision. He asked his managers to specify what they'd be

willing to do within the next forty-eight hours to support the vision. He had his secretary publish that information after the end of the meeting.

He also asked his managers to set some longer-term actions—things to be done within ninety days. He also compiled those and sent them out to everyone.

Paul asked for a report on progress for both the forty-eight-hour and ninety-day goals. He found that 87 percent of the forty-eight-hour actions were accomplished and 82 percent of the ninety-day ones were accomplished.

"The impetus from the immediate burst of activity, caused by the rush to complete the forty-eight-hour actions, really launched my vision," Paul said. "We made lots of believers out of doubters when they saw all that work going on at once."

Short-term actions create a burst of energy supporting your vision. This energy empowers people.

Sixth, *be prepared to handle objections and obstacles.* Watch out for the "yes, but . . ." crowd. There will be managers who can't complete their action steps. There will also be managers who are not quite ready to follow "one more executive fad." In short, there will be disbelievers and critics. Be prepared to handle their inevitable objections.

Sam Benes encountered obstacles when he announced his vision to the management staff. Several people brought up situations in which the actions of executive management contradicted the vision statements. Several others said the vision wouldn't work in their areas.

To deal with these objections, Sam asked his managers to list five obstacles that prevented them from using the vision. Sam compiled them into a report and fed them back to the next management meeting.

Sam chose several of the obstacles over which he had control and set up a specific action plan to remove them, challenging the other managers to do the same.

He said, "Some of the obstacles were the result of individual interpretations. We got rid of those right away because it isn't important that every one carbon copy my view, as long as the general philosophy holds. Most of the real obstacles are being worked on. It may not be perfect, but we are working to do better."

Be prepared for objections and obstacles. Answer them with actions.

In short, empower managers to use your vision by working through the hierarchy, using group management meetings, and being prepared to handle objections.

Your managers are key players in the use of your vision. Your people look not only to you for example setting, but also to their immediate boss as well. Get your management staff using your vision.

Personal Workshop

As you consider how to empower active management support for your vision, ponder the following questions.

1. How can I best use the management hierarchy in getting management actions that reflect using my vision?

What can I ask my direct reports to do? Can they be more visibly involved in living the vision? What's in it for them to live my vision? And how can I get what they want to them?

Can I afford the luxury of cascading the program neatly down the hierarchy, waiting for the higher level to "get it" before bringing it to the next level? Do I need to move more quickly than that will allow?

What is the best way to bring the vision down through the hierarchy? Do I need to carry the message down personally? Or can I rely upon my direct reports to effectively carry the message down? How can I support my direct reports if they do carry the message down?

2. What do my managers really want out of their association with my organization? Do I really know? How can I find out?

Consider spending time with a few managers—at different levels— and practice listening with an open mind to find out what they really want.

143

3. How and when can I hold management meetings to present my vision and get their active support? Is it better to do it in small groups (20–40), or can I handle larger groups (150–200)?

In considering a management meeting, what would make such a meeting appealing? Do slide shows work? Should I use some dramatic event—such as a special speaker? What is the best structure? Are there interaction opportunities to share ideas and clarify thoughts? What would make such a meeting attractive to my managers? How could I find out?

4. If I choose to hold a management meeting, how could I best present the information so that it's both informative and motivating?

Consider the use of visual aids—slides, graphs, pictures, movies— as well as live entertainment—living, breathing customers/employees with stories to share.

How can I get the managers to make individual commitments to action? I'll likely have to set the example with my own action steps, so I've got to be certain that mine are carefully crafted. Consider having them post their action steps on the wall, then sign up to support each other in executing them.

5. How can I set the example in implementing the action steps?

6. How can I anticipate the objections and obstacles that will likely be raised, and have answers for them?

Do I know the problems likely to be raised by my managers? If not, how can I find out? (Perhaps spending some time with a few of your managers might help.) What can I do to remove the obstacles or answer the objections?

7. How can I build in a continuing stream of reports about the managers' actions without creating a paper mill and drowning us all in paper?

EMPLOYEE ACTIONS
THAT EMPOWER THE VISION

It's tough to change. That only happens when everybody pulls together and is empowered to use the vision. And I mean *everybody*. I've only talked about managers thus far. I've saved the biggest and most important group for last—*the employees.* If you don't empower your employees to use your vision—give up! fold up your tent! turn in your badge! You're history.

Empower your employees to use your vision by organizing employee meetings, setting direct feedback, and using key role models. I'll look at all three.

Employee meetings. It would be ideal to meet individually with each employee, explain your vision, and get his/her active support. Unfortunately, you live in a less-than-ideal world. It just isn't practical, except in the smallest of companies. You are forced to use group meetings. Earlier in the chapter I discussed how to structure a management meeting. Employee meetings follow the same format.

At the meeting, personalize your vision. Employees want to know that it's really yours, not some slick PR job. Tell them of your own personal actions to live the vision. Report its personal roots. Highlight the "calling" of the vision. Focus attention on the lofty aims and purposes with which everyone can identify. Recall the "Bringing computer power to the people" vision of Apple Computers, Inc., the "Guest" vision of Disney, and the "To serve God in all we do" vision of ServiceMaster. These are examples of lofty visions that help individual employees think, "I want to contribute to that cause." Make that "cause" clear to employees. Sam Benes did an excellent job of making his company's cause clear to employees.

> When Sam first met with employees in large departmental groups, he put together an audiotape and slide show that showed how one of the division's products saved the life of a young girl in the local community. The young girl actually attended one of the meetings. Sam said, "Here was living, breathing proof of the importance of their jobs and why quality was so important."

A picture is worth a thousand words. A personal visit like the one Sam arranged is worth a million. Real-life examples powerfully communicate the cause and clarify the vision. Deepen the understanding through charts, graphs, and pictures.

End the meeting with a specific action plan from each employee that supports the vision in his/her area. Get both forty-eight-hour actions and ninety-day actions. Summarize and report the actions back to employees and managers. Follow up to make certain that the actions take place. Empower employees to use the vision.

Springfield Remanufacturing Center Company holds weekly employee meetings to discuss specific employee actions to support the vision in each area. Managers review financial and operating results and talk about specific problems/opportunities. Each employee sets an action plan—both as an individual and as part of the departmental team. That plan is shared with all employees and followed up next week for accomplishment. That's empowerment! No wonder their book value has soared more than eighty times in the past few years.[13]

Ben & Jerry's Homemade is a unique U.S. company. For starters they make ice cream—only ice cream. Premium ice cream ("The best ice cream," according to my son). What's more, they're more interested in employees and their community than they are in making money. Their avowed purpose in going into business was to be a force for social change. They've grown in spite of themselves into a $32 million organization.

Ben Cohen—who's the active partner now—works hard to insure that people are "weird" enough before they sign on. He also stays up nights worrying that "funk will not survive the world of big business." That's the world Ben & Jerry's is now entering.

Every week there's an all-hands meeting. Everyone gets together to talk about *everything.* The agenda's open for anyone to say anything. Comments are all taken seriously. If anything comes up during the week, anyone can "ring the bell." When the bell rings, everyone drops whatever he/she is doing and assembles to work on the problem.

Ben & Jerry's is a different place to work—no doubt about that. But it works—well. It's not perfect. They're always fine-tuning, rethinking, and getting weird about this or that. "Our company will change," says Ben. "There's no doubt about that. We just have to make it a good change." Getting employee commitment to their vision through employee meetings is what Ben & Jerry's is all about.[14]

Direct feedback. Build in direct feedback. Find out direct from the horse's mouth both what's happening in using your vision and what difficulties are preventing it from happening. Employee newsletters are excellent ways to get this direct feedback. List your telephone number and your mailing address in the news-letter and urge people to call you directly. Ren McPherson, CEO at Dana some years back, staged a program called "Talk Back to the Boss," where he encouraged employees to contact him directly.

The following shows how Paul Cofino used direct feedback to develop employee actions to support his vision.

> Paul explained his vision at special company meetings. He asked each employee to list two or three actions that would support the vision in his/her area. These were shared with everyone.

> He also asked each employee to write him a "Dear Paul" letter, outlining the obstacles he/she saw in using the vision, along with what each was willing to do to remove/reduce the obstacle.

> Paul received many letters outlining a number of obstacles. He worked on removing the obstacles. Within three months many of the obstacles were being worked on, and productivity was at an all-time high.

Convince people that you care about them. They need to know that before they care about using your vision. Paul's interest in getting direct employee feedback and then acting quickly on it sent a powerful message to his employees. It said, "I really care about what you say. I want to live the vision, not merely talk about it. And I want you to live it, too."

Key alter ego employees. You can't be everywhere. No matter how dedicated and energetic you are, there are space and time limitations. Multiply your presence by training key alter egos. These people can become additional credible role models demonstrating the use of your vision.

Begin by *identifying* the key alter ego employees. Choose the people yourself. Pick respected individuals. Or ask for volunteers, thus getting people who are really dedicated to the task. Either selection process works. Sam Benes, in the following example, used a combination.

> Sam needed a task force of key employees to help develop the widespread use of his vision. He advertised in the com-

pany newspaper for volunteers, offering only the opportunity to do the extra work for no extra pay.

He asked individuals to write a one-page statement explaining why they wanted to serve on the task force. He also established the rule that no more than one person was permitted from each department.

From those who applied, the personnel department selected twenty respected individuals. In addition, several people were urged to "volunteer."

The task force met regularly with Sam. "They were very helpful in both thinking through how we get people to use the vision and in lining up support for the vision throughout the organization," he said.

Give alter ego employees *special status.* Put them in special locations, give them special clothing to wear, or give them special privileges, such as traveling to competitors and/or visiting other locations. These distinctions help other employees use your key alter egos as a reference point—a credible role model to follow in using your vision.

Immerse alter ego employees in your new philosophy. These individuals will be your representatives, your alter egos, your emissaries. Their actions need to reflect your vision. Hans Schleimer went to great lengths to be certain that his key employees were effective alter egos.

Hans was the CEO of a major multinational. He wanted to convert from a technically oriented, product-driven company to a more market-oriented, customer-driven organization.

To develop commitment among his more than 97,000 person work force, he chose 175 informal leaders from across his organization, with heavy concentration from the technical areas, from which he expected a great deal of resistance.

Hans spent three consecutive weeks with his 175 key employees discussing the vision and how it should be used. He wanted to make certain that they understood and internalized it.

They discussed possible obstacles and ways around them.

At the end of the three weeks each person set an action agenda and had a small (three- to five-person) support team to help implement the action plan.

Over the next months Hans remained in close contact with each of 175 alter egos, following up to see what role he could play in keeping them on target. After three months the group reassembled and replanned their agendas.

Hans told me, "The 175 did a marvelous job. I couldn't have done it without them. They were there to answer questions about what words and phrases meant. They were there to model the 'right' behavior. They were all the places I could not be."

Each and every employee must be empowered to use the vision—every time. The welder needs to decide to make the weld perfectly—every time. The reservation operator needs to decide to answer the phone with courtesy—every time. This book is designed to show you how to empower that welder, that reservation operator, to use the vision every time.

Personal Workshop

As you consider how you can empower active employee involvement in living your vision, consider the following questions.

1. What do my employees really want out of their association with my organization? Do I really know? How can I find out?

Consider spending time with several employees and finding out what they really want. Where do they eat lunch? Maybe showing up there a few times will yield rich insights.

2. How can I present my vision so it can be understood by my employees?
How can I use visuals (charts, graphs, pictures) to get my point across? Many of the comments I made in the previous section of this chapter also apply here.

3. How can I present my vision so that it links clearly with some higher "calling" to which my employees can and want to commit?
Can I use some dramatic real-life examples of this higher calling (like the little girl whose life Sam's company's equipment saved)?

4. How can I build in direct personal feedback from employees on their progress and problems in executing the actions that flow from my vision?

5. How can I use the key employee alter ego approach in developing commitment?

What employees would I select? What is the best selection process? How can I give the key employees special status? How can I assure that they internalize my vision?

Empower people to use your new vision. That's what you've read about in this chapter. Unless everyone knows what you want, they can't do it. But then empowering the vision is a more difficult task. Demonstrate it yourself. Point out how it's really working and, therefore, worth using. Get managers to demonstrate it also. And, finally, get the employees to do it.

Whew! What a task. And it isn't over. People need constant reminding of their empowerment. In the next chapters I'll show you how to do that.

8

Expect It or Forget It

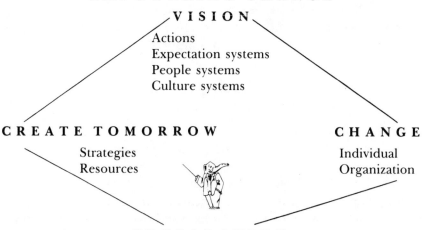

EMPOWERING CHANGE

VISION

Actions
Expectation systems
People systems
Culture systems

CREATE TOMORROW

Strategies
Resources

CHANGE

Individual
Organization

PREPARATION

Getting ready
Anticipating obstacles

People have short memories: they forget easily. Remind your people continually that *they* are empowered to make changes. Or all your work could be washed away like a sand castle at high tide.

Empower your people—every day. Show your vision in action—every day. Talk about the vision's success—every day. Or else—your people will forget and your vision will be history.

Fortunately, you have systems that send clear and powerful messages. Use these messages to reinforce your personal empowerment message. This chapter talks about one of them—the performance management system. The following chapters cover two other systems: personnel and cultural.

The performance management system sends powerful but sometimes confusing messages. Unfortunately most performance systems encourage doing business the same old way. In the 1970s GE failed to install a worker-participation vision in twelve plants. The reason: the performance management system kept sending the "do business the same old way" message. The performance system kept telling managers, "Everything's okay." Without any strong motivation even to consider the new participation system, very few managers did. And those who tried it soon learned that participation was extra work without any extra reward. At GE, as in most companies, "what gets measured gets produced."[1] Participation efforts were neither expected, measured, nor rewarded, so they died a quiet, unnoticed death. The performance system needs to remind people repeatedly that empowerment means *they* do it.

EXPECTATIONS

If you don't expect it—and tell your people you want it—you'll never get it. People are very poor mind readers.

Set specific, numeric expectations. People are motivated to achieve things they can see, touch, and measure. Imagine bowling if you couldn't see how many pins you knocked over. My guess is you'd soon get bored with the game and quit. Expect specific numeric outcomes—and accept nothing less.

Stand firm. You'll get the argument, "I agree with you, but . . . quantifiable goals are just not possible in this situation." The giants in the management studies field all disagree. Professors N. Edward Deming, George Odiorne, and Peter Drucker—to name three—argue that all management activities can be measured. Read the following pages and see for yourself. I believe that every management situation can be measured in one of four quantitative terms—units, money, time, and/or customer/user satisfaction.

American Express is an expert at counting the "uncountable." Amex establishes over two hundred customer-service expectations for its credit card employees, which include application processing time, telephone service time, lost card replacement time, and correspondence response time. In another arena, Amex is working hard to develop a "One Enterprise" mentality. Specific expectations include two multidivision/One Enterprise projects a year on which progress is reported monthly.[2]

In the U.S. hair salon business, John McCormack uses exact numeric expectations to empower the intangibles of his vision. To encourage excellent customer service McCormack expects his stylists to build a request-by-name clientele. He pays an extra 10 percent commission when that happens. When that happens 50 percent of the time the bonus increases an additional 10 percent, and at 75 percent the bonus kicks up another 10 percent. When the particular hairstylist is among the top fifty requested in the chain (McCormack publishes a monthly request standings report), he pays another "superbonus."

To encourage high profitability, McCormack expects his hairdressers to sell hair care products (on which there's a much higher margin), for which he pays another 15 percent bonus. The product bonus can be used to buy various benefits, including health care insurance (rare in the salon business), vacation trips, training sessions, and personal meetings with top fashion and hair care professionals.

Every perk, every benefit, every penny of compensation, are the results of some specific quantifiable achievement for *everyone* in the company—receptionists, trainees, and managers. Everyone has measurable targets, takes personal responsibility for achieving them, and earns everything he/she gets.

Do these specific expectations empower the vision? Absolutely! Hairstylists in McCormack's operation earn three times the industry average in the U.S., with top producers earning as much as seven times. And McCormack stores outperform the industry in almost every measure: double the industry average in average sales per customer, quadruple the industry average in retail product sales, and less than one-third the industry average in employee turnover. Specific, numeric expectations—backed by a real-time computerized feedback and a rich reward system—empower the vision for visible differences—and create win-win experiences for everyone: employees, customers, and owners.[3]

And keep the expectations short term in nature. T. J. Rodgers, president of U.S. Cyprus Semiconductors in San Jose, California, uses a weekly goal-setting activity to empower his people to live his "every employee an entrepreneur." Every Monday each of the 670 employees meet in their ten-to-twenty-person project teams and mutually decide on weekly goals and priorities. These are entered in a computer; the status is updated continually. By Tuesday each of the forty-five managers reprioritizes employees' goals to get hot projects moving faster. Each Wednesday VPs meet with Rodgers to review progress. Continually reviewed "short stroke" goals empower every employee to continually make individual entrepreneurial decisions.

Does it work? In 1986, while most semiconductor firms were awash in red ink, Cypress earned $13.4 million on sales of $50.9 million. Cypress introduced 33 percent more chips than other similar-size firms, 90 percent of which worked correctly the first time—more than double the industry average. No wonder Rodgers calls his system "Turbo MBO"—it turbo-empowers his people to use his vision and produce better products, faster, with high profit margins.[4]

It even works in government. One city manager in California has each of his employees set specific, measurable expectations for customer service and quality. These goals are measured each week and charted next to the employee's work area. So do several branch managers for the employment development department at the state level and the highway maintenance crew chiefs at the county level. A social service department manager in a local government in Holland helped his people establish service and quality levels with their customers. These levels are reviewed at the weekly staff meeting attended by all employees.

Relate to strategic advantage. What is your strategic advantage—around which your vision is based? Is it customer service? quality? fast delivery? flexibility? new product development? Whatever it is, clearly spell out a specific numeric expectation in that area for *every* job. If customer service is your competitive edge, *every* job in your organization needs a specific quantifiable expectation about that person's contribution to customer service. No exceptions!

In 1980, it became clear to U.K.'s Rank Xerox what they had to do to succeed. They found themselves 50 percent behind their Japanese competitors on such criteria as final product quality and inventory size. They established the "Leadership through Quality" program and organized quality project teams to improve operations. Each group established a benchmark and then worked to achieve it. For instance, in 1980 there was one defect in every machine. The benchmark for 1988 was two per 1,000 machines. In 1980 Rank Xerox held three months of inventory. The benchmark was set at one half a months of inventory for 1988.

The benchmarks focused action. By 1987 final product defects had fallen to six per 1,000 and inventory had fallen to eighteen days. In both 1984 and 1985 Rank Xerox won the British Quality Award. Measurement related to strategic advantage produces results.[5]

For the U.S. Tactical Air Command (as previously discussed), the competitive edge is very clear cut: flying and fighting. General Creech built those twin expectations into every job under his command. Wing commanders (executives) were ordered to resume flying and wear their flying suits around the base. Sortie expectations were set for every squadron, as were maintenance levels, number of hours each plane was in the air, and number of planes combat ready. Every squadron member—and that included every member of TAC—knew precisely what he/she had to do to meet the flying/fighting expectations. An average annual increase in sorties of 11 percent during General Creech's six years of command combined with a total reduction of 40 percent in the budget testifies to the empowerment of specific expectations—even in a glacial environment like the military.[6]

Sometimes flexibility and hustle are *the* principal competitive advantages. Financial service firms like Goldman, Sachs and Morgan Guarantee regularly outearn their competitors—not with proprietary products or economies of scale—but with superior execution and aggressive opportunism. Each employee in these firms knows that quick action and hustle are the ways to win. They are clearly expected to demonstrate these characteristics and are empowered to do so by the clarity of the expectations.[7]

Efficiency is the key competitive advantage at the Springfield Remanufacturing Center Company. Every employee knows that efficiency is his/her responsibility—and gets reminded of that at the weekly departmental meeting. At that meeting each employee takes specific responsibility for efficiency improvements of the operation. Progress is reported at the next week's meeting.[8] That's empowerment! It means that every single individual knows what he/she needs to know to measure the real or reinforcing effect of his/her work on the total output.

Quality is *the* watchword at IBM these days—for internal as well as external customers. To meet this general quality expectation, corporate accounting agreed with their internal customers on a specific set of expectations for internal data transfer, including specific accuracy expectations, procedures to check data accuracy before transfer, and feedback mechanisms to correct errors. Errors dropped more than 80 percent to less than 1 percent once the specific expectations were agreed upon—the result of empowerment—or giving people the tools and data to do what had to be done.[9]

Customer service is a major strategic thrust of Apple Computer, Inc., these days. Managers are expected to staff the consumer toll-free telephone number regularly. Managers who participate get a commemorative listening certificate—with a gold star if he/she actually answers one or more calls. In this way, Apple executives put forth expectations that empower and reinforce customer service behavior.[10]

The Boston Celtics are the class act in U.S. basketball. They've won more championships than any other team. They've got good players—and even one or two great players—but their competitive edge lies in their ability to play together as a team. There's a clear expectation on the part of everybody that they will play together. Larry Bird, the acknowledged star, said on the eve of a big game, "I'll be ready and the other guys will be ready and *we're* going to win this thing." Red Auerbach, long-term coach and now president, said, "One day Bill Walton told me he was down in the dumps. I asked him what was wrong, and he said he didn't feel like he was contributing to the team. . . . I told him that we didn't care what he scored. All we were interested in was what he contributed. Did he roll down? Did he play defense? Did he run the court? Did he pass? . . . From that point on he was a different guy. . . . And he never looked to see what he scored. All he looked at was, did we win? And it was 'we,' not 'I.' "[11]

Look for what will give you a competitive edge. What you want depends on how much and how clearly you empower your people to deliver. If quality is your competitive edge, then set such numeric expectations as scrap, rework, part-per-million defect rate, unscheduled machine downtime, customer complaints, warranty expenses, and service calls.

If new product development is your competitive edge, then set such numeric expectations as total launch time for new products, product and process development milestones, key characteristics of new products in comparison with customer needs and competitors' design, and customer satisfaction with new products.

Link specific numeric expectations with your strategic advantage. Strategies come in four varieties. There's the innovation variety, where new and different is vital. Harvey-Armstrong Jones built ICI based upon that approach. Then there's the low-cost variety. Amstrad, the successful U.K. PC producer, buys the cheapest Asian components for its no-frills PC. Then there's the market share variety of strategy, practiced successfully by the Japanese. Last, there's the quality strategy; take care of quality and the rest takes care of itself. IBM, Shell, and Merck are examples of this.[12] Whatever your strategy, translate it into specific expectations for each and every employee.

Translate your vision into specific numeric expectations. Express these expectations in terms of *time, money, units,* or *customer/ user satisfaction.* Let your people know that you expect them to use the vision. If you don't expect it—and communicate your expectation clearly—your people will never know it—or do it.

Personal Workshop

As you consider the design of your expectations, please ponder the following questions.

1. What are the performance expectations now in my organization?

Do people know what's expected of them? How can we share more of these expectations? Do these current expectations encourage people to reach for the best they can be, or are they the "foxhole" type (keep your head down, don't try anything new, and hope your competition gets shot being too adventurous)?

Ask a few of your colleagues and direct reports and then go two or three levels down in the organization. Do you get the same answers?

2. How specific are my expectations for myself and my direct reports?

Do your expectations spell out dates, times, money, number of units, and what will count when it comes to those who have to sign off on the output?

How specific are the expectations of others in your organization? What can you do to help others be more specific?

3. Do my expectations for myself and my direct reports relate to my strategic advantage?

How do your expectations encourage focus on that strategic advantage? Are they realistic given resource and external conditions?

Do the expectations of others in your organization agree with that strategic advantage? What can you do to encourage people to do what contributes to your strategic advantage?

4. Does everyone in the organization have a set of specific, numeric expectations that support our strategic objectives?

MEASUREMENT

Measure it—or forget it! That's the watchword for this section. What gets measured gets empowered and produced. So measure the behavior you expect. In bowling you roll the ball down the alley and count the number of pins still standing (hopefully none!) to see whether you met the standard.

As it is in sports, so it is in business—in theory, at least! "But how can you measure the intangibles?" so many managers ask. "After all, it's how you accomplish the task that matters just as well—maybe more." Again, there are many ways to quantify intangible behavior.

"Service" and "friendliness" can be measured—in an awesomely powerful way. There are a number of excellent observable measures of customer service, for instance, as Jan Courtlander, the branch manager for a regional banking chain, discovered.

As part of the bank's new commitment to customer service, Jan was charged with the responsibility of improving the branch's level of customer service. Her boss told her that the number of account closings would be his way of measuring Jan's success in this area. She wasn't completely happy with that measure—as many things beyond her control affected account closings—but that was her boss's measure, so she was stuck with it. She also knew that the number of account closings meant little to the bank tellers, so she couldn't use that measure with her people.

For several weeks she puzzled over how to measure improvements in customer service by her tellers. Then she hit upon the idea of asking her tellers for their ideas. They flooded her with many ideas—which boiled down to the following five measures:

1. Smile.

2. Use the customer name.

3. Maintain a neat, businesslike appearance.

4. Make at least one nonbusiness comment.

5. Say "Hello" in the beginning and "Thank you" at the end.

Employees agreed to evaluate their fellow workers daily using those measures or a 1–5 scale. Jan took all those who got 90 percent 4 scores or better for a week to a special lunch. Within weeks she noticed a distinctly friendlier and warmer atmosphere in the bank. Her regional manager commented on the friendly feeling as well.

Jan knew that her bank was not rate competitive, so she felt that a lot of the impact of the improvement in her tellers' customer service was washed away. The number of account closings fell somewhat, though not as much as either Jan or her manager expected. But her branch was the only one in the thirty-seven-outlet chain to show a decrease in closing during this period.

Jan teaches us several lessons. First, *ask the people closest to the job* to come up with specific measures. They often know good jobs from bad ones, many times even better than the manager.

Also, use *different measures at different levels.* Bank teller measures will be different from branch manager measures. But for any level, provide short-cycle feedback based on the production cycle. Daily feedback helps empower employees.

Design measurements that provide clear, direct feedback on a few strategic advantage measures. Focus attention on vision-supporting behaviors. Empower your people to use your vision.

Use few measures. Keep it short and simple (KISS). Measure only what you *really* want. And what you really want are those few activities that support your new vision.

Define the best measure of the most important task for *each* employee. No exceptions! Measure *every* employee on those few most important activities that contribute to your new vision. A few basic questions help. *Ask employees,* "How does this job help us live the vision? Can it make us win?" And then, "How do you know when you're succeeding or failing?"

Ask customers also. In his recent book *Passion for Excellence,* Tom Peters cites the example of Todd Frazer (not his real name) in the plumbing supply business.

> Several years ago Todd was determined to become the "best service company" in his business. To figure out what that meant, he asked his forty branch managers. They told him to offer more brand-name products, spruce up the looks of the branches, and hire a higher-caliber (and more experienced) salesman. . . . Todd did it all. And then he waited. And waited. Nothing happened.
>
> A couple of years later his frustration reached the boiling point. . . . He simply visited his customers and asked them what they wanted. . . .
>
> . . . Here's what Todd heard. The problem for the plumbers was the cost of labor they wasted waiting for an order from Todd (or one of his competitors) to arrive. So Todd promised one-hour service when the local industry standard was (then) one-half day. . . . He promised a maximum wait of fifteen minutes for service fulfillment if the plumber came to the branch. . . .
>
> The results are history. . . . In the last couple of years Todd has added 50 percent to his revenues, in a no-growth market, and is able to charge premium prices.[13]

Customers tell you what's really essential. And how about *internal customers/users?* 3M, GTE, IBM, Bell Canada, Shell Oil, and Westinghouse ask internal customers to evaluate the importance and quality-service levels of staff departments. Staff members and customers then negotiate contracts for service levels and measurements.[14] Sounds like what Todd did, doesn't it? Empowering people through clear, numerical "scores" and "goals" will probably work for you also.

How about combining employees, external customers, and internal customers/users? That's what Warren Rodgers, president of Monroeville, Pennsylvania, Computer Specialists, Inc., does. Twice a year Warren has his people fill out evaluation sheets on their own performance and on the performance of their internal suppliers. He then asks his external customers to do the same evaluation.[15] People meet to talk about the ratings and resolve any differences.

CEO Gault knows what keeps the bounce in Rubbermaid's performance. It focuses on four key factors—sales growth of 15 percent, earnings growth of 15 percent, sufficient new product introductions so that 30 percent of sales are from products no more than five years old, and 90 percent success rate for new product introductions. Gault carefully measures these four factors—which taken together give Rubbermaid its competitive advantage—and every employee can recite them from memory. For Rubbermaid these four measures are the best indicators of their most important tasks.[16] They empower people to follow Gault's vision.

Chairman John Ashcroft grew Coloroll, Inc., from a 3 percent market share in wall coverings in Britain in 1978 to a market leadership position of 30 percent in 1986, while increasing profits eighteen times. Ashcroft says, "The easiest way to make money is to cut costs." So he relentlessly measures . . . measures . . . measures controllable costs. Everyone has a coffee mug imprinted with ten cost questions, including orders, production, inventory, cash, lost orders, and profits. Ashcroft says, "The trick is not how many questions you ask, but how frequently you ask a limited number of questions—and the ten questions on the mug are the ones the guys know I'd be asking if I were around." Ashcroft knows what gives him a competitive edge, and he measures it with fervor, thus empowering people to act on them.[17]

Mrs. Fields Cookies is one of the sweetest success stories in recent years. Over five hundred stores in thirty-seven states produce a "feel good feelings" (what her stores sell, according to Debbie Fields), selling cookies with 50 percent chocolate by weight and a profit margin to match. How do you empower employees—mostly young and part-time—in such a far-flung empire to live the vision—fresh, warm, wonderful cookies served up by smiling, productive, honest people? Few organizations would willingly take on such a formidable task.

Debbie, and her husband and partner, Randy, have the simple answer—detailed, computerized measurements. Every store, every hour, gets a detailed report, complete with action recommendations, based on the measurement of last hour's sales. The report includes when to prepare cookie mixes, what cookies to prepare, when to bake, crew staffing, suggestive selling ideas, and ways to drum up new business.

Store managers and employees know exactly what's expected—what gets measured in their hourly computer report. Clarity empowers action—and produces "feel good feelings" for employees, customers, managers, and owners alike.[18]

Use *nonfinancial measures* as well. In the U.S., Westinghouse's College Station, Texas, appliance plant is the most cost-efficient of its kind. Its productivity is six times that of its sister plant in Baltimore. They measure two key nonfinancial factors that contribute to their competitive edge—skill levels of employees (they pay for skill level, not seniority) and team performance as evaluated by team members. These measurements empower performance on these two critical-to-success factors.[19]

Diamond International Corporation's Palmer, Massachusetts, egg carton plant is in a very cost competitive industry. To encourage productivity they measure employees on such nonfinancial factors as attendance, formal discipline actions, lost-time injuries, cost-saving or safety-improving suggestions, departmental performance, and participation in community activities. On each of these measurements, employees earn points which are then redeemed for jackets and other prizes. Productivity rose 14.5 percent in the first year of the measurement-reward program and kept up a steady 2.7 percent annual improvement ever since.[20]

Tax man Henry Block uses a different nonfinancial measurement system to evaluate his employees. Henry listens for the "thank-yous." When a customer leaves and says, "Thank you," to the employee, Henry knows that customer feels he/she got good service. Taxpayers who feel they got good service are most likely to come back next year. Henry trains his managers to listen for the thank-yous. Perhaps that's why his H&R Block is the most successful franchised tax preparation services in America.[21]

Keep it short and simple, though. Too many measures confuse people. Charlie Dinsmore, an engineering department head for an equipment design and manufacturing firm, learned that lesson the hard way.

Charlie's company vision stressed multidisciplinary teams working together to provide excellent equipment. He announced eleven measures ranging from cooperation scores given by other departments to unit costs and on-time delivery. After three months he noticed very little movement in his measures and relatively little interest in the company's vision.

I urged Charlie to simplify his measures. His people came up with the following three measures:

1. on-time, on-budget delivery of multidisciplinary efforts;

2. complimentary customer letters;

3. number of requests to work with department members on future team efforts.

Almost immediately Charlie noticed a much more cooperative, harmonious working relationship with other departments and with customers. Over the next six months each of the three indexes rose dramatically.

Tie in your few measures with your *strategic advantage.* Be sure you have useful information and figures that relate to your strategic advantage. Unfortunately too many internal information systems fail to provide such data. Why? Most internal information systems grew out of the financial reporting system. The financial reporting system measures factors of interest to bankers and financiers. The result: too many systems relate myriad financial numbers that bear little relationship to operations.

Furthermore, most management accounting grew up in the 1920s when manufacturing was the dominant industry. Accounting systems were built on the premise that what got made in one time period was sold in the same time period. Neither of these two assumptions is correct today.

Professors Robert Johnson and Thomas Kaplan, in their book *Relevance Lost,* argue for a new approach to cost accounting. They call it an activity-based or transaction-based accounting system. They cite the example of a hydraulic valve manufacturer with thousands of items in its product line. The company had a typical sales distribution: 20 percent of the products accounted for 80 percent of revenues, 60 percent accounted for 99 percent of revenues, and the 40 percent of the products that generated 1 percent of the revenues had the highest gross margins according to the accounting system, which allocated overhead (better than 75 percent of total costs) on the basis of sales volume. Activity-based costing showed a very different picture. The low-volume items (75 percent of the line) were losing money. The 25 percent of the products that made money generated more than 80 percent of the sales and 300 percent of the profits.[22]

Let's not get lost in the world of accounting systems. That will sidetrack us. My message here is, *Measure the indicative costs* in order to get *good measures of your strategic advantages.*

Direct feedback. "Don't wait," is the best advise in giving empowering feedback. Give feedback as close as possible to the behavior you want. Immediate feedback reinforces the behavior—and increases the probability that the behavior will be repeated. If you want to empower good customer service, measure it and tell people how they did on it as soon as possible after they do it.

As you recall, Springfield Remanufacturing Center Company uses a red flashing electronic message board to give its employees feedback on key measures that tie in to their competitive advantage. Each employee sees every day the results of key efficiency measures for that day's production.[23]

Build in short-cycle measurement feedback, even in complex, long-cycle tasks. Q. T. Wiles is a turnaround specialist. He's a partner in Hambrecht and Quist, a leading Silicon Valley venture capitalist. He resurrects the problem companies in Hambrecht and Quist's portfolio. When he takes over, Q. T. measures ten key items to help him empower the long-term restructuring of the business. He does weekly P&Ls and project/product status reports to empower short-term actions to identify and correct problems. He also insists on weekly trip reports and "what I learned from customers" reports to empower people to more rapidly respond to changing conditions. To ensure that information empowers action, Q. T. asks for weekly reports on the five most important tasks accomplished. His monthly reports focus on the "top ten accounts," the top ten customers who owe money, head count, and recruiting lists, which leads to the monthly activity report. These magic ten measures empower people to support the "get well quickly" vision.[24]

Furthermore, maximize empowerment by getting the word directly to the person for whom it is intended. Get it directly to the person as quickly as possible. Imagine how frustrated you'd be if every time you bowled a ball down the alley you had to wait several hours to find out from the alley manager how many pins you knocked down. You'd probably give up the game quickly! Most people do the same thing at work.

The highly successful Domino's Pizza uses a TIPO (team/individual performance objectives) program to provide weekly and monthly feedback on performance to *all* employees in the chain. Both individuals and teams establish key customer satisfaction levels and reduce it to some numerical value. The team and the supervisor establish priorities and expected service levels. Results are feedback weekly and bonuses paid monthly. This real-time feedback empowers employees to keep their eye on the customer satisfaction ball.

Domino's TIPO measurement system uses real-time, short-term direct feedback to accomplish long-term strategic objectives. Domino's realizes that "a pizza is a pizza is a pizza." Eventually all pizza places will deliver. Domino's encourages customers to buy Domino's tomorrow by providing superior service today. Customer loyalty, purchased through superior service, is Domino's long-term strategy, which they empower by the TIPO series of short-term, real-time feedbacks.[25]

McDonald's understands the need to give short-stroke feedback in order to empower its vision. Field consultants visit outlets regularly. During their visits they give immediate feedback on operations. "Great hash browns, but watch those biscuits. They're a little stale." Field representatives are the embodiment of the McDonald's vision of "Service, Cleanliness, Quality, Value." They measure managers' performance in living the vision and give real-time feedback. Store personnel know that the next customer in line, ordering a Big Mac, could be one of those opportunities to find out how well they're living the vision.[26]

Talk about short term. Remember Debbie Fields of Mrs. Fields

Cookies, who measures store performance *hourly.* Or John McCormack, who measures hairstylists' performance daily. Or T. J. Rodgers, who measures over 4,500 employee goals daily.

Empower your people to use the vision. Measure and provide real-time, direct feedback on those actions that support the vision.

Personal Workshop

As you consider the design of the measurement system, please ponder the following questions.

1. How do I know when I'm really succeeding?

What are the key data points that tell you that you're on or off track?

2. Do my direct reports have measurement data that tells them how they're doing?

3. Do all the people in my organization have data that tells each of them how they're doing?

REWARD

What gets measured, gets produced. What gets rewarded, gets produced again. So empower people by rewarding using the vision. It's so simple—and so many companies don't do it. Fairness and equity seem more important than performance. Don't fall into the "let's give everyone the same" trap. Discriminate unabashedly—on the basis of performance.

Empower your people by rewarding the "right" behavior—using your vision. Use many different rewards, reward all those who use your vision, and individualize rewards.

Many different rewards possible. Find ways to reward those people who regularly use your vision. That empowers people to use your vision. Use formal and informal rewards, including instant cash bonuses, pictures on bulletin boards, and personal lunch dates. Demonstrate graphically, publicly, and systematically that using the vision consistently *really* matters.

166

Money is always a good reward. Instant cash *bonuses* remind people about using the vision. Dr. David Martin, vice-president of research for U.S. company Genentech, writes "Genenchecks" for up to $1,000 to those who develop new applications.[27] Psicor (supplying equipment and professionals called perfusionists for open heart surgery) provides bonuses for specific activities such as bigger caseloads and out-of-town assignments. IBM pays awards of $10,000 or more for outstanding innovations. John McCormack links specific performance—such as being requested by customers at least 75 percent of the time or selling at least $300 worth of hair care products a week—with specific rewards—such as health care insurance, trips, and special seminars.[28] Link vision using activities with bonuses as a way to empower people.

Pay *individual or group incentives* to reward using the vision. Worthington Steel and Nucor both "pay by the pound." They give group incentives based upon the productivity of the group. They also pay individual incentives based upon company profitability. Dana Corporation is a leader in the use of the Scanlon plan. This plan is a group and individual incentive program built around an employee participation system for determining production standards. Lincoln Electric pays its people on an individual incentive system based both on productivity and methods improvements. Lincoln's costs have fallen faster than any other competitor, and employees earn up to 50 percent above the area average.[29] The Au Bon Pain chain of restaurants and bakeries pays store managers a modest flat salary and then shares profits fifty-fifty above $170,000.[30] More than seven hundred U.K. companies have pay-for-performance or profit-sharing schemes. Productivity bonuses at British Steel, for example, have boosted workers' pay from $213 per week to $414, while keeping unit costs steady.[31]

Even the government is infected with the pay-for-performance virus. Using quantifiable financial and service-level delivery goals, managers in many public jurisdictions can gain or lose up to 20 percent of their base pay. When you want to empower performance—pay for it!

Pay systems often get stuck in concrete. If yours is, use *moneylike* rewards. Arrange for *free tickets* to the local amusement park or movie theater for those who stayed all night to complete the rush project. Distribute *gift certificates* to people using your vision. Treat staff members who regularly use your vision to *special lunches.* The list goes on and on. There are a host of small but impressive monetarylike rewards you could use to empower people who consistently use your vision.

Watch out, though! Don't overemphasize the importance of monetary rewards. No doubt many people in your organization talk a lot about money—or at least how little they have of it. It's easy to be persuaded that giving everyone a big salary increase would instantly empower your people. Those of us who've given large salary increases know that they do bump performance—for a short while! But then performance sags again to close to the original level. Both research and practical experience indicate that money is a poor long-term motivator for most people. Money is a powerful demotivator, particularly when people feel underpaid in comparison with others. Once a sense of parity is achieved, however, additional money does little to empower using the vision. So don't get caught in the trap of overfocusing on the mostly nonchangeable monetary reward system.

Promotion is another good reward. *Dual technical and managerial promotional ladders* prevent losing good technical people. IBM's Fellow Program—where technical people are given five years to do what they want—is widely copied. Promote those people who use your vision—and be certain that everyone knows it.

Recognize those who use your vision with visible and tangible rewards. Here's some recognition ideas.

- **"Feather in the cap" award at Delta Airlines annually for the person who does the most in customer service.**

- **Top U.K. salespeople for Hewlett-Packard join the President's Club and fly to Palo Alto to meet president John Young.**[32]

- **Sam Walton, one of the richest men in America and president of Wal-Mart (30-plus percent return on shareholder equity over the past twelve years), shows up with coffee and doughnuts at two A.M. on the day preceding an opening to recognize those people who are working extra hard to make the opening a success.**

- Ward Wheaton was division manager for a Minneapolis Honeywell group that won a $100 million contract. He rented an ice-cream truck—bought ice-cream cones for two hundred engineers—and had their picture taken eating their cones. Many veterans of that project still proudly display that photo many years later.

- Jack Welch—the present CEO for General Electric—installed a special telephone in his office and asked purchasing agents throughout his company to call him when they cost-reduced a product. Whenever the phone rang, Welch interrupted what he was doing to take the call, personally thank (recognize) the person for what had been accomplished, and dash off a handwritten congratulatory note to the individual. Some of those notes are still framed in GE offices.

- Neil Stratton, a police captain in Walnut Creek, California, gives out "champion cards" whenever he (or his supervisors) catches someone doing something right. Several other city departments and police jurisdictions now use the technique.

- George Slocum, president and CEO of Transco Energy in Houston, uses a quarterly "bragging session" where individuals report to all employees the progress they've made in reducing costs, improving services, or reducing absenteeism. George figures to save $18 million as a result of these sessions over the next two years.

- Robert Arnold and Daniel Boyce, owners of a Palmer, Massachusetts, egg carton plant, offers points to employees for perfect attendance, accident-free work, discipline-free record, grievance-free record, cost-saving suggestions, and community work. The reward? A jacket. And the people treasure it.

- Red Auerbach is the former coach and current president of the Boston Celtics—the most successful basketball franchise in history. Talking about motivating players, he said, "Pride, that's all. Pride of excellence. Pride of winning. I

tell our guys, 'Isn't it nice to go around all summer and say you're a member of the greatest basketball team in the world? . . .' The biggest motivating force you can have is the championship ring."

Find a thousand ways to give recognition both personally and through various programs.[33] Let your imagination run free.

Autonomy is a powerful reward. People love not to have to "check with the boss." Delegate autonomy to those who demonstrate using the vision.

Preferred work assignments are another strong reward. Give people work they love to do, and they'll do it well. Give people the work they love to do when they use your vision, and you empower them to use your vision. Peggy Wilton, a nursing floor supervisor in a large hospital, learned that lesson.

> Peggy's floor was the best in the hospital—best in terms of absenteeism, quality of patient care, and patient customer service.
>
> The hospital administrator asked Peggy how she did it. "It's easy," she said. "I get the group together once a month. We do it usually at my house or someone else's clubhouse. We share the good and the bad things that are happening—applauding the good and figuring out how to fix the bad.
>
> "We then list all the work that needs doing over the next month, and people volunteer for assignments. That way people get to do what they like to do—and the chance to change every month. If all the work doesn't get done—or several people want the same assignments—we either swap out—you do the first two weeks and I'll do the next—or we draw straws to decide.
>
> "It's easy since I don't have to make the tough decisions and choose among people. They decide and are much more dedicated to their decision than they'd ever be to mine. Management is easy. Now if we could only do something about the paperwork . . ."

Choose any one of a number of different rewards—money, promotion, recognition, autonomy, and preferred work assignments. Empower people to use your vision by rewarding those who do.

Reward everyone who uses your vision. Reward everyone who uses your vision. *Everyone!* The porter, the secretary, the programmer, the warehouse man, the assembler, the purchasing agent, the accounting clerk, the technician, the engineer, the manager—all need to be rewarded for using the vision. Some managers go to great lengths to reward everyone.

Jan Carlzon, president of SAS, wanted to reward his people for returning SAS to profitability and improving service to the level where they were chosen the "best business class airline in the world" by its passengers. So he threw a Christmas party for all employees. He rented private limousines to transport employees to and from the party. At the all-you-could-eat-and-drink party, Carlzon gave each employee—all sixteen thousand of them—gold watches to thank them for their contribution.

Carlzon's action may be a little extreme for you. Maybe you'd prefer IBM's practice, where 80 percent of the salespeople attain the 100 percent club (indicative of attaining 100 percent of their quota) and get to spend three days at a resort with their partners. Or perhaps you don't have IBM's budget, so you might consider adopting a version of what Johanna Jansen, department manager for a retail store, did for her employees.

> Johanna and her twenty-four clerks (ten of whom were part-timers) decide on sale goals—for the department as a whole and for each individual—every month. If the department meets its goals, Johanna takes all employees who meet their individual goals to lunch at a good restaurant in the area. She's arranged a trade-out with the store manager. She sells clothing to the restaurant manager and his employees at the employee discount and he gives her meals at cost.

Rewarding those who consistently use your vision empowers others to use it also.

Individualize rewards. Different strokes for different folks. People get turned on and motivated by different things. One person's reward is another person's insult. Maximize the power of your rewards by giving the right reward for the right performance to the right person. But what's the right reward? Do you need to be a seer or soothsayer to discover the right reward for each individual? What an incredibly difficult task!

171

Or is it? Don't make too much of this individualization. Put away your crystal ball and Ouija board. Why not ask each employee the rewards he or she wants? Why not offer a cafeteria of rewards and allow employees to choose for themselves? Ed Roy, president of a service franchiser company, took that approach, and it worked well for him.

> Ed was tired of trying to guess what his people wanted. He'd just run a big contest with the prize being an all-expenses-paid trip to Hawaii. The crowning blow was when the winner asked for the value of the trip in cash, rather than taking it.
>
> In a fit of desperation Ed listed all the possible rewards he could think of—the list came to 114. Some were monetary, some were merchandise, some were recognition, and some were professional development activities. He gave the list to the people and asked them to decide what they wanted in the next sales incentive contest. He was surprised when he got twenty-seven different choices from his twenty-seven people! Keeping his word, he promised each person his/her favorite reward.
>
> After awarding the reward, Ed expanded upon the idea of offering rewards to everyone who qualified, rather than one big reward to a grand winner. Since the listing idea worked so well before, he listed eighty-seven different (smaller) rewards and asked his people to choose again. Again he got twenty-seven different rewards from his twenty-seven people, including many individuals who shifted their interest from the last choice. Not surprisingly, twenty-four of the twenty-seven qualified for the reward they chose.

Let your people tell you what reward they want. Then empower your people by being certain that when they deliver the performance you want, you deliver the rewards they want.

Personal Workshop

As you consider your reward system, please ponder the following questions.

1. What is rewarded now in my organization? What pays off for employees now in my organization?

2. What rewards am I using now to reward using the vision? How can I use more rewards?

Money?

Promotions?

Autonomy?

Recognition?

Personal/professional development?

3. How can I individualize rewards?

Empower people to keep using the vision. Use your performance management system to do it. Expect them to use the vision. Spell out your expectations in specific, numeric terms and relate them to your strategic advantage. Measure the few most important behaviors, and give real-time, direct feedback on them. Reward using the vision. Use money, promotion, recognition, autonomy, and preferred work assignments. Reward everyone. Individualize the reward system. Empower your people by managing their performance.

Don't forget—*your actions are the key to success.* Set the example by personally specifying expectations, determining measures, and building in rewards for those who use your vision. For it is ultimately true that the only testament worth giving is the living testament.

9

People Are the Key

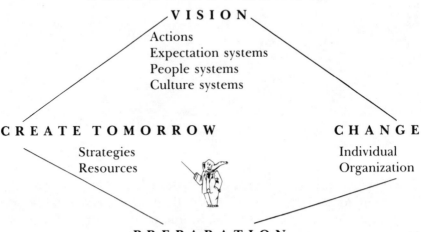

EMPOWERING CHANGE
VISION
Actions
Expectation systems
People systems
Culture systems

CREATE TOMORROW
Strategies
Resources

CHANGE
Individual
Organization

PREPARATION
Getting ready
Anticipating obstacles

Listen to the editors of *Business.* This leading British management journal helps us see why people are the key in today's competitive environment. They wrote:[1]

> We are moving from the set piece trench warfare of Flanders in 1914–1918 toward the quick response jungle war of Vietnam. Seventy years ago great armies moved on detailed instructions of supreme commanders and their general staffs. Today we need the flexibility of response seen in a well-led fighting patrol, harnessed within the vision that ensures a victorious campaign.

Pay attention in the Pentagon and the Ministry of Defense—and every other organization. Flexible bands of disciplined people focused tightly on a vision: that's the key to success in the jungles of Vietnam, the sands of Iran, and the marketplace.

But people forget the vision easily. The new vision is unfamiliar and uncomfortable. People look for reinforcement that they are doing the right thing.

Empower the "use the vision" message through your organizational systems. They tell your people what's valued and expected.

You read about one powerful system—the performance management system. That message was simple and straightforward. Expect, measure, and reward using the vision. Now here's another powerful system—your personnel system.

People see whom you hire, how you orient them, train them, and pay them. These personnel actions send important messages about the seriousness of your commitment to using your vision. And if you're not serious—why should anyone else be? Donna White's experience with personnel policies that depower using the vision is, unfortunately, all too typical.

> Donna was the branch manager for a small office in the employment development department for a large state in the U.S. She instituted a "quality first" vision using many of the ideas we've spelled out in this book. There was widespread enthusiasm for her effort, and most indices indicated positive results.
>
> After a year or so, Donna noticed a loss of enthusiasm. She discovered that several personnel actions were sabotaging her efforts. One employee told her, "We didn't get any raise this year. Why? Our office did great. Just because the legislature overspent, why should I suffer?"
>
> Donna also discovered that a number of new employees who were hired in the last year didn't even know about the vision and what it meant. No one had bothered to tell them about it when they were hired.
>
> Another employee complained, "We've been asking for some training in statistics so we can do a better job in our quality circle, but we can't get anyone to listen. The office manager says she's too busy hiring to do any training right now. I guess quality circles aren't important enough."
>
> Performance began to slip, and Donna noticed that some of the old ways were coming back.

Empower using the vision with your personnel system.

IT ISN'T EASY—BUT IT'S POSSIBLE

Personnel policies often seem set in concrete, impossible to change. In fact, they are designed to be difficult to circumvent and/or modify. They ensure consistent and fair treatment of all employees—porters in Buffalo, New York, and engineers in Manchester, England.

External pressures keep personnel policies inflexible. Union rules force rigidity. Governmental regulations contribute their share of concrete. Industry traditions and past organizational cultures slow down the possibility of change.

Yes, it's tough to change personnel policies—even for the CEO. Yet it's absolutely possible—and essential—if you are going to empower your people. Anyone can do it—at any level. Let me show you how.

RECRUITMENT

Hire the "right" people. But who are the "right" people? They are people who both want to and have the skill to use your vision. It's a lot easier to hire skilled, willing people than it is to develop those skills and/or willingness. A successful venture capitalist put it this way: "If you want a company full of eagles—hire eagles. No matter how much you train them—no matter how much you pay them—no matter how hard you work to motivate them—a turkey will never soar like an eagle. Rather than soaring, all you'll get is lots of wing flapping, frenetic running around, and gobble gobbles."

Recruit and select people who believe in your vision. Don't miss this golden opportunity. You have maximum freedom during selection. The easiest way to empower your people is to select newcomers who want to and can contribute.

How?

Begin with a *selection profile* that includes characteristics that support your vision. In other words, select individuals who are most likely to use your vision. I used this approach in working with a U.S. midsize regional bank. The bank wanted to upgrade its customer service.

As part of the bank's vision of superior customer service, I modified its selection profile. In addition to looking for neat, well-groomed people with good numerical skills, we added the following:

- **Prior successful service activity—those activities involving people-oriented services such as waitressing or canvasing**
- **Prior people interaction involvement—clubs, athletics**
- **Pleasant, smiling demeanor**

We found it took longer to find people with everything we wanted, but we had the patience to keep looking. Within a short time new people formed the majority in the bank. Customer service evaluations improved until we had the best scores in the area. As a bonus, account closings fell and cross-selling activities doubled.

Another experience with a department in a U.S. state government showed how to select the right people in a civil service environment. The department director wanted to improve the customer service elements of her department.

> She held a meeting with all of her managers and explained her vision—which they all shared enthusiastically. She also asked the director of the Civil Service Commission to attend the meeting and talk with them about how the department could hire more service-oriented individuals.
>
> The managers appointed a "tiger team" to recommend revised selection procedures. Sixty days later the team issued its report at another manager meeting. Revised profiles, on-the-job preemployment experiences, and team member interviews were adopted.
>
> The new procedures were implemented throughout the state. They survived an early legal threat. Within a year customer ratings zoomed from 5.6 (out of a possible 8) to 7.1.

The people at Sewell Village Cadillac in the U.S. know all about selecting the right people. They spend days interviewing potential employees. They put potentials through a rigorous battery of psychological tests. According to owner Carl Sewell, these tests are designed to measure "intensity, aggressiveness, intelligence—and stamina." All this for a maintenance mechanic's job to work in Carl Sewell's service department.

For Carl Sewell, his service department is the centerpiece of his vision of customer satisfaction. Carl pampers his customers—everywhere, but particularly in the service center. He loans cars to service customers, furnishes comfortable lounges for them to wait in, and assures them their car will be fixed correctly. What a difference between Sewell and the ordinary car dealer service center—in terms of the way customers get treated, its profitability, and the pay and attitude of its employees. Sewell's people work long hours and earn good money—an average of $50,000 per year. Sewell is one of the most profitable dealerships. And it consistently ranks near the top in customer satisfaction evaluations.[2]

Sam Walton knows all about hiring the right people to empower his vision. Sam's the CEO and guiding light behind Wal-Mart, a 35-plus percent Return on Investment retailer—and the largest single creator of jobs in America. Sam hires bright young people as clerks at 10 percent over the minimum wage. He spots the best talent early by delegating responsibility and evaluating performance frequently. He then encourages them to stay by providing up to $2,500 to help pay college tuition. No wonder 40 percent of Wal-Mart's managers began as trainees.[3]

"Big Brown"—United Parcel Service—follows a similar "get them young, look them over, and keep the best" strategy. UPS hires more than forty thousand college students as part-time sorters. Part-timers who demonstrate commitment to hard work and identification with the company are offered full-time jobs when they graduate. Sixteen dollars an hour and high regard in the company are the initial attractions, plus the opportunity to move into management and become a stockholder. At every level UPS screens, screens, screens to get the best person—the person who will use the vision. UPS rigorously defines the "right" person and searches for that individual assiduously.[4]

Bernard Marcus and Arthur Blank of Home Depot also look for the "right" people. Their right people—in the tough do-it-yourself discount warehouse retail market—are knowledgeable salespeople, expert enough to demystify plumbing, electrical, and construction problems for Mr. and Mrs. Layman.

These full-time employees—in an industry characterized by part-timers—attend weekly product knowledge classes in the full range of products carried by Home Depot. In return, these employees earn higher-than-average salaries and are covered under a full benefits plan. Marcus and Blank also benefit. Home Depot's grown an average of 82 percent per year since 1979. Average store volume has also grown by an amazing 18 percent—in an industry where 5 percent is considered extraordinary. Providing top-flight service at bargain-basement prices is possible—when you get the "right" people.[5]

Thomas Melohn, president of North American Tool and Die, also looks for the "right" people. He defines the right people as "people with traditional middle-American values and the old-fashioned barn-raising spirit." He sees the selection process as a series of increasingly smaller screens. He starts with applications. He screens out applications that are crumpled, incomplete, soiled, or contain spelling and grammar errors. He looks for extracurricular activities such as community projects and Boy Scouts. From the culled pile, he and several other people in the company interview prospects. Only then do they choose.[6]

It takes time to find the "right" person. But it takes even longer to correct, pay for, and eventually get rid of the "wrong" person. Harvey Mackay, author of *How to Swim with the Sharks and Not Get Eaten* and president of Mackay Envelope, spends up to two years finding the right person. He observes people in several different settings and is a fanatic about checking out the person with people he knows in the industry.[7]

The managers at Au Bon Pain spend four to six weeks in the recruitment process. In addition to the traditional interview, they also have employees in similar jobs interview the candidate. Surviving that, the candidate spends several days working in a store to see what it's really like. It takes time—and energy—to find the right person.[8]

Select people who are likely to use your vision. You can do this at any level in the organization. You don't need corporate approval either.

Change the vision and you need to change the people you hire. That's what executives at Westinghouse's College Station, Texas, appliance plant did. Turnover skyrocketed to 22 percent when the plant adopted a team center approach. So they hired different people—recruits with initiative, ability to take advice, and creativity—all skills/attitudes required to use the new "team center" vision.[9]

Next, *train others to use that profile.* Empower everyone doing hiring to look for the "right" skills/attitudes. Fill your organization with these people—get supporters everywhere. In a unionized engine plant installing a new vision, for instance, a committee of two manufacturing supervisors and two union stewards interviews all recruits. Using the profile of attitudes/skills required, this committee makes the final selection decision.[10]

At Johnsonville Foods, a sausage maker, potential teammates do the interviewing and selection. Team members understand the job—often better than the manager. Team members select people with whom they can work, thus assuring initial acceptance into the team of the new member. Furthermore, the first few days of work are easier for the new employee since he/she knows the people in the team from the interviews.

Even outsiders—such as assessment centers run by local colleges—can do selection using the profile. An axle plant installing a new team center approach sent all their applicants down to an eight-hour assessment center run by a local community college. The plant union and management committee trained the community college assessors in their profile. Then the assessors designed the assessment center experience.[11]

Many large U.K. employers of college graduates use assessment centers. Managers from British Telecom, British Airways, Shell, and Sainsbury usually meet with the assessment center staff to review requirements. The assessment staff then designs the two- or three-day experience including simulations, group discussions, and in-baskets, and checks it with the company before involving candidates.[12]

Also, *use recruiters who reflect your vision.* Send out recruiters who embody your vision in action. At IBM, for instance, young, aggressive marketing types were sent out to recruit other young, aggressive marketing types. Recruiting is a natural selection, weeding-out process. Applicants look at the recruiter and ask themselves, "Do I want to work in an organization filled with people like him or her?" At the same time recruiters are examining the applicant and asking themselves, "Do I want to work with this individual?" Likes attract. So you'll likely hire more people just like the recruiter. Be sure that your recruiters are the kinds of people you want more of in your organization.

Even better, use your employees as recruiters. Integrated Microcomputer Systems, Inc., a $20 million software development company in Rockville, Maryland, relies extensively upon employee referrals. More than 60 percent of its current staff were referred by current employees. Referring employees earn bonuses for suc-cessful placement and retention (at least four months)—from $300 for administrative jobs to $800 for technical jobs and $1,000 for managerial and highly skilled jobs.[13] People recommend people who are like themselves. Good people recommend good people. Tap the rich vein of your own employees' network to get more of the "right" people.

Communicate your vision during the interview process. Tell every applicant what it takes to be successful in your organization—namely, to use your vision. Share stories of empowered individu-als—and even a failure or two. Paint a picture for every applicant of your vision in action.

At a U.S. unionized engine plant, all applicants—including inter-nal transferees—go through a four-hour briefing. The joint union-management committee reviews their vision of the new team approach and what each job requires. The union representatives in particular want each applicant to know what he/she is getting into.[14]

Thomas Melohn of North American Tool and Die spends a great deal of time during the interview process telling about NATD's philosophy. He says, "I begin to convey some of our basic tenets: honesty, product quality, treating fellow employees as we want to be treated, and respect for the person running the ma-chine. I talk about our ESOP, our low turnover rate, our job ro-tation plan, and opportunities for advancement. I explain that NATD has no policy manuals because we don't need them. . . . In effect, I'm selling NATD's strengths. . . ."[15]

Applicants listen intently during recruitment. It's a good time to tell them your vision when the soil is particularly fertile.

Shape your selection process to hire people who will most likely use your vision. Empower others to use your vision by demonstrat-ing your serious commitment.

Personal Workshop

As you think about your recruitment policies, please ponder the following questions.

1. What personal qualities and prior experiences would be most supportive of using my vision?

181

2. How can I include those personal qualities and prior experiences as part of the selection profile for my unit?

3. When can I train/instruct all people who do recruitment to use my revised profile?

4. Which of my employees best embody my vision, and how can I get them involved in the recruitment process?

5. How can I be certain that my vision is actively communicated during the interviewing process?

ORIENTATION

My venture capital friend says, "Once you hire eagles, be certain that you keep their eagle mentality alive." Capture the first few days and use that time to reinforce your eagle's mentality. The first few days on the job are the most important. The new hire is most impressionable during this time. You never get a second chance to make a good first impression. Yet I'm amazed at how few managers seize this rich opportunity.

At very least, *tell your vision in the orientation program.* Seize the opportunity to tell the new recruits about your vision. Selwyn Roberts, the president and founder of a small, growing U.K. software and systems firm, found that his orientation program was the ideal place to recapture his "lost spirit."

> Selywn founded his firm in 1978 on the basis of "integrity." To him that meant treating customers and employees fairly and equitably—always giving the extra measure. As long as he stayed in personal contact with all customers and employees, his vision was alive and well.
>
> As the company grew to forty-five employees, and Selwyn no longer saw every employee or customer, his vision blurred. He told me, "We lost sight of what we stood for. We still did good work. But not good enough work. The newcomers didn't have the same 'spirit' as the old-timers, and soon they constituted the majority.
>
> "I decided that it was important not to lose sight of our vision, so I changed my orientation program. I now take a

whole day for newcomers to tell them what we stand for. I even get a customer to come in and talk to them about 'integrity.' We've got the 'spirit' again."

Schlumberger is the class act in the oil field services business. They have the highest profit-to-sales ratio and largest market share of any company in its business. They've achieved this record in the face of one of the most challenging tasks: maintaining standards among two thousand geographically separated geological engineers working on mobile rigs equipped with sophisticated gear worth more than $1 million. How do they do it? Each year Schlumberger recruits the brightest and the best engineering graduates. Then these "special" people go through a grueling several-month orientation program. One engineer graduate said, "Indoctrination is just as important as technical training." Schlumberger's orientation program equips its people to work independently—often in remote areas of the world—with its vision clearly in mind.[16]

Personally teach a portion of the program to demonstrate your seriousness. Selwyn joins a very impressive list of company presidents who do, including Andy Grove, president of Intel; Bernard Marcus and Arthur Blank, leaders of Home Depot; and Jim Treybig, president of Tandem computers.

Or why not have employees teach the vision? Bill Gore at W. L. Gore and Associates does. His lattice, nonhierarchical organization is based on the premise of each person finding how he/she can best contribute to the success of the firm. That poses significant mental adjustment for many individuals raised in the "tell me what to do and I'll do it" world. Employees volunteer to sponsor newcomers. Every newcomer must have a sponsor. In Gore's words, "The sponsor's commitment is to get them where they are earning their pay as quickly as possible. The sponsor provides instruction, training, and feedback."[17] What a great way to empower the vision in all newcomers.

Sequent Computer Systems, Inc., of Beaverton, Oregon, uses a similar approach. Each new employee gets a sponsor who spends thirty minutes a day for the first several weeks showing the new recruit around. Teamwork is a crucial part of Sequent's vision. So helping people get to know people faster helps newcomers internalize the vision faster.[18]

Reflect the vision in your orientation period. Give people an opportunity to *learn how to use it.* IBM piles on the work during its orientation program. The trainee is in classes until nine P.M. Individual and collective assignments keep them going until one or two A.M. The newcomer soon learns to rely on others to help—and to be a reliable helper for others in return. Teamwork and camaraderie result. And this shared experience builds a network of relationships that lies at the heart of IBM's ability to quickly marshal people from diverse parts of the organization—to solve customer problems. This empowers IBM's "excellence in service" vision.

William Wilson of Pioneer/Eclipse Corporation of Sparta, North Carolina, uses a unique approach to orienting new executives. As a rapidly growing company, Wilson frequently hires experienced people from the outside. He wants to be certain that his new executive really understands his business's values and products. So as part of the orientation program, every executive spends a night working with the company product—a floor cleaning system. Wilson wants to be certain that the newcomer doesn't think the work is "beneath him or her, because that's not the kind of people we need."[19]

The Phillips organization—the Dutch electronics giant—gives its recent college graduate employees a real organizational problem to investigate. They end their course with a report and recommendation to the company's highest managing council, the managing board. This task is in addition to the normal twelve hours of instruction. The chairman of the board intends the assignment to empower the new hires to use the teamwork that characterizes his organization.

At Morgan Stanley new employees go through a one-year program during which they work twelve to fourteen hours a day, plus at least one day on the weekend. Lunches are limited to one-half hour, eaten in the company cafeteria. All of this is in preparation for the extensive work that is required—often into the night and on weekends—when putting together an investment deal, the task these new hires will be undertaking once they "graduate."

Build in the use of your vision even in short programs. The president of a small software house in the United Kingdom assigns all new employees to work the help desk during their first week with the company. This gives the trainee a quick initiation into the customer service vision of the company. Whether the orientation program is two hours or two years in length, empower the vision by mirroring the skills and attitudes required by your vision.

Extend the orientation process. Have the *immediate supervisor prepare a specific job orientation program* that includes "How we use the vision in this department." Steven, the division manager for a wood products plant, requires his supervisors to file a one-page statement for each new employee, spelling out the steps he/she will take during the first thirty days to orient the new person. Included is the use of the vision in that department. Steve follows up with each supervisor to check that the plan is being followed. I've seen similar plans work at all levels of government.

Stay in *personal touch* with the new hire. There are lots of ways. Schedule breakfast after they've been on the job several months. Stop by during your wandering and see the employee at his/her workplace. Arrange for formal meetings several months after the orientation program. Reemphasize your personal interest in using the vision.

Orientation is a golden opportunity. Shape your orientation program to empower people to use your vision. It's a lot tougher to convert an "old hand" to your new vision than to have your vision adopted by a "new employee." And any supervisor, at any level, can do it.

Personal Workshop

As you review your orientation practices, please ponder the following questions.

1. How can I add vision explanation to the current formal orientation program?

2. When can I redesign my orientation program to both reflect my vision and give new employees an opportunity to use it in real situations?

3. What simple procedures can I design (or have designed) to ensure that the immediate supervisors of new hires stress the use of vision in their departments?

4. How can I best maximize my contacts with new hires to send the message personally about the importance of using the vision?

TRAINING

Train people to use your vision. IBM lost focus on its vision—and fell on hard times as a result. Chairman Akers uses training to remind his people about the IBM vision. All new employees (including old employees who are in new jobs) receive eighty hours of training. All management and professional employees get a minimum of forty hours. Training at IBM empowers individuals to use the vision and build vision-relevant skills.

Train/retrain how to use the vision. Continually empower *managers* through training to use the vision.

Follow Henry Block's lead. Every manager in his more than nine thousand income-tax return preparation offices has started on the bottom and been trained—extensively—for his/her current position. Every manager worked first as a preparer, then as an assistant manager, then as a manager, then as a district manager, and so forth—no exceptions. At every step Block provides extensive training to prepare the individual with the needed technical and managerial skills. His unparalleled success is living testimony to the wisdom of his training investment.[20]

Mercedes-Benz knows a good thing when it has it—and uses training to preserve it. More than half of the Mercedes' 170 U.K. dealerships are family run. These family-run dealerships are friendlier and provide better service. Smoothing the transition from one generation to the next while enhancing the quality of the customer service provided by these family-owned dealerships will be Mercedes' future competitive edge.

But, succession is difficult within a family business. All too often parents cede control only under great pressure and after considerable intrigue and destructive behavior. Palace revolutions can leave organizations spent and demoralized. Mercedes wants to avoid the potential loss of its service delivery to customers during any family squabbles. To develop the dealers of the future (and retain its tradition of superior customer service), Mercedes offers a six-week Family Business Programme for the sons and daughters of current dealers. In addition to the traditional corporate management and business development topics, Peter Padley, head of personnel and training for Mercedes, also focuses on such family relationship matters as handling sibling rivalry, peer group resentment, paternal mistrust, and maternal intervention. If you can learn to handle dad and mom today you should be more than equipped to handle any customer tomorrow. Good thinking, Mercedes.[21]

Empower *employees* through training, also. Motorola spends one percent of sales revenues in training employees in quality. Employees get up to forty hours of instruction in technical skills (such as statistical quality control and technology developments) and working-together skills (such as teamwork, communication, and problem solving). Motorola realizes thirty times its training investment in direct quality savings. This training empowers Motorola's quality vision.[22]

Training reinforces the vision. Ask UPS. More than 80 percent of the full-time staff—employees and managers—show up for voluntary after-hours workshops on the company's competitive challenges. These workshops reinforce the employee's commitment to the vision of customer service and efficiency.[23]

Remember Home Depot? Employees receive up to twenty hours of training a month, including off-site courses taught by vendors. "The classes taught by fellow employees are the more real world, because they know the questions that customers are asking," says Steve Noren, regional manager for northern California. Does it pay off? You bet. Sales margins and returns are two to three times the industry average.[24]

ServiceMaster, the most successful commercial company in the world during the last fifteen years, empowers its vision through training both managers and employees. The CEO stated, "Before asking someone to do something, you have to help them *be something.*" (Emphasis added.) His organization spends more in training and development than any other company to help people "be something." Managers get extensive training culminating in a "master's" program taught partially by the chief executive. Employees meet weekly to discuss new ideas and get additional education. Recently, when a hospital under contract to ServiceMaster hired a deaf employee, the local manager authorized sign language training for employees so they could work with the new employee.[25]

Retrain employees—rather than lay them off. It pays. Dan Ward, a GTE human resource executive, found that retraining was more cost efficient than laying off and rehiring. Here's a few examples of firms that have done that:[26]

- **Digital Equipment Corporation had too many assemblers, product technicians, and managers and not enough process controllers/designers and programmers. Volunteers underwent a nine-to-twelve-month retooling program. About 3,800 people successfully made the transition. Six hundred left rather than go through retraining.**

- **When they switched over to a new technology, General Motors in the U.S. gave employees at the Fort Wayne, Indiana, truck plant more than four hundred hours of instruction in using the new equipment, which cut across traditional trade lines, and in communications and problem-solving skills so they could participate in the weekly production meetings.**

Empower your people with the attitudes and skills needed to use your vision.

Devote some portion of every training to how we can use this information/tool to enhance our vision. At Hewlett-Packard every training course includes a discussion of "how we can use this tool to manage more effectively in the H-P way." At the very least, ask attendees to write a brief statement after the course about how they will adapt course material to use the vision.

Empower your people with training in the right tools and attitudes. Target your training activities clearly on using the vision. And you can do most of it on your own—at any organizational level—without formal approval.

Personal Workshop

As you review your training and development policies, please ponder the following questions.

1. When and how can I offer training to my people in using the vision?

2. How can I ensure that all training—internal and external—gets related back to the use of my vision?

CAREER DEVELOPMENT

People change—jobs, companies, locations, and even careers. Show your people that your new vision will contribute to their long-term development. Empower them to use your vision by showing them that it's in their long-term best interests.

Use *career planning* activities to empower your vision. Encourage employees to systematically and frequently talk about their career and job preferences. But don't make it a paper mill. Ask four simple, direct questions.

- **What job/occupation would you like to have in three to five years?**

- **What skills, experiences, and competencies are required by the job?**

- **What are you planning to do to prepare yourself for that job?**

- **How can I support your efforts?**

Empower the vision by showing employees the relationship between using your vision and achieving their long-term career objectives.

Use *job rotation* to broaden perspectives and implement career plans. Many organizations, like AT&T, IBM, 3M, Hewlett-Packard, Siemens, and Matsushita, rotate individuals every several years. Job rotation provides personal broadening and builds long-term career development. John Akers, CEO of IBM, rotated through several line and staff jobs on his way to the top spot.

Promote people who *reflect your vision.* Promoting those people who use your vision empowers others to do the same. One company passed over an executive with an outstanding financial track record because he hadn't consistently used the company's vision in his management activities. The message was clear—advancement goes to those who manage using the company's values and produce excellent financial results as well.

Use the dual career ladder to retain competent technical people and reflect your vision of technical excellence. Many high-tech firms use dual career ladders to encourage their technical employees to remain in their technical fields. It is not uncommon for scientists and engineers in firms such as Xerox, Honeywell, IBM, and Texas Instruments to earn as much as or more than managers. Advanced technical education offerings also induce technical employees to remain within their technical areas of expertise.

High-tech firms aren't the only ones using the dual career ladder to empower their excellence vision. William Cash, vice-president of consultants Cresap, McCormick and Page, reports the following low-tech applications:[27]

- **A bank set up a dual promotion ladder for their portfolio managers and bond traders that enables them to make as much money as managers.**

- **A direct sales organization revamped its sales compensation system to pay salespeople as well as sales managers. This should prevent good salespeople from leaving the field to become poor sales managers, just so they can earn more money.**

- **A fast-food organization created senior technical advisers at the level equivalent to vice-president of operations. They placed individuals in the job who were particularly effective in working one on one with franchisees. This should keep intact the strength of the organization—its relationship with franchisees.**

Empower your vision by demonstrating that using it contributes to long-term career success. Encourage career planning and job rotation that fosters this long-term view. Use promotions to reinforce the shorter-term perspective. Any manager can do it. You don't need to be CEO.

Personal Workshop

As you review your career development policies, please ponder the following questions.

1. How can I use career planning activities to further empower the use of my vision?

2. How can I encourage job rotations and promotions that reflect my vision in action?

PERFORMANCE APPRAISAL

Use your performance appraisal system to empower your people to use your vision. Every organization's got a performance appraisal system. Most are corporatewide. Rather than changing the current system (which may be too difficult in the short run), *evaluate how the person is using your vision.* Barbara Castle, finance director in a small local government, successfully modified her performance appraisal form.

> Barbara saw she couldn't change the citywide performance appraisal form, so she asked her employees to add a separate page and answer two questions: "How am I currently using the vision?" and "How can I use the vision more effectively?"
>
> All eleven people submitted the separate page. Using the answers from these two questions, Barbara discussed with each person how he/she could use the vision more effectively.
>
> Barbara told me, "Encouraging my people to evaluate their use of the vision—and, of course, I did the same—created lots of discussion and focus on how the vision was being used in the department. This increased awareness led to greater use of the vision."

Evaluate what you want—because what gets measured, gets produced. Westinghouse's College Station, Texas, plant wants to encourage employees to learn all the jobs in their work module. Multiskilled teams are essential to their team center vision. So they evaluate employees on the basis of skills mastered.[28] Nissan's Smyrna, Tennessee, plant does the same,[29] as does a General Motors engine plant.[30]

If customer service is central to your vision, measure that as part of your performance appraisal. 3M, GTE, and Westinghouse evaluate white-collar workers using a program called Productivity Map. The program asks employees to identify and evaluate performance on key services delivered by their department. Internal customers do the same. Discrepancies and similarities are discussed during the performance appraisal.[31]

Get *employee input* into the evaluation process. Teams at Westinghouse's College Station, Texas, plant evaluate daily their own performance—including that of each member—and how it compares with those of other teams in the plant.[32] At the Woodwood Governor Company—a $200 million U.S. aerospace components manufacturer with margins twice that of its competitors—each employee evaluates everyone in his/her department (including supervisors). Supervisors do the same. The evaluations are sent to the fourteen-person member evaluation committee, which ranks all 2,750 employees. These rankings determine base pay and bonus.[33]

Tap *employee attitudes* as grist for the appraisal mill. IBM, General Dynamics, and Hewlett-Packard gather employee attitude survey data that taps whether individual managers are using the vision. Each manager sees the results, which are included in his/her personnel file.

Empower people to use your vision. Send the clear message that using the vision pays off and not using the vision doesn't.

Personal Workshop

As you review your performance appraisal policies, please ponder the following questions.

1. How can I include in my performance appraisal an evaluation of the use of my vision?

2. How can I conduct employee attitude surveys or get employee input in some way to check if my managers are using my vision systematically?

COMPENSATION

If you want it, pay for it! Put your money where your vision is! But be creative! When dealing with the typical rigidly structured pay system, you have to be innovative in order to succeed. Let me give you some ideas.

Pay for knowledge. Westinghouse's College Station, Texas, plant does, as do several GM plants. Employees pass tests—usually agreed upon between the union and the company—to qualify for higher base pay. Reduce the number of job classifications to make this team module approach work.[34]

Pay for specific vision-related performance. Reward key behaviors called for in your vision—big. Ball Corporation—a $1.1 billion U.S. manufacturer of diversified products from canning jars to satellites—pays management bonuses based upon specific accomplishments tied in to the company's vision of efficiency. Foremen, for instance, can earn up to 20 percent of their base salary for keeping machine downtime under budget.[35]

Domino's pays bonuses to all employees—even staff types—based on customer service performance. Domino's empowers the customer service that they believe is their key competitive advantage and is a central part of their vision.[36]

Merrill Lynch pays its 10,400 brokers bonuses based upon the accumulation of assets rather than maximizing trading profits. Merrill cut commissions on small trades and substituted its new bonus plan. This new bonus plan directly empowers Merrill Lynch's new vision of managing assets.[37]

Psicor is a small Michigan provider of perfusionists (specialists for open heart surgery). It's a competitive labor market, with good people in very short supply. To keep his best people and reward the "right" performance, founder Michael Dunaway pays quarterly raises of 5 percent (based solely on performance). He also pays additional bonuses for specific vision-related activities such as higher caseloads, out-of-town assignments, and professional certification.[38]

American Express's new vision calls for integration of their many different financial services—"One Enterprise," they call it. CEO and chairman Jim Robinson pays special bonuses to executives and managers who contribute to the vision.[39]

Share gains. Several thousand gain-sharing programs exist now, usually as Scanlon plans. In fact, 26 percent of U.S. firms have some form of gain sharing. Under the typical Scanlon plan, employees set objectives, work to improve performance, and receive some percentage of the gains (typically 7 percent). Herman Miller, Inc., and Dana Corporation are two widely known examples of Scanlon plan successes.[40]

Pacific Bell in 1986 negotiated a non–Scanlon plan gain-sharing agreement with the Communications Workers of America. Under the plan a certain amount of profit will be set aside to pay to groups of workers who meet specified performance goals—like getting phones installed quickly.[41]

Worthington Steel and Nucor Steel, two of the most successful minimills in the U.S., "pay by the pound." Base wages are considerably lower than union contract scale. Yet last year, when Nucor's mill in Darlington, South Carolina, advertised for eight openings, over 1,300 applicants applied. Why? Is it so desirable to work in this hot, smelly, physically demanding job? Hardly. It's a matter of money. At Nucor workers earn weekly bonuses based on the number of tons of quality steel produced by their team. With these bonuses Nucor employees earn more than their unionized counterparts. How can Nucor afford to pay more? Last year Nucor turned out twice as much steel per person as industry giants USX and Bethlehem.

Everyone shares in the gains at Nucor. Department managers earn bonuses based on return on assets, plant managers on the basis of return on equity.

Carrier, a unit of United Technologies, is another firm believer in gain sharing. Six months after installation of the gain-sharing program productivity was 24 percent higher and rejects fell by more than 90 percent. Carrier established the benchmark of 1.8 man-hours to get a finished product out the door. When the plant exceeds that, the savings are split fifty-fifty—by everyone from managers to janitors. As an indication of the success of the plan, in early 1988 a water main broke, creating sink holes into which several pieces of equipment fell. People worked day and night to get the equipment up and running again so they wouldn't miss the weekly bonus.[42] (They didn't.)

Firestone knows gain sharing works—over time. Their Wilson, North Carolina, plant has had a successful gain-sharing program since 1977.

3M is also a believer in gain sharing. They encourage gains in productivity by sharing one-half the gain over a moving average. 3M's orthopedic division in Irvine improved productivity by more than 65 percent since the plan was instituted in 1983. Employees earn an average of 10 percent bonuses over base quarterly earnings. Ten of the more than one hundred plants report similar success stories.[43]

Gain-share with groups where you can identify the gains to be shared using objective, measurable criteria. Be prepared for heavy employee involvement. At both the Firestone and Carrier plants, for instance, regular employee meetings are an integral part of the program. Consultant Mitchell Fein says, "Management must be willing to do two things—share and listen."

In addition, focus on several objectives. Emphasize productivity alone and you may wind up getting more junk produced. In the U.S., Walter Riley, CEO of G.O.D., Inc., a Kearny, New Jersey, overnight freight forwarder, found this out. He originally paid his dock loaders for each shipment handled. Shipments soared—but so did errors and breakage. To fix the new situation, Riley added a 25 percent bonus for error-free performance. That represented more than $150 extra a week for dock workers averaging $600. That number got their attention. Today, 85 percent of all workers earn the bonus. Profits also doubled—after bonus payments.[44]

But it can be expensive. You might have to pay gain sharing even when you don't make a profit.

Springfield Remanufacturing Center Company (SRC) pays gain-sharing bonuses based upon specific goal accomplishment. In 1985 they set two goals: reduction of plant overhead to $32 per hour and increase operating income to 15 percent of sales. They made the first goal but missed the second, so only a 7.8 percent bonus was paid rather than the possible 10 percent.[45]

Sometimes you get to share the pain as well as the gain. SRC discovered this other side of the coin. In 1987 SRC lost a major

GM contract. No matter how Jack Stack and his managers worked, they couldn't figure out how to avoid laying off one hundred employees. They went to the entire 350-plus work force and gave them the choice of the pain they wanted to share—either one hundred people go now, or the company works to find fifty thousand additional hours by taking on marginally profitable work that would reduce (or eliminate) their bonus. And if the company couldn't find the extra work, two hundred persons might have to be laid off. The employees voted overwhelmingly to gamble on the two-hundred-or-nothing option. The good news is that through extraordinary hustle Stack found enough work to keep everyone and add one hundred new people. The bad news is that the lower margin work cut the bonus in half to 3.4 percent. Share the gain—share the pain—two sides of the same coin.[46]

Gain sharing also works in government. Several cities identify potential areas for improvement, set base standards, and share productivity gains with employees. One city in California established base standards in their road maintenance area and paid employees a gain-sharing bonus of 20 percent of the savings. Costs were reduced 31 percent, and employees earned 50 percent more in wages. They became the highest-paid road maintenance employees in the area. The city council bragged about it in area newspapers, pointing out how the public benefited. Rather than the feared public outcry, newspapers and public opinion alike congratulated the council on its foresightedness.

Share profits. This must be a good idea. Half a million U.S. companies have profit-sharing programs, as do more than seven hundred U.K. firms. That represents more than 30 percent of all U.S. firms and 17 percent of U.K. firms.[47] Lincoln Electric is often cited as an example. Lincoln pays 6 percent to its shareholders first, sets aside investment money, and pays the rest to employees, who earn from 20 percent to more than 100 percent of their already wage-competitive base pay. This policy empowers the use of Lincoln's efficiency vision—and the creation of the most cost-effective company in its industry.

Keep your profit-sharing formula simple. Ron Shaich and Len Schlesinger, owners of the Au Bon Pain restaurant and bakery chain, know all about the need to keep profit-sharing plans simple.

They worked for several years to get a profit-sharing program in place that would encourage their store managers to manage their store the way Ron and Len wanted them to. They were unsuccessful. Finally, when they saw how Pete Harmon ran his successful Kentucky Fried Chicken franchise, they threw out their thirty-page document in favor of a simpler four-pager that basically outlined a fifty-fifty split of the profits over controllable costs. Managers understood what was expected and what they could earn.

Results improved dramatically. Store turnover shot up 37 percent, overall company sales rose 40 percent, and profits grew an even larger 60 percent. Average partner store manager's earnings doubled to $65,000, with several managers making in excess of $90,000. Most significant, Ron Shaich now no longer deals with crises but has the time for strategic planning.[48] Share profits and watch them grow.

Or how about using profit sharing to raise money. That's what Reinhard Mohn, president of the German media empire, Bertelsmann, did. When his expansion plans outran the banks' willingness to underwrite, Mr. Mohn encouraged employees to buy nonvoting profit-sharing certificates in the company. He raised DM 371 million (approximately $150 million) in equity capital. His employees now receive annual interest (15 percent in 1989) plus a nest egg continually enriched through profit-sharing contributions. Talk about a win/win.[49]

One-time bonuses. Give special monetary recognition to special performers. More than 20 percent of the firms surveyed by Hewitt Associates gave one-time bonuses to white-collar employees. And a BNA survey showed that 20 percent of union contracts called for lump-sum payments.

Herb Miller, marketing director for a midsize U.S. steel mill, was able to convince his boss to enable him to grant up to $5,000 in one-time bonuses for outstanding work. His boss gave him $25,000 to spend during the year for that purpose. Herb used his bonuses to reward teams and individuals who achieved outstanding results using his vision. Herb showed the best sales and marketing penetration growth of any year in the company's history, and he credited his bonus plan for much of his success. IBM would agree. They give $10,000 or more for an outstanding innovation.

Pay for performance in government. The pay-for-performance virus has found its way into government as well. In the city of Long Beach, California, managers can gain or lose up to 20 percent of their base salary, depending upon performance against numeric fiscal and service targets. Two people are even making more than the city manager.[50]

Nonpay rewards also work. Don't lose sight of the other, nonpay rewards that keep the people empowered to use your vision. Pay is important. No doubt about it. Pay people less than they think they are worth, and they will either give you what they think you are paying for or leave. But pay isn't everything. There's a host of nonmonetary rewards that work—well!

Personal Workshop

As you review your compensation policies, please ponder the following questions.

1. What compensation policies can I mold to empower my vision?

Can I give one-time bonuses?

Gain sharing?

Profit sharing?

Pay for knowledge?

2. How can I more directly link pay for specific vision performance?

Empower your people to keep using the vision. Use your personnel policies to keep the vision constantly in the forefront of your people's thoughts. Do it at all—and any—levels in the organization. You don't have to be the chief to make personnel policies support your vision.

Recruit people who want to and have the skill to carry out your vision. Inculcate the vision through your orientation program. Reinforce the vision through training and career development activities. Reward use of the vision through performance appraisal and compensation practices.

People learn slowly and forget quickly. Performance management systems help you empower your people. Personnel systems further that empowerment. Yet it may not be enough. Some people need more. Let's look at another way to empower your people to use your vision—the cultural system.

10

Culture Is It

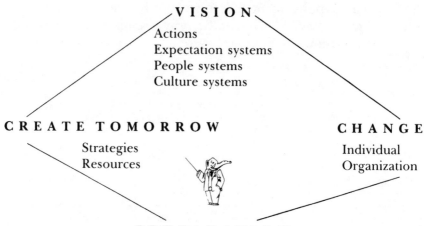

EMPOWERING CHANGE

VISION

Actions
Expectation systems
People systems
Culture systems

CREATE TOMORROW

Strategies
Resources

CHANGE

Individual
Organization

PREPARATION

Getting ready
Anticipating obstacles

Empower! Empower! Empower! People need a lot of it if they're going to use your vision—consistently. Performance systems and personnel systems need to keep up the steady drumbeat—empowering people at every turn. And despite the power of these two systems, it still isn't enough.

People are particularly sensitive to messages. Empowering messages come from the performance system about what you really want. Empowering messages come from the personnel system about what you're really willing to reward. Empowering messages come from the culture system about what's "right." Of these three, people listen most to the messages from the cultural system. You can't see or touch the cultural system. Yet it's there all the same. You know what it is (mostly). And more important, your people know it very well. The law of the culture outweighs any other law. It is the strongest empowering message of all.

CULTURE IS IT!

The story is told too often not to be true. A president, after attending a meeting in which corporate culture was the topic, turns to his vice-president and says, "This culture stuff is great! I want one by Monday." The sad truth is that the president already has a culture—but maybe not the one he wants.

Every organization has a culture. Every department has a culture. Every little informal work group that works together for even a few days develops a culture. So everyone's got one. The key question is, do you have one that empowers the use of your vision? Ken Brice, the president of a midsize regional bank, realized too late the impact of the wrong culture on the success of his vision.

> Ken saw that the coming revolution in the banking field required his bank to become much more marketing-oriented. He wanted his branch managers to become more sensitive to the customers' needs. He initiated a major advertising effort—in both public media and throughout the branches—built around his new vision, "Your personal banker."
>
> Initially new account business climbed as the public responded favorably. Ken was pleased with the results.
>
> After several months Ken noticed that account closings continued at their high level, as did the customer complaint letters.
>
> Upon closer investigation, Ken found that very little had really changed in his bank. Tellers were still treated as third-class citizens—and they treated their customers the same way. Branch managers went out to get new business but didn't really follow up with a new account once it was in the bank. The old banking mentality hadn't changed.
>
> Before Ken could take significant action to remedy the situation, the accelerating account closings pushed his board into asking for—and getting—his resignation. "Next time," he told me, "I'll pay more attention to changing the mentality first."

Every organization has a culture that shapes behavior. Sometimes the culture works for you. Culture worked for Johnson & Johnson when it hit the Tylenol crises in 1982 and 1985. When news of the problem came in, managers used the company vision to make decisions. The company's vision states (in part), "We believe our first responsibility is to the doctors, nurses, and patients, to mothers and all others who use our products and services. . . . We are responsible to the communities in which we live and work and to the world as well." Using these statements as empowerers of their behavior, Johnson & Johnson managers recalled every package from every shelf in the world. Managers were applauded for taking responsibility and the dramatic short-term financial loss.[1]

Culture calls the tune. What happened at Johnson & Johnson happens everywhere. In the previous anecdote Ken discovered that the wrong culture can sabotage your vision efforts.

What is culture, anyway? The answer of a programmer in a large aerospace company says it best: "Culture? That's just the way we do things around here." Every organization has a standard way of doing things governing virtually every aspect of working life—from how long coffee breaks are to how you sell your products and services. Culture is the sum total of all the standard ways people are supposed to (and actually do) act. You are surrounded by culture. No wonder you have difficulty seeing your culture. It's so close to you, and so second nature, that you hardly think about it.

Create the culture you want—one that empowers using the vision. I'll show you several ways to do that.

Personal Workshop

As you review your current culture, please ponder the following questions.

1. What is my current culture?

How would I describe my culture? In other words, what's really important in my organization?

Ask five other people—including several individuals at different organizational levels—and see what they say in response to that question.

2. What aspect of my current culture empowers my new vision? What aspects don't?

MARK THE PASSING OF THE OLD WAY

Your new vision is new. That means something else has passed—namely the old vision. Empower the new vision by creating a passage ritual. Stress the good points of the past and optimism for the future. The English do it. At the funeral for a fallen monarch, the English chant, "The King is dead. Long live the King!" This ritual marks the passage of the old ruler—"The King is dead"—and the empowerment of the new ruler—"Long live the King!"

Our culture is filled with similar empowering transitions. New Year's Eve parties symbolize the ending of one year and the hope to be found in the one just beginning. Funerals are times to remember the good points of the loved one and the hope for new beginnings elsewhere. Parties given to retiring or leaving employees are celebrations of the ending of the employee's past status and the hope for the new opportunities to be found in the new status.

Organizations create similar empowering transition rituals.[2]

- **When AT&T's breakup was announced, workers throughout the system put on black armbands to symbolize the death of a family member (Ma Bell).**

- **When the Massachusetts voters passed a tax control law that severely cut school funds, students named hallways after laid-off teachers and held rallies to honor their finding new jobs.**

- **When computer terminals were introduced into a large urban newspaper, reporters passed around a bronzed old-fashioned typewriter to the person who'd get the new terminal next.**

- **When IBM took over Rolm, John Opel, the chairman of IBM, showed up at the usual Friday bash wearing the casual clothes typical of the Rolm culture—and very atypical**

203

of the IBM culture. At the same time, the president of Rolm showed up at the annual employee party dressed in the Charlie Chaplin outfit of the IBM television character.

Demonstrate to your people—dramatically and visibly—that the old order is passing and a new one is coming that promises better times. Signal people that things will be different—without denigrating the past. In working with Mark Julian, an operations manager for a newly reorganized data processing department in a local government, we successfully used a passage ritual to empower his people to use his vision.

Mark developed a new customer service vision. Previously, his 325 people had a very poor service reputation. They were known for their arrogance and extremely late delivery.

Mark followed many of the steps spelled out on the previous pages. But while most of his people supported the new vision enthusiastically, much of the conversation around the department still used the old arrogant language.

Mark decided to symbolically "bury" the arrogant and poor delivery image. He held a diagnostic journey—a "trip through customer land," he called it—visiting customers, conducting surveys, gathering data about what customers thought about their service. There was a lot of criticism and some positive aspects.

Mark reviewed the results with his people. He stressed taking positive action to correct the bad points and reinforce the good ones. He coined the phrase "on-time service" as the watchword for his "new" division.

All of this stirred quite a bit of interest in the department. It was the topic of conversation for weeks, particularly since the employees talked a lot about the new slogan. After a while the slogan fell into disuse, but Mark never heard his people slip back into the arrogant language again. These and other actions helped him establish an excellent reputation for service and on-time delivery.

Empower your employees to leave the past behind and use your new vision. Here's the steps to build an empowering passage ritual:

1. *Remember the glory of the golden past.* Recall some time in the distant past when things were very good (which can be contrasted with the recent past or current situation that is not as good). Remind people that they are part of a proud tradition. It may have slipped some in the present, but it can be attained again. AT&T executives did this consistently during their breakup period.

2. *Promise a better future.* Draw the inspiration from the golden past. Look beyond the gray present. Focus attention on the better tomorrow-to-be. Your people need to see that better tomorrow and believe they can attain it. Each executive in the newly formed "baby Bells" stressed the "better tomorrow" for their individual operating units.

   Ma Bell could have learned from her offspring. While cutting more than sixty-six thousand employees, AT&T made a number of grievous errors. For example, executives confided in Wall Street analysts about the pending massive job cuts. They neglected to tell their employees. Result: Employees read about it in the newspaper. The grapevine went berserk. People spent more time worrying than working. It took years for employees to see a future in their jobs.

   Contrast AT&T's faux pas with the massive communications efforts of Ford, Bethlehem Steel, and Bank of America. Both Ford and Bethlehem flooded their employees with electronic messages from their in-house television networks. Bank of America relied upon personal visits from senior executives to carry the message about the bank's future. Robert Beck, senior vice-president for human resources, personally screened and trained executives to deliver the empowering message. He looked for people who were neither condescending, evasive, nor overly pessimistic. He wanted the executives to paint a clear picture of a better tomorrow—but one that was not guaranteed.[3]

3. *Pose moderate risks.* Don't make it too easy. Present real risks and hardships. Consider the Indian ritual of sending a young brave out to survive three days in the wild on his own to prove he was a "man." Or the Bar Mitzvah passage for Jewish boys who must master several biblical passages and give a public speech

to the congregation. Or the demanding orientation program at Morgan Stanley, which requires the novitiate to work six days a week, twelve to sixteen hours a day.

4. *Remind all employees of common values.* Bind your people through a common set of values. AT&T executives talked constantly about the common values of customer service and excellence in phone service that would continue despite the breakup.

5. *Celebrate the new way once the passage is complete.* Celebrate once you're on the path to the new. AT&T, for instance, held many farewell parties to say good-bye to colleagues who were being "spun off." These spun-off employees then held welcoming parties to celebrate their new status.

Professor Noel Tichy's transformational leadership program helps restructured employees build a successful passage ritual. "Unless you acknowledge a certain period of mourning as being normal and legitimate," he says, "you won't be able to do a new beginning properly." So his workshops enable employees to express their grief at the passing of the old way. He also encourages managers to express their emotion as well. "If you can't do the 'soft' stuff as well as the tough stuff," he says, "you'll never get people's total support." GE, Exxon, and Chase Manhattan were previous clients. IBM's taking the cure now—helping its people pass through the old ways and be empowered to use the new.[4]

Sometimes you need to destroy the old way before you can empower a new future. Ed Brennan, the CEO of Sears Roebuck & Co., is an expert at tearing down before building up. He shuttered more than fifty stores and cut employment more than 20 percent, including more than 1,500 career executives who were offered an "early out" program.

But Brennan loved the old Sears culture. His entire family had worked for Sears. The Sears brand was on his forehead. Once he cleaned out the underbrush, he set out to empower his "Store of the Future." He knew his remaining people needed a better future to look forward to. He personally reviewed every item in every merchandise line to be certain that they attracted customers. He personally visited stores to constantly remind managers and employees alike of their golden past and their promised future. He stressed their common values in serving customers. His Sears label was evident for all to see—and follow.

The Sears saga is far from over. Brennan reversed the precipitous decline in market share—even though it took seven years. There's a new, more modern Sears vision in place. It's beginning to work. But the Wal-Marts, Limited, and K marts of the world keep nibbling away.[5] There is no rest.

Change is inevitable. Most people look back with nostalgia at the "good old days" and view the past through rose-colored glasses. Help people leave the past by encouraging the mourning that is necessary to cleanse that past and empower the new way.

Personal Workshop

As you consider the various ways in which you might ceremonially mark the passing of the old way and the coming of your new culture, ponder the following questions.

1. How can I help my people remember the glory of a golden past?

2. How can I promise a better future with my vision?

3. How can I build in passage rituals that contain a moderate amount of risk but encourage success?

4. As the passage is taking place, how can I remind my people of the common values that bind them together?

5. How can I celebrate when the old order has passed?

DEVELOP SHARED ACTIVITIES
BUILT AROUND YOUR VISION

"The family that prays together stays together," is a common billboard sign. I'd modify that slogan to read, "The people who work and play together share a common vision."

Build work activities that use your vision. Demanding orientation programs (as with Morgan Stanley and IBM) empower people to adopt the culture of teamwork and striving for excellence. Demanding project team assignments (as with Texas Instruments and Phillips) require using corporate values.

Capitalize on the empowerment generated from all your vision-building activities. Ted Powers, the division general manager for a pharmaceutical distribution company, used shared work experiences to empower his people to use his vision.

> Ted had a glimmer of a vision—built around the slogan "Working together for good health." After several meetings with a small brain trust of trusted lieutenants, he gathered twenty-seven volunteers to help him develop the specific wording. After many meetings the group came up with a one-page statement. Ted wondered if the words were clear enough to everyone, but he decided to proceed anyway since the volunteer group felt so strongly about them.
>
> He next met with all managers to secure their participation in executing the vision and ended the meeting asking each one to write down three specific action steps he/she would take in the next thirty days to use the vision. He published the action steps and followed up with periodic meetings to discuss them. He was not totally pleased with many of the steps, feeling they were too vague, but because the individuals were so committed to doing them he continued the activity.
>
> He next met with all employees in departmental groupings to explain his vision and again asked for actions to live the vision. The employees were generally enthusiastic, but not as totally committed as Ted thought they should be. He got more "Yes, buts . . ." than he expected.
>
> Productivity began to pick up and quality improved as customer complaints nosedived. Ted was pleased with the results, so when several employees asked him to continue the group meetings he easily agreed.
>
> Ted told us, "I didn't realize it at first, but as the meetings went on it became clear to me that the meetings themselves were causing the change. People love to be included. They love to have a hand in shaping the effort and knowing that their input made a difference. I was focusing on the impre-

cise words and generalized actions and missing the important process going on. I tell you, without those meetings
we'd never have been successful."

Use the power of shared work activities to empower your people
to use your vision consistently.

That's what Hewlett-Packard CEO and president John Young
did in the U.S. He saw that a tenfold increase in quality was required to be competitive with the Japanese. People thought he was
crazy. Events proved he wasn't.

H-P has a long tradition of building products for the person at
the "next desk." H-P engineers were acculturated to leave work on
their desk so passing colleagues could fiddle with it and contribute
to its development. William Hewlett—one of the founders—urged
engineers to develop products useful to the "person at the next
desk," then sell them to all the "next desks" in the world.

John Young capitalized on this "next desk" orientation. He
added shared work activities to empower his quality vision. He
stressed that every employee was both a customer and a supplier.
Circuit board assemblers, for instance, have chip and hardware
"suppliers" and subassembly component "customers." He asked
customers and suppliers to work together to set mutual expectations, standards, and measurements that improved the quality of
the product at every stage. "Don't make or accept junk," he
urged.

The results are dramatic. Empowered by the shared work activities using the quality vision, H-P increased quality levels nine times
in a few years. In just two areas, for instance, H-P saved $542
million in manufacturing inventory costs and $150 million in
money owed by customers. Shared work activities empowered employees to use John Young's quality vision.[6]

Use *shared play activities* to empower your people to use your new
vision. Tandem Computer and Hewlett-Packard use Friday afternoon beer bashes as a vision empowerer. The values of equality
and individual respect are experienced every Friday.

Meals bring people together and empower using the vision.
Northwestern Life gives free lunches, for instance. Employees can
ask questions, get information, and work together to solve problems. The Limited (the highly successful specialty realtor) gives

free popcorn in the afternoon to encourage individuals to get together informally.

Special events celebrations empower people to use the vision. IBM's 100 percent Club celebrations and Golden Circle bashes remind everyone that selling pays in IBM. SAS's 1982 Christmas bash shared the fruits of living their customer service vision in a fun setting. The Limited's President's Club meeting held every August in Colorado for the top branch managers presents awards at the top of the mountain, symbolizing that these people have reached a summit of performance.

Personal Workshop

As you review the various ways you can develop shared activities to empower your vision, please ponder the following questions.

1. How can I build in shared work activities that demand use of the vision in order to complete?
   a. Can I use orientation activities?
   b. Can I generate project team assignments?

2. How can I build in shared work activities around my vision?

3. How can I develop shared play activities that empower my vision?
   a. What can I do on a regular basis—such as Friday afternoon beer or midafternoon popcorn?
   b. What can I do to celebrate the special events so as to empower my vision?

DEVELOP SHARED SAYINGS
AROUND THE VISION

Words are powerful empowerers. Leaders from the dawning of time have used words to empower their followers. From the Bible, encapsulating the spoken words of Abraham and Jesus, founders of the Judeo-Christian faiths, to the Magna Carta, the Declaration of Independence, *Mein Kampf,* and *Das Kapital,* words have empowered behavior and fundamentally shaped our world.

Words communicate purpose and empower actions. John Patterson, the founder of the U.S. company NCR, realized the value of communicating his vision. He developed the first regular sales training school (at which he regularly taught), along with the first sales training manual. When he died in 1922, NCR held 90 percent of the U.S. cash register market.

Patterson's star pupil, Thomas Watson, Sr., used a similar approach. Watson used formalized sales training and constant written and oral communication of his vision to shape IBM into the dominant force it is today. And IBM is not alone. The vast majority of the one hundred best companies for which to work in America, reported by Levering, Moskowitz, and Katz in *The 100 Best Companies to Work for in America,* have written vision statements that are repeated frequently to employees. Written statements are included in employee handbooks, emblazoned on company notebooks, repeated frequently in memos, and spoken about often at training sessions.[7] Constantly communicating the vision empowers the use of that vision as the answer to the question "How do we do things around here?"

Begin with the crafting of the words. Repeat your words frequently—so your people see it as "gospel." Use the same words in different formats. Thomas Watson wrote about the importance of his vision—respect for the individual, customer service, and excellence in execution—in every memo, and he talked about it with every person he met in his office or in the field. He personally taught sales training and management development classes in which he stressed these three cornerstones. In short, he took every opportunity to insure that his vision was shared by everyone in his organization.

John Sculley, in another computer company, is an expert in developing shared sayings. When he won the power struggle with Steve Jobs for control of Apple Computer, Inc., he saw the need to move the company in a radically new direction.

> What I had to do was convince people that we were in a crisis, and that we weren't going to pull out of it unless we pulled together. . . . The thing that was going to be . . . difficult was finding a new direction for the company that people at Apple could continue to feel excited about. How were we going to hold on to the roots of Apple?

The only way I knew how . . . was to get groups of managers together to sit down and talk it through. . . . We went over the mistakes and the successes. And we tried to figure out what things were really important to us. It meant sitting down with many, many people.

Out of these many soul-searching meetings came Apple's new empowering vision.[8]

Be similarly obsessed with developing a set of shared sayings in your organization built around your vision. You want your vision to be repeated in the hallways and talked about over lunch. By developing your vision into a set of shared sayings, you empower people to keep using your vision. Shared vision sayings empower vision-supporting actions.

Personal Workshop

As you consider how you can develop shared sayings built around your vision, please ponder the following questions.

1. How can I craft the words that reflect my vision? How can I get groups of employees—formally or informally—to help me develop words that can be widely shared?

2. How can I repeat the words frequently? In what settings—formal and informal—can I send the message? How about at orientation programs? training sessions? employee handbooks? bulletin board messages? letters to the home?

USE STORIES ABOUT HEROES
WHO EXEMPLIFY YOUR NEW VISION IN ACTION

Stories tell the tale of what an organization stands for. Every country has its national heroes. America has its stories about Daniel Boone, George Washington, Abraham Lincoln, and John Kennedy. In the U.K. there are stories about King Arthur and his Knights of the Round Table (particularly Sir Lancelot), King Richard "The Lion Hearted," Queen Elizabeth I, William Shakespeare,

Thomas Beckett, Queen Victoria, and the Beatles. Germany has its Bismarck, France its Napoleon and de Gaulle, Turkey its Ataturk, and Holland its Michel de Ruyter, Prince Willem van Oranje, and Floris de V. In each country these heroes embody the values and visions citizens hold dear. Stories about these people empower the country's ideal.

AT&T has its stories—linemen working two consecutive days in freezing weather or a telephone operator staying on the job to maintain the vital connections while a fire roared around her. These heroes reinforce the "service to the customers" vision of the old Ma Bell.

IBM has its stories about heroes—the warehouse man who noticed the error in a customer's shipment and corrected it without asking permission, the repair crew that worked all night to get the computers up and running to meet the eight A.M. payroll run, and the systems engineer who designed a solution for a customer after the competitor said it couldn't be done.

Other companies have their stories about heroes as well. Ray Kroc found a fly in a condiment jar at the Winnipeg franchise. The franchisee lost his store two weeks later. This empowers McDonald's "Quality, Service, Cleanliness, and Value" vision. Don Vlcek (president of Domino's Pizza) rolled up his sleeves and corrected some lumpy dough. This action empowers the company's commitment to quality. Sir John Harvey-Jones' blowing up Stone Mountain—the original building and company headquarters for U.K.'s Imperial Chemical Company—empowered his company's commitment to radically change its ways of doing business.

Hero stories are told and retold again and again. They play a prominent role in orientation sessions for new employees, at training sessions for continuing employees, and in hallway conversations. They are empowering evidence that the vision lives. Stories are a criteria against which to measure present performance. Employees ask themselves, "Does my current choice match what these heroes would do in a similar situation?" "Am I keeping the faith?"

Create heroes who exemplify your new vision in action. Begin by *gathering stories* of individuals using your vision. Ask employees to send you success stories. You'll be surprised at the flood of responses. Or use special project teams to collect stories, as did Bob Landau, head librarian in a large U.S. eastern city.

Bob appointed a team with the prime responsibility to draft an employee handbook that included stories of employees successfully using the vision. The team gathered fifty stories initially.

To increase the number of stories, the team posted large notices listing the names of employees who contributed a story and urging each of them to find one or two other employees with examples. The team expects to list the names of those 150 or so employees on large notices and urge each of them to find one or two other employees with examples. They plan to repeat the process until they've collected at least five hundred stories for inclusion in the employee handbook.

Then, *widely publicize* stories that reflect the successful use of your vision. Use such formal systems as columns in employee newsletters or monthly employee memos. Use your daily contacts to tell the stories ("Did you hear what X did? . . ."). Communicate these stories compulsively. Your aim—raise the story of Sarah going out of her way to help this customer to the level of belief surrounding the legend of George Washington chopping down the cherry tree.

Celebrate your heroes. Give your new heroes special status. Bank of America is striving to convert its conservative culture into a more entrepreneurial one. At the annual meeting of all managerial personnel, those managers who exemplify the new entrepreneurial culture (the heroes) were called up to the stage. In front of all their peers they were given a leather briefcase as a special award. As their stories were told to the assembled group, each was asked to open his/her briefcase. It was filled with $10,000 in cash!

Celebrate your heroes at regular meetings. Jean Simmons, the purchasing agent for a large U.S. midwestern city, used several mechanisms to develop new heroes who exemplified her new vision.

Jean crafted a new vision built around the slogan "Helping you achieve success," using many of the techniques laid out in previous chapters. It was received enthusiastically by her employees and her customers.

To gather information on those who were using her vision, Jean ran an "ad" in the employee newspaper asking for stories that illustrated her people providing excellent service. At her monthly staff meeting she also asked her own twenty-one-person staff to send her stories.

She received eighteen stories. The editor of the employee newsletter agreed to publish one of these every month for the next year. She published the other stories in monthly memos she sent to all 2,800 employees in the city.

She got each of the heroes a special Oscar-type statue and awarded it to them at a special luncheon she gave her department. She talked often about these heroes and retold their stories to each new employee.

Jean knew her vision had arrived when the chief financial officer told his boss—the city manager—one of the stories as evidence of the significant strides his division was making in improving customer service.

"I figure," Jean told me, "that the stories are now part of my departmental culture. They really helped me to empower my people using my vision."

Tell stories about heroes using your vision. Empower your people to use your vision.

Personal Workshop

As you consider ways to find and celebrate heroes to empower your people to use your vision, please consider the following questions.

1. What stories are currently making the rounds in my organization? Are they supportive or destructive of my vision?

2. Who is currently using my vision successfully? Can I identify who he/she is and find out what he/she is doing and with what success?

3. How can I gather stories about those who are using my vision? Can I advertise in the employee newspaper? Request stories from my direct staff at the meetings? Ask all my managers at a managers meeting to send me stories? Put a notice on the bulletin board asking employees to send me stories? Can I ask all the people I meet in the hallways to send me stories?

4. How can I widely publicize the stories once I get them? Can I get the editor of the employee newsletter to print stories? Can I publish a newsletter highlighting these heroes? Can I get some of these stories into the orientation program or the training programs? Can I put up bulletin board notices?

5. How can I celebrate my heroes? What regular events can I use to celebrate these users of my vision? Can I acknowledge them during my regular staff meetings or my regular management and/or employee meetings? What special events can I construct to highlight these special people?

HANDLE DIFFICULT TIMES USING YOUR VISION

"Hard times bring out the best in people," Winston Churchill wrote, "and the worst." And it also brings out your real values and visions.

Most vision statements are crafted in the sunshine of good times. It's easy to be in favor of such things as working together, providing real-time rewards, transfers rather than layoffs, challenging work, and the other noble-sounding values when the cash is rolling in and the future looks bright.

But bad times come even to the best of companies. How you handle the tough times will send an unmistakable and unforgettable message. Handle the problems using your vision, and you empower your people. But waffle—for the hundreds of good reasons we all have heard so often—and you'd better plan a funeral, because your vision is dead.

The organizations that successfully empower their vision stick to it during the tough times. IBM, for instance, encountered unexpected difficult times in 1985, 1986, and 1987. Every other computer company laid off employees. Not IBM, where continuity of employment is a cornerstone. It probably cost IBM the chance to continue year-to-year earnings growth. But it wasn't even a decision. At IBM short-term economic results have a lower priority than the continuity of vision.

During the recession of the early 1970s, in Silicon Valley all electronic companies laid off employees—except one. That company went on a nine-day fortnight (employees worked nine out of every ten days) to preserve employment for all employees. That organization today is still viewed as one of the premier companies in America.

A disaster the dimensions of the Tylenol issue might have destroyed most companies—or at least led to the all-too-familiar double-talk defensive stonewalling so characteristic of car and tire companies. But not Johnson & Johnson. They relied upon their vision, immediately recalled all Tylenol, destroyed current stocks, redesigned tamper-proof sealed bottles, and even discontinued capsule production. Today their market share is higher than ever.

Chairman John Gutfreund of Salomon Brothers knows all about handling disasters, particularly those of his own making. The story about the closing of Salomon's U.S. municipal bond department was leaked to the press and published in the weekend edition of *The New York Times*. Gutfreund wasted no time on Monday morning. He called a general meeting on the trading floor first thing. He told those who were departing about the generous severance packages they'd be receiving and reassured those who were staying about their future. His people-oriented vision saw him through that particular difficult time.[9]

Contrast Salomon's actions in handling bad news with BHP's action when they cut back operations in Houston a few years ago. All employees were called into a room and given an envelope with an A or B on it. The B's were invited into another room and informed they were history. Morale and productivity has yet to recover.[10]

A number of AT&T managers also committed serious errors while they were laying off people. In cutting back, many managers conveyed the message, "I'm still needed around here and you're not. Nyah, nyah, nyah." It's difficult to say how much of AT&T's continuing soap opera of missed opportunities is a consequence of depowering people to use its new vision, but it's probably a lot.[11]

It may never come back for AT&T executives—or any other executive who abandons the vision during tough times.

Empower the new vision by shaping your culture to support it. Culture is a major empowerer of your vision's success.

Mark the passing of the old way. Clarify the better future that builds on a glorious past. Develop shared activities that give people a chance to use your vision. Enable people to experience the empowerment of project teams, vision-crafting activities, and orientation programs that use your vision. Develop shared sayings that encapsulate your vision and become grist for the conversation mill throughout your organization. Identify heroes using your vision, and tell stories about them. Last, use your vision during the tough times—that's when it really counts.

Culture is it. People listen carefully to the messages sent by the Pied Piper of culture. Shape the culture to empower people to use your vision.

11

Empower Individual Change Agents

EMPOWERING CHANGE
VISION
Actions
Expectation systems
People systems
Culture systems

CREATE TOMORROW
Strategies
Resources

CHANGE
Individual
Organization

PREPARATION
Getting ready
Anticipating obstacles

It's exciting to think about a new vision, particularly when you're the creator/driver of it. You see the need clearly. You feel the urgency in your stomach. You're motivated to change. You see the fire with your own eyes. You smell the smoke in your own nostrils. The tent is on fire. You have to change.

Why are others in the organization so lackadaisical? Don't they smell the smoke? Don't they see the fire? Don't they feel the urgency to change? Unfortunately, no. It's not so exciting to think about a new vision when you're the recipient of it. In fact, from that vantage point it is downright threatening.

Convert the threat into an opportunity. Enlist the broadest number of individual change agents—empowered people at all levels—to champion your vision.

How?

Bring the change process—and your new vision—down to the gut level for each and every individual. Focus every person on

219

using your vision to solve the biggest job-related issue confronting him/her.

How? That's what this chapter is all about.

Too many change activities reflect the old Chinese proverb, "Lots of noise at the top of the stairs, but no one coming down." When change is driven from the top of the organization—without significant across-the-board participation—it is a recipe for failure. Remember the third principle, way back in chapter 1? Participation empowers the vision. How to do that is what I'll cover in this chapter.

IT ISN'T EASY
TO EMPOWER REAL PARTICIPATION

Everyone needs to play their best. Implementing your vision is like playing the NFL Chicago Bears. Field a whole team—and get everyone to play their best—or get the bandages, whirlpools, and excuses ready.

Unfortunately most organizations don't work that way. Organizations are not built to get everyone to play his/her best. There's a miserable record of empowering real participation.

The current management headsets rob many empowerment efforts of their substance. What's often left is the form of participation, without any real content. A quality circle leader at a GE defense plant said, "The group felt that management had the plans and was only bringing them to the worker improvement group to get them approved."[1] And what happens if "they" revolt and don't approve management's plans? Many companies answer, "Stop the process. 'They' are not willing to be fixed."

Furthermore, years of "I'll think and you do" programming leave a residue of dependency throughout the organization. In many organizations managers are so trained to wait for instructions from headquarters that they are incapable of making independent decisions.

How can you empower change agents throughout the organization? Basically, link your vision tightly to the performance of their job. Demonstrate how using your vision deals with the realities of their everyday activities. Use the following process: identify strategic business issues, develop customer-supplier contracts using your new vision that specify deliverables for each issue, and frequently measure progress on the contracts.

IDENTIFY STRATEGIC BUSINESS ISSUES

Identify the critical strategic issues confronting the business unit. Link your vision with their solution. Every unit—whether in sales/marketing, personnel, finance, engineering, product development, or customer-focused/product-based—has a handful of issues—strategic business issues (SBIs)—that will determine its fate for the coming period. So does every individual. Show clearly how your vision leads to the successful resolution of these SBIs.

Where to begin? *Identify the few critical SBIs.* Sue Akins, division manager for a computer software and services company, identified her small handful of critical SBIs in the following way.

Sue's fifty-six-person group sold, installed, and serviced a customized software accounting package. She had more than four hundred customers in her urban area. Sue spent most of her time handling key accounts and resolving customer problems.

Sue recognized that her division was in deep trouble. Margins were slipping (and even falling into the red), and customer complaints were growing rapidly. "We need to do something," she told me.

Sue got her group together for a one-day meeting. She invited the company president (there were nineteen product divisions like Sue's) to talk about the biggest problems facing the overall business. He identified three: getting/keeping more customers, being more efficient so that margins improved, and being more customer service–oriented so that current customers felt they received greater value for the package. Sue's employees agreed that those were the same issues facing them as well.

"To fix these problems is a tall order," Sue told her group. "Let's see what we can do about it." Sue reminded the group of their commonly-agreed-upon vision—"Quality, Service, and Accuracy." "Let's see how this vision helps us meet these strategic issues," she said.

Individuals first identified the most pressing problems confronting them in their jobs that contributed to the overall division's issues. These were shared within the entire group and agreed upon by the end of the meeting. Before the meeting broke up that day, individuals identified the five most important "customers/users" they serviced within the division.

During the next week customer-supplier dyads met to identify their biggest problems (those that contributed to the overall company's issues) and discuss how they could work together to solve them. These agreements were then reduced to writing and shared with the entire division through the electronic mail system. This weekly process of setting goals and reviewing results continued for several months.

During the weekly dyad meetings there was considerable discussion about the need to maintain quality standards, provide excellent service, and have a first-time accuracy approach. "As long as we keep asking ourselves, 'Is this quality, service, and accuracy?' we stay on track," one programmer told me.

Sue noticed an immediate spurt in productivity and customer focus. She was amazed at the interest and enthusiasm. Complaints from external customers fell off almost immediately. By the third month margins began to creep back up.

"Getting people to see how they could concretely contribute to better performance was the key," Sue told me. "All too often we talk in generalities and leave people wondering what they can really do. Also, we focused on a few issues that were manageable. All too often the tendency is to want to improve everything at once with the result that nothing ever happens. We've got a whole organization of people who feel empowered to live the vision now."

Link vision to the resolution of the SBIs. Focus on the few most important SBIs that facilitate this empowerment process.

Sue also reminds us to *stress individual concrete contribution.* Too many times we urge people to "do better" and never define "better." Show people how the vision works in their little corner of the universe. Demonstrate how the vision helps them solve their biggest, most important problem.

Worse, management defines "better" for the individual, rather than letting the individual define it. So "better" becomes management's agenda, not the individual's. No wonder "better" happens so infrequently.

Use a little *drama* to encourage individuals to step forward and identify their SBIs. One airline with which I worked asked for volunteers to work with the president in improving the airline's customer service ratings. Just about 9 percent of the airline personnel volunteered even though the president promised no additional wages or benefits. To each of the volunteer groups he posed the following question: "What do we need to do in your area to live the vision—the best business-class airline in our region?" He authorized trips on competing airlines to gather competitive information. This little bit of drama, combined with earnest working at their recommendations, resulted in the airline being chosen "Airline of the Year."

Involve every function. It's easy to identify strategic issues for traditional line activities. Lots of people in staff-type jobs resist similar "specification." Joan Walters found a way around that.

> In 1983, the CEO of a *Fortune* 500 company stood in front of his executive committee and said, "We must change the way we do business—or risk losing it." Five years later a new CEO stood in front of much the same committee and said, "We need to launch the process of continuous change in our organization, or else we may not be here by the year 2000." In the intervening time, little besides the identity of the CEO had changed in that organization.
>
> Recognizing the need for a new approach, the CEO turned to the senior vice-president of human resources and said, "And, Joan, I want your group to empower change throughout the organization and implant the process of continuous improvement." That's when Joan called me.

To launch the process, Joan called together the division HR heads. At the start of the two-day conference, each HR person called his/her senior division executive officer to identify the significant business issue(s) (SBI) confronting his/her division—both operational (short term, less than a year) and strategic (longer term, more than a year). The HR person also identified the HR contribution wanted by that senior executive.

The results were startling. For the first time many of these individuals came face to face with the business realities of their organizations. All too often staff people live in a world all their own, disconnected from the pressing realities with which their operating colleagues deal on a minute-by-minute basis.

Furthermore, almost none of these HR people had ever asked, "How can I contribute to the unit's performance?" "I always thought I knew—better than anyone else. I would never have thought he expected me to do *that!*" was the comment of one HR division head.

The combination of both of these pieces of information triggered considerable discussion and soul searching within the group. The SBIs were the first topic. It was particularly difficult for many of the HR career types to grasp the real meaning of the SBIs and their relationship to HR responsibilities. In one unit, for instance, 99 percent first-time quality was the operational SBI. Currently more than 50 percent of the unit's output required rework. The division HR head said, "I agree it's terrible. But what can I do about the fact that the typical product reaches the end of the line with more than five hundred yellow 'exception' tickets on it? It's a technical problem, not an HR problem."

The biggest obstacle, however, was the philosophical debate over whether HR programs *should* be designed to meet division management's expectations, or whether there wasn't a higher "professional" calling. This is the classical professional-business controversy that plagues many staff groups. Accounting people, for instance, face similar questions. Does the division finance manager serve the operating official? the senior corporate financial official? the stockholders? or even some vaguely defined professional group? These controversies hobble the effectiveness of staff groups—and lead them to be left out of significant business decisions.

Who is the real HR customer? Is it the line management? Is it the corporate HR person? Is it the people in the unit? Or is it the HR profession? After much intensive discussion most members of the group agreed that HR needed to serve the business's SBIs. For several of the participants, that represented a significant shift in thinking.

With the target now fixed, next came the question of how HR could best contribute to the unit's SBI accomplishment. The common theme throughout the divisions' SBIs were cost reduction and productivity, quality, and service improvements. It was clear that none of that would happen unless there was a substantial change in current ways of doing business. HR had to develop ways to empower change in the organization.

Each participant then drafted a program for the coming six months to empower change in his/her organization. Reviewing the sheets on the wall showed that there was a big gap between knowing you had to do "something" to create change and knowing the right "something" to do. Many of the proposals were traditional personnel programs, wrapped in new language. They had to see how their traditional personnel systems—recruiting, orientation, training, performance appraisal, career development, and compensation—impacted service, quality, and productivity levels. These people needed to know how to use their systems to empower change. New input was necessary.

The ensuing two-hour lecture covered three topics. First, Joan cited examples of high-performance companies using traditional personnel systems to empower significant change. Singapore Airlines' recruiting and training practices, for instance, which significantly upgraded their service levels. Or American Express's service measurements, which yield 99.5 percent statement accuracy. Many of the participants could immediately see how they could directly contribute to improved service levels.

Second, Joan went beyond traditional personnel systems. She stressed the empowerment in performance systems—expectations, measurements, and rewards. She talked about how other organizations were using these systems to empower change.

Cypress Semiconductors, for instance, uses an MBO-type performance system to generate weekly prioritized goals and actions that focus on quality and shortening the development cycle. Using their system, Cypress generated 90 percent first-time performance for custom-designed chips (significantly better than the industry average).

Third, several members of the group shared experiences working with new kinds of empowering structures. They discussed several examples of decentralization in engineering, production, and marketing activities. There were at least three locations experimenting with New United Motors Manufacturing, Inc.-type work group structures. At least one entire division had reorganized on the basis of natural work groups to handle rapid changes in their environment.

Joan challenged the HR participants to apply these new insights—gleaned from the lecture and the experiences of their own colleagues—to serving their unit's SBIs.

Now she got a much different list. Many of the action items dealt with measurement—how to measure service, quality, and productivity. There was a significant absence of real-time realistic measurement of quality, cost, and service throughout the organization. Participants set out to facilitate the creation of new measurement systems for the organization, using their own department as the test case.

Reorganization into more customer-focused structures was another popular action theme. Most of the HR people committed to reorganize themselves from their traditional functional structure into a more customer-based one. There were also several commitments to facilitate new work group structures, first in pilot sites in their organization, then spreading throughout the unit.

Almost everyone used the medium of "customer contracting" to drive their new direction. This process is used by IBM, Volvo, and Hewlett-Packard. Participants agreed to meet with their major in-house suppliers and customers to determine short-term and long-term deliverables, standards of performance, and measurements.

But that's not the end of the story. It's one thing to commit to doing something at a seminar. It's something else to produce that "something" in the reality of organizational life. To bridge this gap, Joan asked individuals to identify the constraints and bottlenecks that prevented them from accomplishing their goals. She used Eli Goldratt's *The Goal* as the basis for the discussion. Although Goldratt focuses on manufacturing, with minor modification, she was able to apply his concepts to administrative activities.

Joan identified three major constraints—those resources whose capacities were less than demand. Staff training and capability was the major constraint. Most functionally trained HR personnel were not capable of facilitating change. To fill this hole, major retraining activities were planned, along with selective new hiring.

The second biggest constraint was the lack of knowledge of customer needs. Most staff groups operate behind thick walls. Active solicitation of customer needs was planned to bridge this knowledge gap.

Last, the pressing work load of other "traditional" personnel activities left little time/people resource for these "new" responsibilities. Each HR head left with the commitment to offload or eliminate up to 35 percent of current activities.

Above all, *work at empowering your vision continuously.* It's difficult to turn the tables, *asking the question,* "What can you do to execute this new vision?" *rather than giving the answer,* "Here's what I want you to do." Your people will not believe you when you say, "I really want you to decide." They've heard those words before. In the past those words have generally been followed by criticism, carping, and, finally, announcing the "right" (the boss's) way. It won't be easy. But, then again, change never is easy—just necessary.

Start the process by identifying the critical strategic issues confronting the organization. Involve every level and function. Get everyone to specify specific and concrete contributions to the overall SBIs.

Personal Workshop

As you think about how to identify your SBIs and link them with your vision, please consider the following questions.

1. What are the few critical strategic business issues (SBIs) facing my business in the coming year?

2. How can my vision help to resolve these SBIs?

3. How can I help each person identify for his/her function those SBIs that contribute to the overall SBIs?

4. How can I get each person to identify concrete contributions to his/her unit's SBIs?

ESTABLISH CUSTOMER-SUPPLIER CONTRACTS

Everyone in the organization *has a "customer."* It may be the person at the next desk. It may be the person in the next department. It may be the manager of the department or the secretary. Everyone has a set of internal customers, because everyone produces "outputs" (ideas, papers, data, approvals) for someone else in the organization.

Everyone also *has suppliers.* It may be the person at the next desk. It may be the person in the next department. It may be the manager or the secretary. Everyone has suppliers because everyone gets "inputs" (ideas, papers, data, approvals) from others in the organization.

The organization is an *interdependent system* of groups, departments, and individuals. The *web of customer-supplier contracts* binds all the components together to produce an organization. Link your vision to the successful execution of these contracts. That's how to empower individual change agents to use your vision. For example, Tony Amaya, shift supervisor for a metal machining plant, sees it this way:

I supervise nineteen people. My biggest suppliers include

1. Jose, the shift supervisor in the next department, who gives me partially machined parts that my group finishes.

2. Dennis, the process engineer in my area, who gives me instructions about the right processes to use—speeds, feeds, and so on.

3. Sharon, the manufacturing engineer for my area, who gives me the right drawings and parts specifications.

4. Mike, the production control expediter, who gets me the parts and subassemblies I need.

5. Paul, the personnel representative, who gets me the people I need.

6. Alan, the shift supervisor on the last shift, who gives me the work load every day.

There are many more, but these are the most important now.

As for customers, the most important ones are

1. John, on the next shift, whom I set up to finish what I can't get done.

2. Sheryl, the general foreman, whom I have to please.

3. Dave, the quality control supervisor on my shift, who inspects and accepts or rejects my parts.

4. Linda, the cost accounting supervisor, who gets my time cards and job allocations.

There's more customers too, but these are the important ones these days.

I meet regularly with each of these customers and suppliers to establish "contracts" of how I help them do their job (in the case of customers) and how they help me do my job (suppliers). At these meetings we frequently talk about the department's SBIs and make certain that our agreements contribute to them. We also have posted our vision statement on the wall and sometime during the meeting one of us will ask the standard question, "Is this in keeping with the vision?"

It's weird sometimes when the same person is both a supplier and a customer. For instance, manufacturing engineering supplies me with drawings and specifications, while I supply them with producibility data. Linda in cost accounting is my customer when I give her weekly status reports. She's my supplier when I make up the annual budget. It works okay. It's just strange to think about.

Tony's experience underlines another important dimension—contracts are based on *what I need to make my contribution to the SBIs.* As either a customer or a supplier, the basis for the contract is the contribution to the SBIs. Consider the words of Ric Ross, production control supervisor in a metal fabrication plant.

My principal suppliers are

1. Michele in purchasing, who gets me the material I need.

2. Henry in quality assurance, who approves the incoming material, both external and internal.

3. Manufacturing engineering, including John in tooling, who gets me the right tools; Sheryl in planning, who gives me the proper work sequence; and Jose in industrial engineering, who gives me the methods sheets.

My job is to ensure that parts needed today are on the floor. That's necessary in order for us to meet our SBI of first-time quality units, on schedule, at budgeted cost. In order to do that my group controls inventories, capacity planning, and the MRP system.

My principal customers are

1. Jim, my counterpart in assembly, to whom I deliver the finished parts.

2. Sui, the fabrication foreman, for whom I get the package of parts and materials.

3. Vern, the general superintendent, whom I have to please.

4. Shelley, in MIS, who maintains the MRP system and to whom I supply performance-to-schedule data.

Whatever we do, though, it has to support our vision. I believe very strongly in our department's vision, "Keep the line running, minimizing inventory and costs."

It's clear in a manufacturing environment how the network of contracts is based on contribution to the SBIs. It's also clear in a commercial environment. Here's the situation faced by Sharon Peterson, a contracts coordinator for the leasing arm of a large computer company.

My principal task is to do all the prework so that accurate invoices get out in forty-eight hours. In that way customers receive their computers quickly and we shorten the float time between billing and collection.

I contribute to the company's SBI—maintaining margins in the face of increasing price competition—by turning the paperwork around quickly and making certain that it's accurate. If I do my job correctly, we can collect monies owed us faster, thus reducing interest costs.

My principal customers are

1. Customers to whom I provide the data upon which their invoices for leased hardware is based.

2. Sam, my boss in the contracts office, to whom I provide backlog and delivery information.

3. Barry, in the finance office, to whom I provide data about projected cash flows, backlogs, and lease income reports.

4. Wayne, who runs the invoice processing group, to whom I provide the data for the preparation of the invoice.

My principal suppliers are

1. Sheila, in the contracts department, who supplies me with information concerning each customer, including sales and delivery.

2. Shasta, in the finance department, who supplies me with tax information and other accounting data.

3. Rick, in operations, who gives me all the detailed hardware listing for each customer.

We also live our vision, "Grow people and financial results." I work hard to build positive relationships that stimulate people to be more responsible.

In any situation, in any job, at any level, the contribution to the
SBIs and the execution of the vision are the basis for the supplier-
customer contract.

Insist upon *specific quantifiable short-stroke "deliverables."* It's all too
easy to slip off into the never-never land of "trying," not delivering. Shaun Nelson, purchasing agent for a local government, fell
into this trap.

> Shaun saw the need to improve his department's perfor-
> mance, given the tight city budgets. He got his people to-
> gether and crafted a vision, "Serving the best with the best,"
> using many of the processes outlined in this book. Everyone
> from the city manager on down was enthusiastic about the
> change.
>
> To launch the vision, Shaun got his group together again
> and asked the city manager to identify for them the strategic
> issues facing the city. The city manager identified internal
> efficiency (doing more with less), upgrading city services,
> and improving the image of the city employees with the
> general public.
>
> Shaun's department then identified their departmental
> strategic issues as improving internal efficiency, securing
> higher-quality purchased parts and services, and being
> more customer-oriented toward their suppliers. Each per-
> son identified his/her key customers (both internal and ex-
> ternal), met with those customers, and set monthly goals
> and expectations.
>
> There was an initial spurt of interest and enthusiasm.
> People talked a lot about the process. They seemed univer-
> sally to like talking with customers. Unfortunately there
> seemed to be little concrete improvement in the depart-
> ment's performance.
>
> Shaun noticed that many of the agreements between cus-
> tomers and suppliers were vague and nonspecific. The
> buyer of janitorial services, for instance, contracted with the
> supplier to "notify the supplier as soon as possible about

changes in office assignments." The supplier, in turn, agreed to "do a better job of cleaning the offices." Despite the good intentions of both parties, the press of other business often meant delays in notifying the supplier about office changes (so new offices went uncleaned for weeks while abandoned offices were cleaned) and sometimes sloppiness in cleaning offices by the supplier.

When Shaun brought up the subject at the weekly staff meeting, it was greeted with universal criticism. "We're doing the best we can," his people said. "If you want better performance, get more resources." Shaun reemphasized the vision and everyone's role in supporting it. But it was too late.

"I downplayed the contracting process and got involved in the other phases of systems and actions to implement my vision. It's worked fairly well. But it's been much harder than I expected. Tell everyone else, *be specific.*"

The second step in the process of empowering individual change agents is to develop the web of customer-supplier contracts. Involve everyone in this interdependent system. Base the contracts upon contributions to the SBIs. Use your vision to resolve the SBIs. Identify short-stroke, specific, quantifiable deliverables. These contracts form the basis for empowering change agents.

Personal Workshop

As you consider setting up customer-supplier contracts, please ponder the following questions.

1. Who are my principal customers? my principal suppliers?

2. How can I meet with these customers/suppliers and establish concrete, quantifiable, short-stroke contributions to SBIs?

3. How can I encourage everyone in the unit to engage in this customer/supplier contracting process?

4. How can I be certain—without creating a paper mill or a KGB—that this contracting process is alive and well in my organization?

MEASURE CONTRACT PERFORMANCE

What gets measured gets produced. So measure the outputs of each contract—frequently. That's how to get them produced—regularly.

We've already talked about the importance of measurement in chapter 8. Ask the people closest to the job—customers (both internal and external) and employees. Use different measures for different jobs. Use a few measures. Measure religiously. Stress short-term measures. Use nonfinancial measures. Tie in the measures to your strategic advantage. You remember, I'm sure. No need to review them in depth again.

Just two elaborations. First, *customers and suppliers establish measures.* Customers (those who use the product) know best what they want and when they get it. So they determine the measures, since they do the measuring. Suppliers (those who create the product) are the next most knowledgeable group about what constitutes a good/bad outcome. The key: get these two most knowledgeable groups together to mutually establish the "right" measures.

Chuck Meiser supervises a design drafting section for a machine tool manufacturer. He established the following measures in conjunction with his major customers-suppliers.

> First I met with the design engineering department to get the statement of work required and engineering specifications for new products. I'm their major customer. We established that I needed complete engineering orders (all the specifications and product designs) at least four weeks before the product release date with an accuracy level of 100 percent. We also agreed that there would be zero complaints from the draftsmen in my section who worked with the package. Those were good measures, we both thought.
>
> I also met with the marketing department to get any unique customer requirements. We agreed that the absence of final commercial customer complaints due to leaving out special requirements would be the best measure.
>
> Then I met with my customers. First I went to the operations department, who use my drawings. We established

234

what they wanted the drawings to look like—form, content, and procedure sheets. Then we established the timetable for drawing releases. We agreed that the best measures were zero complaints from operators about nonusability of the drawings, on-time delivery of drawings, and conformance of 100 percent of the drawings with guidelines in the manual.

Then I went to the manufacturing engineering section head. She takes my drawings and turns out process engineering instruction sheets for operations. We agreed that the best measures were conformance of 100 percent of the drawing with manual guidelines, on-time delivery of the complete package, and zero complaints from engineers using the drawings. She also suggested that there be no more than two rework requests on the project, but I convinced her that the zero-complaint measure covered the rework contingency.

All of these contracts contributes to our SBI of "reducing engineering time by 50 percent," which tied in with the overall company SBI of "getting new products to market faster." It also helps us live our department vision: "Quality, reliability, and accuracy."

Second, *relate measures to SBIs and vision.* Service and quality play central parts in many SBIs and visions. If that's true for you, include measures of service and quality. Measures might include accuracy, complaints, completeness, timeliness, availability, rework required, callbacks, repairs, uptime/downtime, inventory turnover, percent of specifications met, and usability.

Sharon Pebble supervised the documentation section in an engineering department for a large municipality. The city's overall vision was to provide the best service—"#1 in citizen satisfaction." Her engineering department set its SBI as "100 percent first-time quality work on time and on budget." Her group set their SBI as "on-time, on-budget release of all engineering documentation with 100 percent first-time quality." Each of her people established contracts with their customers that contributed to these SBIs.

Measure it—or forget it. Measure contract performance and relate it to the SBIs and the vision. Measurement empowers individuals at all levels to be change agents for your vision.

Personal Workshop

As you consider how to measure contract performance, please ponder the following questions.

1. What specific measures can I establish for my contracts?

2. How can I encourage others to establish specific quantifiable measures for their contracts?

Everyone must support your new vision—at all organizational levels—in all departments. Empower individual change agents throughout the organization. Identify SBIs that relate your vision to units' significant business challenges. Develop customer/supplier contracts that use the vision to handle these SBIs. Measure contract performance and progress toward the SBIs.

Change isn't easy. There are significant obstacles to overcome, not the least of which is inertia. Individuals must smell the smoke in their own nostrils. They must see the fire with their own eyes. They must experience the urgency to change in the pit of their own stomach. Heighten that urgency by linking change with the critical strategic issues facing each person. Empower change agents throughout the organization. Do it—or forget it.

12

Change Happens—The Elephant Learns

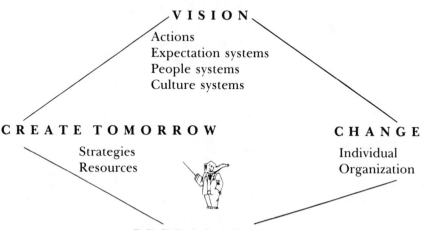

E M P O W E R I N G   C H A N G E

V I S I O N

Actions
Expectation systems
People systems
Culture systems

C R E A T E   T O M O R R O W

Strategies
Resources

C H A N G E

Individual
Organization

P R E P A R A T I O N

Getting ready
Anticipating obstacles

This is hard work. Change isn't easy. John Diebold, famous computer consultant, said, "We face two options: either renewal and reform or revolution and ruin." Given those two options, is there any choice?

The tent is clearly on fire. Smell the smoke. See the flames. Feel the urgency. "To change or not to change?" is not the question. "How to change?" is the question. That's what this book is about.

Be assured, change is happening. From the rust belt in America, to the green belt in Germany, to the island of Singapore, empowered people are making significant changes. The winds of change are blowing through City Halls, factories, and offices across the globe. It is happening—everywhere.

As I review our journey, I am haunted by a series of visual images. One-liners come to mind, such as "The process is the product," "The change begins with me," "Questions empower vision," "The vision is the focus," and "The urgency is the energy." Let me share these intermediate thoughts with you.

THE PROCESS IS THE PRODUCT

We are obsessed with results. The process of achieving those results often is less important.

Grades drive our education system. My students tell me all the time, "Recruiters look at grades. I've got to do well to get into graduate school. The 'Big Eight' accounting firms only hire people with GPAs of 3.5 and above. My folks won't support me unless I get a B or better."

The visual image that fills my mind is my office packed with panicked students searching frantically for five more points on a test answer.

Managers are equally obsessed with results. The most frequently asked question is, "What's the bottom-line impact—this quarter?" How many executives can afford to show consecutive quarters of no growth (or declines) before the sharks start circling? Not many.

Fixating on profit is like a player riveted to the scoreboard during a football game. Ken Blanchard—*The One-Minute Manager*—points out that you don't score many points looking at the scoreboard. The game is won or lost on the field. The scoreboard only records the results. Understand how to score touchdowns, not how to record them. The processes by which you manage is the game. The profit and loss statement is the scoreboard.

Coach Vince Lombardi understood. He stressed "winning." "It's the only thing," he's been quoted as saying. But for Lombardi, "winning" meant being proud of your performance. He stressed that if you did your best—played "110 percent of your effort for 100 percent of the game"—you'd likely have more points on the board by the time the gun went off. But the way to win was to be proud of what you do. How's that for a process focus? Lombardi understood how to win games on the field. By understanding the linkage between "A" (blocking, tackling, and carrying the ball) and "B" (winning games), he won big. He kept his focus on the process field, not on the scoreboard of results.

The process attitude works in business as well. Mark Basich, a worker at the Quasar Plant (owned by Matsushita), wrote the following prize-winning slogan: "Are you proud enough to buy what you build?" Lombardi would understand Mark's words.

Work constantly to prevent the demand for short-term results from driving out longer-term process considerations. Karen Wilding's anecdote reveals how easy it is to allow short-term considerations to overpower longer-term process considerations—and what you can do to prevent it.

Karen's vision was

"1. Improve quality—improve the process to achieve better quality.

2. Meet schedule consistently.

3. Develop personnel—communication, leadership, initiative."

Karen admitted that she'd been less than supportive of education activities for her people. Despite her vision statement, training activities were almost always the first casualty in a cost-reduction drive.

"Had my people been more educated," Karen told me, "they would be more productive. There's an entire set of new tools in my business. I've been so busy getting the current work out that I haven't taken the time to train the people in these new tools. It's a catch-22 situation. I'm just barely making the schedule now. I can't afford to take the time out to do the training. Yet if I don't, we'll never get ahead. As long as the pressure is on to make the current schedule, there isn't the opportunity to invest in the future.

"Despite all the pressure, I decided to take the time to do the training. I invested five days in new tools training. Within weeks I could see the productivity improvement. I only wish I had done it sooner."

Process considerations act as *reality checks.* Doug Rawlings, assistant managing editor for a large U.S. urban newspaper, discovered this important role of process considerations as reported in the following anecdote.

Doug's vision was "to make a difference in the lives of our readers through full, probing news coverage of local, national, and international news. To grow with our employees in our commitment to excellence, accuracy, fairness, and truth."

Doug developed and implemented his vision using many of the processes outlined in this book. He was pleased with the results. "We're on track. People seem genuinely motivated to ever-increasing standards and toward serving our readers." Then a situation arose that reminded Doug about the value of his vision.

A reporter heard from a confidential source that a popular politician had accepted some questionable home improvements from a local builder who was trying to get several zoning approvals through the city council. The facts were unclear, though innuendos indicated that perhaps the politician had gotten a special price from the builder.

The reporter came to Doug with the potential story. She wanted to dig in and get more information. Doug questioned her closely about her sources and the veracity of the suspicions. He was satisfied that there might be something to the allegation. But, as he told me later, "As I sat there talking to her, I wondered to myself, Is this fair, accurate, and truthful? It bothered me that the evidence was flimsy and all hearsay. I was determined to be certain that we kept focused on our vision and avoid looking like we were out to get somebody.

"She did a thorough job of researching the story. We talked several times. Each time I reminded her of our commitment to accuracy, fairness, and truth.

"The evidence was far from conclusive. The price for the work did seem a little low. This builder had never done similar work for such a low price, though other builders had charged similar prices for similar work. Furthermore, the politician had been a strong supporter of the zoning changes requested not only by this builder, but also of other builders.

"I thought about it for a long time. I didn't want us to get so caught up in getting the story that we neglected to go back to the touchstone of our vision and good common sense. I kept asking the process questions: 'Is this accurate, truthful, and fair or just a suspicion?' 'Are the interests of our readers really served by this story?'

"I finally decided to talk directly with the politician to get reaction and validation before I broke the story. He was both angry and thankful. He explained that he had gotten competing bids from several builders. This one builder was the lowest. In retrospect, he felt that maybe it wasn't a good time to do the remodeling. 'But,' he asked, 'is there ever a time when there aren't zoning changes pending before the council? And if I chose to exclude anyone who had changes pending before the council, I'd remove all the good builders from consideration. That certainly doesn't seem fair, does it?'

"We ran the story, along with the politician's explanation. We even gave him space to explain his side. The story generated a lot of discussion. I was particularly pleased with the quality of the discussion. I believe that we served the interests of our readers. Maybe we didn't sell as many newspapers as we could have had we sensationalized the story. But we were true to our vision. And asking those process questions kept us on track."

Emphasize vision to generate a process focus. Reread the vision statements in chapter 6 and you'll hear the process orientation.
Remember Honda's vision?

1. Quality in all jobs—learn, think, analyze, evaluate, and improve;

2. Reliable products—on time, with excellence and consistency;

3. Better communication—listen, ask, and speak up.

All pure process considerations.
Remember Hershey Chocolate's vision?

1. Protect and enhance the corporation's high level of ethics and conduct;

2. Maintain a strong "people" orientation and demonstrate care for every employee;

3. Attract and hold customers and consumers with products and services of consistent superior quality and value;

4. Sustain a strong results orientation coupled with a prudent approach to business.

Also all process considerations.

Process considerations include customer service, quality, employee growth and development, communication, ethics, on-time delivery, and time to market. In his book, *Kaizen,* Masaaki Imai, a Japanese management expert, says that the process-oriented manager focuses on[1]

1. Discipline;

2. Time management;

3. Skill development;

4. Participation and involvement;

5. Morale;

6. Communication.

Measure process activities as another way to focus on process. What gets measured gets produced. So measure process activities. At the Bridgestone Tire Company, their salesperson measurements emphasize such process considerations as amount of time spent calling on new customers, time spent on outside customer calls versus time spent in the office on clerical work, and percentage of new inquiries successfully closed.[2]

Too often results considerations even creep into our process activities. Quality circles are primarily a process activity, designed to improve quality, another process concern. We rob the process of its vitality when we use only results measures to evaluate its success. Process measures for a quality circle might include number of meetings held, participation rate, number of problems solved, and number of reports submitted.

Imai cites the quintessence of a process-oriented measurement system.[3]

At one of Matsushita's plants, the waitresses in the cafeteria formed a quality circle and studied tea consumption during the lunch period. . . . They noticed that tea consumption differed greatly from table to table. Therefore, they collected data on the tea drinking behavior during lunch. For one thing they found that the same people tended to sit at the same table. After taking and analyzing data for days they were able to establish an expected consumption level for each table. Using their findings, they started putting out different amounts of tea for each table, with the result that they were able to reduce tea-leaf consumption by one-half. How much were their activities worth in terms of actual amount of money saved? Probably very little. However, *they were awarded the Presidential Gold Medal for the year.* (Emphasis added.)

Review the list of possible measures included in chapter 8 and you'll find mostly process concerns. To measure the process concern of quality, use such numeric measures as scrap, rework, parts-per-million defect rate, unscheduled machine downtime, customer complaints, warranty expenses, and service calls.

To measure new product development—another process concern—use total launch time for new products, product and process development milestones, key characteristics of new products in comparison with customer needs and competitors' design, and customer satisfaction with new products.

Management is about "how." Management is about process. Become obsessed with "what" and you forget "how." When you don't know "how," you can't consistently produce the "what."

This is particularly true about change. Change is a process, not a destination. It never ends. Regardless of how successful you are this year, there is always next year. Merck has been extremely successful in the late 1980s. The chairman knows that they can't afford to rest on their laurels and coast. He's increased R&D expenditures and added muscle to his marketing organization. He's increased training activities as well to insure that his people are ready for the competitive 1990s. The chairman knows there is no rest. There is no ending. Change is a process.

Don Shula's words are apropos one more time here (he's the

coach of the Miami Dolphins NFL team): "Success isn't final, and failure isn't fatal." Change is a lifetime process.

The visual image that haunts me is that of Ralph Stayer talking with a group of executives. (Stayer is president of Johnsonville Sausage, which Tom Peters calls "the most advanced employee involvement company in the world.") Ralph leans forward and says, "We talk mostly about individual growth at Johnsonville. I keep asking about new skills, new knowledge, new activities. It's my experience that those kinds of questions get me the best bottom line." As Ralph speaks the heads shake up and down, pens write furiously, the eyes burn brightly. Another group of converts.

In successful companies—as for successful people—process is the product. Understanding "how" precedes reproducing "what."

Personal Workshop

As you consider how to enhance process considerations, please ponder the following questions.

1. What are the important processes in my organization?

2. How can I get good measures of these important processes?

3. How can I encourage my people to be more process-oriented?

CHANGE BEGINS WITH ME

Vaughn Beals, Jr., CEO and president, chairman for Harley-Davidson, looks straight into the camera and says, "We tried all the usual solutions—the culture routine, the robot routine, the low-wage routine—and none of them worked. We couldn't avoid the inescapable conclusion. We—the management—were the problem." Prophetic, insightful words, born of desperation. And the beginning of one of the great American success stories of the middle 1980s.

In the early 1980s Harley was flat on its back, leveled by Honda. Honda was selling motorcycles for less. To add insult to injury, Honda had better styling—and theirs didn't leak oil. It looked as if Harley had a one-way ticket to the corporate graveyard.

Then, Vaughn Beals woke up. He realized that his fundamental problem was not Honda, or the unions, or whoever was the excuse that week. Rather, his biggest problem stared back at him in the mirror every morning. As Michael Jackson sang, world peace begins with the "man in the mirror."

Beals empowered his people. He organized them into teams and gave the teams responsibility for scheduling, quality, and production line design. He slimmed down the hierarchy and got supervisors out of the way of the people so they could do the job they needed to do. He put in a "Just In Time" inventory system. By trusting his people, he even made it work. Today, Beals says, "The power from those teams is damn near infinite." What a turnaround—in the way he thinks.

Empower change by looking squarely in the mirror and asking, "What am I doing that either empowers people to change or prevents them from changing?" Make a list. Don't be surprised if your empowering actions list is a whole lot shorter than the disempowering list. I know mine was when I first started. Then do more of the empowering behaviors and fewer of the disempowering ones.

It won't be easy. You've got many years of programming and education to overcome. I know. We in the academic universities turn out thousands of managers a year with the misguided philosophy that their job is to "fix problems." Virtually all of your previous successes have come from "fixing problems." Unfortunately, those that got you here will not get you farther. Remember the elephant analogy. Previous success in "fixing problems" is the rope, attached to nothing, that prevents us from changing.

Seek help. I did. So did Ralph Stayer of Johnsonville Sausage. I asked my people to give me a sign when I was overpowering them, which I did frequently. It took me a while to accept that feedback—without getting angry. It's still difficult. I also tape-recorded my interactions and held frequent replays. Try it yourself. Listen to yourself and ask, "Did my behavior really help to empower others?" "What else could I do to help my people take responsibility?" "What else could I do to get out of the way?" But be ready. It'll take time to change.

Often, the whole world seems against you. You are harassed by systems that reinforce the wrong behavior, systems that systematically cripple your vision efforts. Ken Brock confronted one of the most difficult system problems—and licked it when he decided to take charge and change himself.

Ken was manager of the drafting department for a large airplane manufacturing company. His company was experiencing considerable difficulty. Production was a year and a half behind schedule. Work in process had literally climbed to the top of the six-story building. There were 1,800 open engineering change orders waiting to be approved by the Engineering Review Board, which processed about 180 change orders a month. To say that there was a problem is to understate the reality.

Ken's section, though, was highly rated. They met more than 98 percent of their drawing release dates. That record earned him and his people performance bonuses.

Ken was in one of my workshops. At that workshop he admitted that his section issued blank drawings in order to meet scheduled milestone delivery dates. "We don't have time to do the job correctly, so we assign the proper drawing number and turn out a white sheet. We finish the job when we can and issue a request for an ECO (engineering change order). In the meantime, as we finish them, we issue revised drawings so the materials department can get on with ordering parts and manufacturing engineering can get on with issuing process control sheets. All the while, these ECOs wait in the queue and eventually get handled.

"As long as we issue blank drawings we are contributing to the demise of the plant. But what am I going to do? Our bonuses are based on meeting that schedule. If we don't meet that schedule, it costs us in the department several thousand dollars. Everyone else does it also. Each department meets its goals—and gets its bonus—but the whole plant is sinking."

During the workshop Ken agreed to stop issuing blank drawings and take the consequences. I was certain that his unwillingness to continue to play the game would precipitate a major confrontation. I was correct.

Ken called me several weeks later with his report. "I stopped issuing white drawings as soon as I got back. I got calls from everyone trying to find out what was going on. My people all stood behind me. They saw that someone had to have courage to stop the farce. After several big meetings we finally confronted the system issue. The department heads all got together and we worked out a way to handle partial releases so that the other departments could get on with their work. We also found several ways to shorten our work cycle. The short story is that we found a way to change the system that everyone previously said was set in concrete. President Jackson was correct: 'One person with courage makes a majority.' Thanks for helping me find the courage to change."

Change begins with you. It takes courage to change. Ask Ken, he's an expert.

The visual image that haunts me is that of a software company I visited in the United Kingdom. The managing director spent several hours describing his process of individual change. He'd changed from being a dictator to being an empowerer. His journey reminded me of Ralph Stayer. Then he invited me to check it out for myself.

I attended several of their product team meetings. In the hours I spent with them, I must have heard the word *we* a hundred times. "We" referred to we the team, we the company, we the management and associates (they call all employees "associates"), we our customers and us, we our suppliers and us. I never heard a manager refer to associates as "they." I never heard an associate refer to a manager as "they." I worked with them fourteen hours that day. And I wasn't tired. Their energy energized me.

Personal Workshop

As you consider how you can change your mentality, please ponder the following questions.

1. How do I see my role in relation to employees?
   a. Do I have a "we-they" attitude?
   b. How do I know? What evidence do I have? What would my employees say? my managers? my customers? my suppliers?
   c. How can I find out how they really see me?

2. What do I do now that either encourages or discourages employee empowerment?

247

a. How do I know what I do?
b. How can I find out what I do?
c. Who can help me get better feedback?

3. How can I change to encourage more empowerment?

QUESTIONS EMPOWER PEOPLE

I recall so well the following incident. It happened in a midsize manufacturing plant. The staff was wrestling with the typical production problems—accelerating schedules, cost pressures, mechanical breakdowns. The meeting was already two hours old when this incident came up.

"What should we do?" asks one of the people around the table. Every eye in the room turns in the direction of the boss. The silence hangs heavy for twenty-one seconds. Finally she looks at one of the people at the table and says, "Sam, what do you think we ought to do?"

Unusual? Yes. But becoming more typical every day.

Too many of us still believe that it is our responsibility to provide answers. Talk about a restraining bracelet that traps you as the tent burns down. Providing answers got you where you are today. As you climbed the ladder your quick on-target response—being an instant expert—led to promotion after promotion. You were rewarded for having the answers.

Look around now, though. Ask yourself, "Is that still true? Do I still have to give all the answers?" Or an even better question: "Is it better if I don't give all the answers?"

There are lots of benefits to asking questions rather than providing answers. For starters, it *saves time.* I remember my own early management experience running a production plant for Sylvania Electric Products, Inc.

> I'd come in at seven A.M. Ten feet inside the door I'd get my first problem. "Jim, I'm almost out of parts here." I'd answer, "I'll call supply and get you some," and make a note. Two steps later there was another problem. "Jim, this machine's acting up." "I'll call maintenance," was my easy reply, along with another note. By the time I got to my

office—125 or so feet into the production area—my pockets were bulging with notes. I spent the first several hours handling the problems that I picked up on my way to the office. I stayed late. Everyone who gave me their problems went home on time.

It took me some time to realize that something was wrong—and that something was my handling of everybody else's problems. My boss used to introduce me as the person who "had three kids at home and 425 kids in the plant." He was a very insightful man.

Does this sound familiar? Once I started asking questions, and began empowering others, I started to go home at a decent hour.

Doug Gregory, manager for a testware development section for a large computer company, taught me another benefit of asking questions. I wish I'd learned it sooner.

Doug's vision was, "We locate the problem before it becomes one." He'd put it together using many of the suggestions in this book. He was generally pleased with its progress.

A big problem arose in Doug's area. A major piece of equipment developed bugs in the field. Doug's group hadn't found it before shipment. Trauma time.

Doug's boss called. She was furious. "What's going on?" she wanted to know. "I'll call you back with the answer," Doug replied. "You mean you don't know?" she exploded. "There's a group handling it. I'll call you back as soon as I check with them," Doug replied. She banged down the phone.

Doug got the answer and had the team leader reply directly to his boss. The senior vice-president even called and Doug had the team leader reply.

The problem got fixed in record time. It turned out that it wasn't a design problem—the kinds of issues Doug's group normally handled—but was a software-induced glitch. The user had designed his own software, which, it turned out, was not 100 percent compatible. Doug's team worked with the user to solve the problem. They also helped the user modify the software to be compatible with the hardware. At the end the user wrote a strong complimentary letter to the company president, praising the group for their helpfulness.

Doug told me, "I could never have solved that problem. I'm not an expert in that system. All I could have done was create more anxiety, more paperwork, and more meetings. None of that would have worked to solve the problem for the user. I met with the team, asked a few key questions, and gave them their head. They came back several times looking for guidance. I asked some more questions, and they went away with new insight.

"I was working with another team on the new system development. We can't afford to let that delivery date slide. I frankly didn't have the time to handle this problem. Besides, our vision refers to our own internal department operations as well as the hardware systems we test. We work to locate the problem within our own ways of working. We discovered that the best way to locate problems is to ask questions. So we've become great question askers rather than answer givers. It works for us time and again. And it makes my job so much easier. I go home now at six P.M."

Asking questions, rather than giving answers, *develops people.* It helps your people escape the trap of their current paradigm. It helps people develop a broader perspective and deeper skills.

Asking questions also *empowers the vision.* Throughout the book I've stressed the importance of involving people in vision-related activities. Chapter 9 talked about shared activities and sayings built around the vision as a means of shifting your culture. Asking questions facilitates participation.

Remember the Lionel Richie example from chapter 3? Lionel Richie wrote and organized the production of the popular song "We Are the World." He invited the luminaries of the music world to cooperate in the record to raise money for the starving in Africa. He posted a sign next to the studio door that said, "Check your ego at the door." His message was clear. The success of the record depended upon the cooperation of everyone, not the brilliance of a few.

Heed Lionel Richie's message. It also applies to your empowerment of change. "Check your ego at the door" and let others take responsibility. Be less of a guru/hero and more of a facilitator/ coach. Question asking helps. Empower others to live your vision by asking such questions as

1. What goals and actions plans do you have for executing the vision in your area? How can I help?

2. What communication channels can we establish where you can discuss the new vision with your people? How can I stay informed without undercutting other managers?

3. How can I refer questions and comments about the new vision to you rather than answering them myself? How can we together build communication linkages that put you in the direct channel but do not exclude me?

4. How can we communicate constantly about the hero actions of others in multiple mediums? How can we keep up the drumbeat about what others are doing—and their successes using the new vision?

5. How can we ensure that we keep talking about "the team" and "our vision" and "our results"? How can we guard against the use of such disempowering words as "us," "they," and "I"?

6. How can we all avoid having answers to all questions/problems/difficulties? What do we have to do to make "I don't know" a legitimate answer in our organization?

Bottom line of this section: Questions empower the vision. The people at New United Motors Manufacturing, Inc., understand. They use the rule of the "five whys." No solution is ever agreed upon until you've asked "Why?" at least five times. By the time you've asked "Why?" five times, you've peeled away the symptoms and gotten down to serious causes. Asking questions prevents you from playing demigod. It develops your people. It empowers your vision. It saves you time.

Personal Workshop

As you consider how to develop the question-asking skill, ponder the following questions.

1. What questions can I ask to develop my people?

2. How can I turn a question into a question? How can I question a person who comes to me for answers so that he/she comes up with the answer rather than relying upon me?

3. How can I answer the six questions posed earlier?

VISION IS THE FOCUS

An inspiring vision is the key to long-term success. This vision is the picture that drives all action. It includes both deeply felt values and a picture of the organization's strategic focus.

A vision clearly identifies for all concerned—employees, customers, and suppliers—exactly what the organization stands for and precisely why they should support it. A vision both enhances an organization's marketplace competitive advantage, such as IBM's "Provide the best customer service," and provides deep personal identification with the organization's work, such as ServiceMaster's "To serve God in all we do." Chapter 6 cites many examples of inspiring visions.

Vision tightly directs attention to the critical factors that produce long-term success. It may be the customer service and employee respect at IBM, or the search for the unshakable fact at DEC, or the new product development at Ralston. Whatever, your vision becomes a decision-making guide. At every juncture employees ask, "Is my action in keeping with the vision?" This focus—and inspiration—empowers people to change.

Frank Peroucci was the manager for an information resource management unit for a U.S. state government. He found how vision provides an important focus.

Frank's vision was

1. Provide service satisfactions and timely response to our customer's needs;

2. Maximize customer operability to help them help themselves;

3. Develop staff self-stature and leadership potential;

4. Implement cohesive strategies providing innovative, cost-effective solutions."

He established this vision using many of the ideas presented in the book.

Frank continually questioned his people about their use of the vision. He installed a "drill" at his staff meeting where he'd review the four vision statements and ask about current activities that either supported or detracted from the vision. After a few meetings, his people got the message. They automatically brought in examples of vision-supporting and vision-detracting activities.

Frank's people put in place a set of measures of the vision activities. These were posted in the cafeteria every Wednesday. He told me, "I'm particularly pleased with the response. Every Wednesday is 'chart day.' There's endless conversation about the progress of the charts—they're all mostly in the right direction. I knew it was working when one of the managers didn't get his chart up in time and got razzed good.

"Equally important, there's been a lot of excellent comments from our customers. We even got a special commendation from the governor. The vision really helped us to focus on the important things for us—and helped us to deliver them to our customers and ourselves."

Vision tells us "what" needs to be done and "how" we will do it. It plants a stake in the ground. It guides decisions. It inspires actions. It keeps us tightly focused on important process concerns.

Vision is needed at all levels in an organization. The supervisor of the mailroom needs a vision for that mailroom. The manager of data processing needs a vision for the DP department. The accounts payable clerk needs a vision for his/her job. Vision—throughout the organization—focuses and inspires effort.

Personal Workshop

As you consider how to use the vision as a focus, please ponder the following questions.

1. What are the critical factors in our success?

2. How can my vision help us focus on these critical factors?

3. How can I help my people measure their progress using the vision to deal with these critical success factors?

URGENCY IS THE ENERGY

Complacency destroys our will. It saps our capacity. "Use it or lose it," is the popular shibboleth. Too many organizations—too many individuals—have not been using it, so they've been losing it.

The record is discouraging. In the Western world we're losing out in market after market. The U.S. trails in almost every measure of productivity. Stagflation fears—inflation combined with high interest rates—spook the stock market, OCED, and many governments.

Remember the elephant training parable. Trainers shackle young elephants with heavy chains to deeply embedded stakes. In that way the elephant learns to stay in its place. Older elephants never try to leave, even though they have the strength to pull the stake and move beyond. Their conditioning limits their movements with only a small metal bracelet around their foot—attached to nothing.

Like powerful elephants, many organizations are bound by earlier conditioned constraints. "We've always done it this way," is as limiting to an organization's progress as the unattached chain around the elephant's foot.

Yet when the circus tent catches on fire—and the elephant sees the flames with its own eyes and smells the smoke with its own nostrils—it forgets its old conditioning and changes. Your task: set a fire so your people see the flames with their own eyes and smell the smoke with their own nostrils—without burning the tent down. And you can set the fire at any level in the organization.

Build a sense of urgency—a fire. People don't change without it! Bad situations create the urgency to change, which creates the empowerment for change. Don't create this urgency, and people feel powerless to change.

Remember chapter 2? We don't visit the dentist until the tooth hurts so much that we can't stand it anymore. We don't change a light bulb until it burns out. We don't leave a "terrible" job until either we get fired or some awful triggering event occurs (such as a big fight with the boss). We don't end a personal relationship until it gets to be unbearable.

Steve Hilts, back office manager for a local bank, learned the hard way about the need to create a sense of urgency and how to do it. His experience helps us all.

Steve's vision was "Obsession with excellence in

1. Employee development and team building;

2. Customer service, including service guarantees;

3. Quality and innovation;

4. Embracing change and improvement."

Steve developed and installed his vision using many of the ideas from this book.

Everyone seemed to be supportive. Yet Steve sensed an undercurrent of nonparticipation. He asked a number of his employees. One of them told him, "Well, I really believe your words—they're good words. But why are we doing it? Everything's going along just fine. We don't need it. And I'm concerned that this will just pile on more work. I certainly don't need that."

Steve tried to explain to his group how this vision was necessary to keep things going well. He also tried to stress how the banking business was changing and how the bank could easily lose its customers. Steve could tell, though, that he wasn't making much progress. That's when he decided to set the tent on fire.

Steve urged his people to do some comparative shopping of other banks and financial institutions. Afterward they came back and discussed what they had seen. He also suggested that each person contact customers directly and ask them what could be done to improve service.

"It was amazing," Steve told me. "People came back and said, 'Do you know what they [some other bank] are doing?

Why can't we do it also?' Customer feedback also motivated individuals to consider changes. It's tough when you ask someone's opinion and then don't act on it. We had a whole series of customer champions emerge out of these customer contacts.

"Once everyone was champing at the bit, I rediscussed the vision and asked everyone how the vision helps them do what they wanted to do. Almost everyone there saw the relationship between the vision and what they wanted to accomplish. It couldn't be better. People now champion the vision as a way of satisfying customers and personally developing. But none of that would have happened had I not created a little crisis by sending people out to find out what the real world was all about."

Urgency is the energy behind your vision. Urgency focuses. Urgency motivates. Without it, change is impossible and extinction is certain.

Don't let up, though. Keep the tent smoldering. Never let the fire of urgency go out. Keep the smell of smoke in the air, the sight of orange flames just over the horizon.

The visual image that haunts me occurred during a visit to a group of airplane manufacturing factory workers. The twelve of them worked together tightening toggle bolts on the wing assembly. They turned out two planes a day. They had posted two huge charts in their area. One chart tracked their quality—number of complaints about their work from quality control or any other operator. (It had been zero for the week I saw.) The other tracked the quality for their next largest competitor. (That chart showed 7 percent errors.)

The hour I spent with them was devoted entirely to them telling me how "those bastards at _____ weren't going to get this contract." They had put up the chart themselves. It was the only one of its kind in the plant. They called the government inspector at the other plant to get the data daily. They kept the charts themselves. These twelve guys knew more about contract negotiations than most executives I'd met in that plant. They were keenly aware of what it took to stay in business. They were determined to meet the continuing challenge.

How can you build a continuing sense of urgency? Let's review. First, *the process is the product.* The process of strategic planning is the most important product. Include wide ranges of people in the process. Tap the knowledge of those people in most direct contact with the customers, the technologies, the developments. Challenge your people to think about the future, to pay attention to marketplace and technological developments and how they will impact the organization. Seeing the challenges and the threats mobilizes action.

One organization I know involves everyone in the strategic-planning process. Everyone scans ten or more magazines a month—mostly from outside of his/her specialized field of interest—clips the articles that seem related to their business, no matter how far afield it may be, and then reviews the contents of this file every six months in preparation for the semiannual all-hands meeting. Four questions are addressed at this company meeting. Where are we now? What's coming? Where do we want to go? How will we get there? The groups discuss these questions and agree on answers that form the basis for the company's strategic plan. People leave there dedicated to carrying out the plan; committed to winning in the marketplace. How has it worked? The company grew tenfold in the last six years. Its margins never sank below 45 percent return on sales (ROS).

Second, to make this kind of empowering process happen, change your own mentality and behavior. Remember, *change begins with me.* Eliminate the "we-they" mentality that builds in adversarial feelings. Stop trying to "fix problems." Work instead on "fixing me." When you successfully change your mentality, others will follow suit.

Third, use *questions* to activate this new mentality. Learn to ask questions rather than give answers. It develops people, saves you time, and *empowers your vision.*

Fourth, *the vision is the focus* of all your activities. The vision helps you focus on process. It gives you a continuing measuring stick with which to evaluate your own personal change. It forces you to ask questions rather than give answers.

Last, *urgency is the energy* to change today and all the necessary tomorrows. Urgency builds the energy to continue the process focus encouraged by the vision, to continue the personal change process, to ask questions rather than give answers. Urgency is the fuel for your rocket trip to the stars.

Underlying all of these is the observation that *many small steps create change.* It's all too easy to focus on the home run and be disappointed with a single. Singles win games, particularly when you get enough of them. Focus on building small wins, making progress consistently. They add up in the long run.

THE LAST WORD

Change is tough—but it happens. The success stories grow in number and magnitude: GM parts plants, motorcycle plants, chemical plants, insurance offices, and local government departments. It's happening all over the world. Elephants are learning to dance. Slowly, haltingly, slipping back sometimes, but learning. It is tough. And *you can do it.*

At the beginning of the book I wrote the following words: "I want to encourage you to act *today* to begin the change process. I want you to talk *today* with your people about the vision you and they would like to see for your organization. I want to encourage you to meet *today* with your people and discuss how all of you can use your vision to accomplish your new strategies."

To the extent that I have helped you to do all this, I have succeeded. Then this book will not be an end, but a beginning.

So now, after this intermediate stop, on with the rest of the journey!

Notes

Chapter 1. Teaching the Elephant to Dance

1. "Competitiveness: 23 Leaders Speak Out," Bruce R. Scott, *Harvard Business Review*, July–August, 1987, 106–123.
   "The Selling of America," Jacylyn Fierman, *Fortune*, May 22, 1988, 54–64.
   "Can America Compete," *Business Week*, April 20, 1987, 45–69.
   "Stark Proof of Japan's Muscle," *Business Week*, July 17, 1989, 188.
2. "Xerox Rethinks Itself: And This Could Be the Last Time," *Business Week*, February 13, 1987, 90–93.
   "Culture Shock at Xerox," *Business Week*, June 22, 1987, 63–67.
3. Donald Katz, *The Big Store* (New York: Viking, 1987).
   "Why Bigger Is Badder at Sears," Patricia Sellers, *Fortune*, December 5, 1988, 56–60.
   "They Buy Their Stocks Where They Buy Their Socks," Steve Weiner, *Forbes*, March 7, 1988, 60–67.
4. "The Great Rebound: Britain Is Back," Richard Kirkland, Jr., *Fortune*, May 9, 1988, 114–123.
5. "Why U.S. Car Makers Are Losing Ground," Alex Taylor III, *Fortune*, October 2, 1989, 97–116.
   "GM's Bumpy Ride on the Long Road Back," *Business Week*, February 13, 1988, 74–78.
   "Make or Break Time for General Motors," Thomas Moore, *Fortune*, February 15, 1988, 32–42.
6. "The Great Rebound: Britain Is Back," Richard Kirkland, Jr., *Fortune*, May 9, 1988, 114–123.
7. "Jack Welch: How Good a Manager?" *Business Week*, December 14, 1987, 38–41.
   "Not Power, But Empower," *Forbes*, May 30, 1988, 120–123.
   "What Welch Has Wrought at GE," Peter Petrie, *Fortune*, July 7, 1988, 25–28.
8. Internal document, McDonnell Douglas, n.d.
9. Internal document, McDonnell Douglas, n.d.
10. "The Joys of Keeping the Company Small," Fritz Maytag, *Harvard Business Review*, July/August 1986, 6–14.
11. "How Do You Follow an Act Like Bud?" *Business Week*, May 5, 1988, 118–119.
12. *Inc.*, July 1988, 43–47.
13. "How Do You Follow an Act Like Bud?" *Business Week*, May 5, 1988, 118–119.
14. "The Joys of Keeping the Company Small," Fritz Maytag, *Harvard Business Review*, July/August 1986, 6–14.
15. *Inc.*, August 1988, 27–33.
16. "Jack Welch: How Good a Manager?" *Business Week*, December 14, 1987, 38–41.
    "Not Power, But Empower," *Forbes*, May 30, 1988, 120–123.
    "What Welch Has Wrought at GE," Peter Petrie, *Fortune*, July 7, 1988, 25–28.
17. "Anheuser-Busch: The Scandal May Be Small Beer After All," *Business Week*, May 11, 1987, 72–73.

18. "Jack Welch: How Good a Manager?" *Business Week*, December 14, 1987, 38–41.
"Not Power, But Empower," *Forbes*, May 30, 1988, 120–123.
"What Welch Has Wrought at GE," Peter Petrie, *Fortune*, July 7, 1988, 25–28.
19. "When the Fun Is Over," Michael Berns, *Inc.*, March 1987, 112–113.
20. "His Trumpet Was Never Uncertain," *Time*, May 18, 1987, 68.
21. "Why the Bounce at Rubbermaid," Alex Taylor III, *Fortune*, April 13, 1987, 77–78.
22. "The Joys of Keeping the Company Small," Fritz Maytag, *Harvard Business Review*, July/August 1986, 6–14.
23. "How Do You Follow an Act Like 'Bud?" *Business Week*, May 5, 1988, 118–119.
24. *Business*, October 1987, 90–92.
25. "Lessons in the Service Sector," James L. Heskett, *Harvard Business Review*, March/April 1988, 121.
"Servicemaster: Looking for New Worlds to Clean," *Business Week*, January 19, 1987, 60–61.
"Cleanliness, Godliness, and Business," Charles Siler, *Forbes*, November 28, 1988, 219–222.

Chapter 2. Getting Ready to Change

1. "Xerox Rethinks Itself: And This Could Be the Last Time," *Business Week*, February 13, 1987, 90–93.
"Culture Shock at Xerox," *Business Week*, June 22, 1987, 63–67.
2. "Why Kodak Is Starting to Click Again," *Business Week*, February 23, 1987, 80–81.
"Kodak Makes an Olympic Comeback," *Management Today*, June 1988, 90–95.
3. "ABB The New Energy Powerhouse," *International Management*, June 1988, 24–30.
4. "Another Day Another Bright Idea," *The Economist*, April 16, 1988, 82–83.
5. Kurt Lewin, *Field Theory in Social Science* (New York: Harper and Row, 1951).
6. Edgar Schein, *Organizational Psychology* (Englewood Cliffs, N.J.: Prentice-Hall, 1980).
7. "When the Fun Is Over," Michael Berns, *Inc.*, March 1987, 112–113.
8. "Rebirth at Rolls-Royce," Stephen Aris, *Business*, March 1988, 36–40.
9. "When the Fun Is Over," Michael Berns, *Inc.*, March 1987, 112–113.
10. "Rebirth at Rolls-Royce," Stephen Aris, *Business*, March 1988, 36–40.
11. "Why Kodak Is Starting to Click Again," *Business Week*, February 23, 1987, 80–81.
"Kodak Makes an Olympic Comeback," Stephen Aris, *Business*, March 1988, 90–95.
12. "Company Doctor Q. T. Wiles," *Inc.*, February 1988, 27–38.
13. "When the Fun Is Over," Michael Berns, *Inc.*, March 1987, 112–113.
14. "When the Party's Over," Byron Acohido, *Inc.*, July 1987, 25–27.
15. "Elephant Can So Dance," Andrew Grove, *Across the Board*, February 1987, 9–14.

Chapter 3. Anticipate the Obstacles

1. "Toys "Я" Us Goes Overseas—and Finds That Toys Are Them, Too," *Business Week*, January 26, 1987, 54–55.

Notes

Chapter 4. Create Tomorrow

1. "IBM's Big Blues," Carol J. Loomis, *Fortune*, January 19, 1987, 34–52.
"Big Changes at Big Blue," *Business Week*, February 15, 1988, 92–97.
"How IBM Is Fighting Back," *Business Week*, November 17, 1986, 152–157.
2. "I Am Betting My Destiny," Jeffrey Tracktenberg, *Forbes*, March 9, 1987, 66.
"From Fuji to Everest," Marc Beauchamp, *Forbes*, May 2, 1988, 35–36.
3. "Life After Lead," Kerry Hannon, *Forbes*, May 5, 1987, 65.
4. "IBM's Big Blues," Carol J. Loomis, *Fortune*, January 19, 1987, 34–52.
"Big Changes at Big Blue," *Business Week*, February 15, 1988, 92–97.
"How IBM Is Fighting Back," *Business Week*, November 17, 1986, 152–157.
5. "Why Kodak Is Starting to Click Again," *Business Week*, February 23, 1987, 80–81.
"Kodak Makes an Olympic Comeback," Stephen Aris, *Business*, March 1988, 90–95.
6. "Why Martin Marietta Loves Mary Cunningham," Thomas Moore, *Fortune*, March 16, 1987, 66–70.
7. "Many Best Ways to Make Strategy," Michael Gold and Andrew Campbell, *Harvard Business Review*, November/December 1987, 70–76.
8. "How King Kellogg Beat the Blahs," Patricia Sellers, *Fortune*, August 29, 1988, 54–64.
"The Health Craze Has Kellogg Feeling G-r-r-reat," *Business Week*, March 30, 1987, 52–53.
9. "Big Can Still Be Beautiful," Walter Guzzardi, *Fortune*, April 25, 1988, 50–64.
"How Borden Milks Packaged Goods," Bill Saporito, *Fortune*, December 21, 1987, 139–144.
10. "Big Can Still Be Beautiful," Walter Guzzardi, *Fortune*, April 25, 1988, 50–64.
11. "Mirror of a Nation," Alexandra Watson, *Business*, September 1988, 48–58.
"The King of Ketchup," Kerry Hannon, *Forbes*, March 21, 1988, 58–65.
12. "How Comp-U-Card Hooks Home Shoppers," *Business Week*, May 18, 1987, 73–74.
13. "The Last Iceman," Jack Willoughby, *Forbes*, July 13, 1987, 183–204.
14. "Sole Survivor," Joshua Hyatt, *Inc.*, October 1987, 65–68.
15. "The New Power in Black & Decker," John Huey, *Fortune*, January 2, 1989, 65–68.
16. "Big Changes at Big Brown," Kenneth Labich, *Fortune*, January 18, 1988, 56–64.
17. "Billion-Dollar Brainstorm," Gail Bronson, *Forbes*, October 10, 1987, 98.
18. "A Sticky Business," Marc Beauchamp, *Forbes*, January 26, 1987, 61.
19. "The Great Rebound: Britain Is Back," Richard Kirkland, Jr., *Fortune*, May 9, 1988, 114–123.
20. "Sun's Sizzling Race to the Top," Stuart Gannes, *Fortune*, August 17, 1987, 88–91.
"Sun Microsystems Turns on the Afterburners," *Business Week*, July 18, 1988, 80–83.
21. "To Catch a Particle," Gary Slutsker, *Forbes*, January 23, 1989, 88–89.
22. "How Borden Milks Packaged Goods," Bill Saporito, *Fortune*, December 21, 1987, 139–144.
23. "The Media Company that Makes Murdock's Empire Look Small," *The Economist*, April 9, 1989, 75–76.
24. "Sony's Challenge," *Business Week*, June 1, 1987, 38–43.
25. "The Vindication of Edwin Land," Subrata Chakravarty, *Forbes*, May 4, 1987, 83–84.
"How Polaroid Flashed Back," Brian Dumaine, *Fortune*, February 16, 1987, 72–76.
26. "Breakthrough Manufacturing," Elizabeth Haas, *Harvard Business Review*, March/April 1987, 75–81.
27. "Buried Treasure," Jack Willoughby, *Forbes*, May 18, 1987, 201.
28. "Food as Fashion," Steve Weiner and Ellen Paris, *Forbes*, September 7, 1987, 106–107.

Notes

29. "Philips Industry Secret," Jerry Flint, *Forbes*, November 3, 1986, 60–63.
30. "The Great American Revival," Joel Kotkin, *Inc.*, February 1988, 52–63.
31. "What Makes a Survivor," Mary Kuntz, *Forbes*, January 26, 1987, 77.
32. "The Great Rebound: Britain Is Back," Richard Kirkland, Jr., *Fortune*, May 9, 1988, 114–123.
33. "How Borden Milks Packaged Goods," Bill Saporito, *Fortune*, December 21, 1987, 139–144.
34. "How to Compete with IBM," *Forbes*, February 23, 1987, 145.
35. "The Great American Revival," Joel Kotkin, *Inc.*, February 1988, 52–63.
36. "ADP Reprograms for the New Wall Street," *Business Week*, January 18, 1988, 70–72.
37. "Time: The Next Source of Competitive Advantage," George Stall, Jr., *Harvard Business Review*, July/August 1988, 41–51.
38. "Breakthrough Manufacturing," Elizabeth Haas, *Harvard Business Review*, March/April 1987, 75–81.
39. "Guess Who Lost," Lisa Keefe, *Forbes*, September 7, 1987, 60–61.
40. "Good Merchandise and a Square Deal," Jan Parr, *Forbes*, July 13, 1987, 416–418.
41. "Back to Basics," Subrata Chakravarty, *Forbes*, December 7, 1987, 40–41.
42. "Portrait of a CEO as Salesman," James Koch, *Inc.*, March 1988, 44–46.
43. "David Alliance Spins an Empire," Cassandra Jardiene, *Business*, June 1987, 88–91.
44. "King No More," John Taylor, *Forbes*, April 18, 1988, 37–38.
45. "Visa's Back-Office Strategy in the Credit-Card Wars," *Business Week*, April 20, 1987, 75.
46. "This Cat Is Acting Like a Tiger," Ronald Henkoff, *Fortune*, December 19, 1988, 70–76.
47. "Make That Sale, Mr. Sam," *Time*, May 18, 1987, 54–55.
    "Wal-Mart: Will It Take Over the World?" John Huey, *Fortune*, January 30, 1989, 52–64.
48. "Cold Competition: GE Wages the Refrigerator War," Ira Magaziner and Mark Patinkin, *Harvard Business Review*, March/April 1989, 114–124.
49. "The King of Ketchup," Kerry Hannon, *Forbes*, March 21, 1988, 58–65.
50. "Metalbashers Revive," *The Economist*, March 12, 1988, 75–76.
51. "Companies That Serve You Best," Bro Uttal, *Fortune*, December 7, 1987, 98–116.
52. "The Big Comeback at British Airways," Kenneth Labich, *Fortune*, December 5, 1988, 103–108.
    "King of the Jet Set," John Lawless, *Business*, February 1989, 46–54.
53. "How AMEX Is Revamping Its Big, Beautiful Money Machine," *Business Week*, June 13, 1988, 34–36.
    "Amex Charges Ahead," *The Economist*, November 28, 1987, 95–96.
    "American Excess," John F. Berry, *Business*, January 1987, 58–61.
54. "Grease Monkey's Dream," Kerry Hannon, *Forbes*, November 30, 1987, 193.
55. "Benetton Learns to Dance," Peter Fuhrinan, *Forbes*, October 3, 1988, 122–126.
    "The Benetton Way," Sari Gilbert, *Business*, November 1987, 128–135.
    "Benetton Is Betting on More of Everything," *Business Week*, March 23, 1987, 93.
    "Fast Forward," Curtis Bill Pepper, *Business Month*, February 1989, 25–30.

Chapter 5. Focus Resources

1. "Marketing's New Look," *Business Week*, January 26, 1987, 40–53.
   "The Fly in Campbell's Soup," Bill Saporito, *Fortune*, May 9, 1988, 67–70.
2. "New Management Pioneer Jim Swiggert," *Inc.*, February 1987, 34–44.
3. *Inc.*, January 1987, 31–38.

4. "Blood, Sweat, and Profits," Rick Reiff, *Forbes,* March 6, 1989, 110–112.
5. Robert Johnson and Thomas Kaplan, *Relevance Lost: The Rise and Fall of Management Accounting* (Harvard Business School Press, 1987).
6. "The Quality Imperative," Jerry Bowles, *Fortune,* October 22, 1988, 29.
7. "Steelmakers Want to Make Teamwork an Institution," *Business Week,* May 11, 1987, 84.
   "The Payoff from Teamwork," *Business Week,* July 10, 1989, 36–42.

Chapter 6. Vision Makes the Difference

1. "Wanted: Leaders Who Can Make a Difference," Jeremy Main, *Fortune,* September 28, 1987, 92.
2. "Getting Rich on Other People's Paychecks," *Business Week,* November 17, 1986, 148–149.
   "How to Build an Inc 500 Company," *Inc.,* December 1988, 41–60.
3. "Lessons in the Service Sector," James L. Heskett, *Harvard Business Review,* March/April 1988, 121.
   "Servicemaster: Looking for New Worlds to Clean," *Business Week,* January 19, 1987, 60–61.
   "Cleanliness, Godliness, and Business," Charles Siler, *Forbes,* November 28, 1988, 219–222.
4. "J. W. Marriott, Jr.," Mike Sheridan, *Sky,* March 1987, 46–53.
5. "His Trumpet Was Never Uncertain," *Time,* May 18, 1987, 68.
6. "The Mission," Mark Roman, *Success,* June 1987, 54–55.
7. "The Mission," Mark Roman, *Success,* June 1987, 54–55.
8. "The Quiet Coup at Alcoa," *Business Week,* June 27, 1988, 58–65.
   "Alcoa: Recycling Itself to Become a Pioneer in New Materials," *Business Week,* February 9, 1987, 56–57.

Chapter 7. Actions Set the Pace

1. "Market Research the Japanese Way," Johny Johansson and Ikujiro, *Harvard Business Review,* May/June 1987, 16–22.
2. "The Joys of Keeping the Company Small," Fritz Maytag, *Harvard Business Review,* July/August 1986, 6–14.
3. "Four Star Management," Jay Finegan, *Inc.,* January 1987, 42–51.
4. "The Turnaround," Lucien Rhodes with Patricia Amend, *Inc.,* August 1986, 42–50.
5. "The Turnaround," Lucien Rhodes with Patricia Amend, *Inc.,* August 1986, 42–50.
6. "Humanize Your Selling Strategy," Harvey Mackay, *Harvard Business Review,* March/April 1988, 36–47.
7. "May the Force Be with You," Bruce Posner, *Inc.,* July 1987, 70–75.
8. "The Year's Best Sale at Macy's: Itself," *Business Week,* January 12, 1987, 136–137.
9. "Leaders Are Not Pussycats," Nancy Austin, *Success,* October 1986, 10.
10. "Why Managers Must Be Facilitators," John Naisbitt, *Success,* April 1987, 12.
11. "The Turnaround," Lucien Rhodes with Patricia Amend, *Inc.,* August 1986, 42–50.
12. "Four Star Management," Jay Finegan, *Inc.,* January 1987, 42–51.
13. "The Turnaround," Lucien Rhodes with Patricia Amend, *Inc.,* August 1986, 42–50.
14. "Forever Young," Erik Larson, *Inc.,* July 1988, 50–62.

Notes

Chapter 8. Expect It or Forget It

1. "The Revolt Against Working Smarter," Bill Saporito, *Fortune*, July 21, 1986, 58–65.
2. "Synergy Works at American Express," Monci Jo Williams, *Fortune*, February 16, 1987, 79–80.
3. "The Hottest Entrepreneur in America," Bruce Posner and Bo Burlingham, *Inc.*, January 1988, 44–58.
4. "Going for the Goals," Steve Jaufman, *Success*, January/February 1988, 39–41.
5. "If Xerox Can, Canon Can," David Brown, *Business*, January 1988, 34–37.
6. "Four Star Management," Jay Finegan, *Inc.*, January 1987, 42–51.
7. "Hustle as Strategy," Amar Bhide, *Harvard Business Review*, September/October 1986, 59–65.
8. "The Turnaround," Lucien Rhodes with Patricia Amend, *Inc.*, August 1986, 42–50.
9. "How a Company Keeps Internal Customers Satisfied," George Labowitz, *Wall Street Journal*, July 7, 1987, 21.
10. Tom Peters and Nancy Austin, *A Passion for Excellence* (New York: Random House, 1985), 9.
11. "Red Auerbach on Management," Alan Webber, *Harvard Business Review*, March/April 1987, 84–91.
12. "Managers Need Milestones," *The Economist*, January 23, 1988, 16–17.
13. Tom Peters and Nancy Austin, *A Passion for Excellence* (New York: Random House, 1985), 96–97.
14. "Software That Rates White-Collar Workers," *Business Week*, June 1, 1987, 48.
15. "Here Comes the Judges," *Inc.*, August 1988, 90.
16. "Why the Bounce at Rubbermaid," Alex Taylor III, *Fortune*, April 13, 1987, 77–78.
17. "Playing by Its Own Book," *Financial Times*, August 22, 1988, 9.
   "The Importance of Being Coloroll," *Management Today*, January 1987, 42–91.
18. "Mrs. Fields Secret Ingredient," Tom Richman, *Inc.*, October 1987, 65–72.
19. "The Plant of Tomorrow Is in Texas Today," Gregory Miles, *Business Week*, July 28, 1986, 76.
20. "The 100 Club," Daniel Boyle, *Harvard Business Review*, March/April 1987, 26–27.
21. "Taxman Henry Block," *Inc.*, December 1987, 35–42.
22. Robert Johnson and Thomas Kaplan, *Relevance Lost: The Rise and Fall of Management Accounting* (Harvard Business School Press, 1987).
23. "The Turnaround," Lucien Rhodes with Patricia Amend, *Inc.*, August 1986, 42–50.
24. "Company Doctor Q. T. Wiles," *Inc.*, February 1988, 27–38.
25. "Pie in the Sky," Tom Monaghan, *Success*, December 1986, 15–16.
26. "Great Hash Browns, But Watch Those Biscuits," Dyan Machan, *Forbes*, September 19, 1988, 192–196.
27. "Balancing Act," Kathleen Hughes, *Wall Street Journal*, November 10, 1986, 140.
28. "The Attack on Pay," Rosabeth Kanter, *Harvard Business Review*, March/April 1987, 60–67.
29. "Right from the Start," Bruce Posner, *Inc.*, August 1988, 95.
30. "May the Force Be with You," Bruce Posner, *Inc.*, July 1987, 70–75.
31. "The Great Rebound: Britain Is Back," Richard Kirkland, Jr., *Fortune*, May 9, 1988, 114–123.
32. "Keyed Up to Bridge the Generation Gap," Alexandra Watson, *Business*, May 1988, 100–101.
33. "Accentuate the Positive," Kenneth Blanchard, *Success*, November 1986, 8.

Notes

"Red Auerbach on Management," Alan Webber, *Harvard Business Review*, March/April 1987, 84–91.
"The 100 Club," Daniel Boyle, *Harvard Business Review*, March/April 1987, 26–27.

Chapter 9. People Are the Key

1. BIM Sounding Board, *Management Today*, November 1988, 5.
2. "Caddy Shack," Joseph Kahn, *Inc.*, May 1987, 80–87.
3. "Make That Sale, Mr. Sam," *Time*, May 18, 1987, 54–55.
   "Wal-Mart: Will It Take Over the World?" John Huey, *Fortune*, January 30, 1989, 52–64.
4. "Big Changes at Big Brown," Kenneth Labich, *Fortune*, January 18, 1988, 56–64.
5. "The Fix Is in at Home Depot," Bill Saporito, *Fortune*, February 29, 1988, 73–79.
   On Achieving Excellence, Tom Peters, June 1988, 2, monthly newsletter.
6. "Screening for the Best Employees," Thomas Melohn, *Inc.*, January 1987, 104–105.
7. "What's Your Hurry," *Inc.*, March 1988, 115.
8. "May the Force Be with You," Bruce Posner, *Inc.*, July 1987, 70–75.
9. "The Plant of Tomorrow Is in Texas Today," Gregory Miles, *Business Week*, July 28, 1986, 76.
10. "People Policies for the New Machines," Richard Walton and Gerald Susman, *Harvard Business Review*, March/April 1987, 98–106.
11. "People Policies for the New Machines," Richard Walton and Gerald Susman, *Harvard Business Review*, March/April 1987, 98–106.
12. "The Chosen Few," Neil Anderson and Vivian Shackleton, *Business*, June 1987, 133–138.
13. "Bring Your Friends to Work," *Inc.*, November 1988, 149.
14. "People Policies for the New Machines," Richard Walton and Gerald Susman, *Harvard Business Review*, March/April 1987, 98–106.
15. "Screening for the Best Employees," Thomas Melohn, *Inc.*, January 1987, 104–105.
16. "Lessons from the Service Sector," James Heskett, *Harvard Business Review*, March/April 1987, 118–126.
17. "The Gorey Details," Michael Milne, *Management Review*, March 1985, 16–17.
18. "Sponsoring a New Hire," *Inc.*, March 1988, 112.
19. "Educating Executives," *Inc.*, March 1988, 115.
20. "Taxman Henry Block," *Inc.*, December 1987, 35–42.
21. "Mercedes Strengthens U.K. Dealer Family Ties," Alexandra Watson, *Business*, May 1987, 104–105.
22. "Motorola Sends Its Work Force Back to School," *Business Week*, June 6, 1988, 60–61.
23. "Big Changes at Big Brown," Kenneth Labich, *Fortune*, January 18, 1988, 56–64.
24. "The Fix Is in at Home Depot," Bill Saporito, *Fortune*, February 29, 1988, 73–79.
25. "Lessons in the Service Sector," James L. Heskett, *Harvard Business Review*, March/April 1988, 121.
   "Servicemaster: Looking for New Worlds to Clean," *Business Week*, January 19, 1987, 60–61.
26. "Cutting Costs without Cutting People," Bill Saporito, *Fortune*, May 25, 1987, 26–32.
27. "Holding on to Technical Talent," Claudia Deutsch, *New York Times*, November 16, 1986, 4F.
28. "The Plant of Tomorrow Is in Texas Today," Gregory Miles, *Business Week*, July 28, 1986, 76.

Notes

29. "A Ford Man Tunes Up Nissan," Faye Rice, *Fortune*, November 24, 1986, 140–144.
30. "People Policies for the New Machines," Richard Walton and Gerald Susman, *Harvard Business Review*, March/April 1987, 98–106.
31. "How a Company Keeps Internal Customers Satisfied," George Labowitz, *Wall Street Journal*, July 7, 1987, 21.
"Software That Rates White-Collar Workers," *Business Week*, June 1, 1987, 48.
32. "The Plant of Tomorrow Is in Texas Today," Gregory Miles, *Business Week*, July 28, 1986, 76.
33. "How to Win the Class Struggle," Robert McGough, *Forbes*, November 3, 1986, 153–156.
34. "The Plant of Tomorrow Is in Texas Today," Gregory Miles, *Business Week*, July 28, 1986, 76.
"People Policies for the New Machines," Richard Walton and Gerald Susman, *Harvard Business Review*, March/April 1987, 98–106.
35. "A Passion for Fine Tuning," Robert McGough, *Forbes*, May 4, 1987, 44.
36. Tom Peters and Nancy Austin, *A Passion for Excellence* (New York: Random House, 1985), 88–89.
37. "The Attack on Pay," Rosabeth Kanter, *Harvard Business Review*, March/April 1987, 60–67.
38. "The Attack on Pay," Rosabeth Kanter, *Harvard Business Review*, March/April 1987, 60–67.
39. "Synergy Works at American Express," Monci Jo Williams, *Fortune*, February 16, 1987, 79–80.
40. "Here Come Richer, Riskier Pay Plans," Nancy Perry, *Fortune*, December 19, 1988, 50–58.
41. "Watching the Bottom Line Instead of the Clock," *Business Week*, November 7, 1988, 134–135.
42. "Here Come Richer, Riskier Pay Plans," Nancy Perry, *Fortune*, December 19, 1988, 50–58.
43. *On Achieving Excellence*, Tom Peters, August 1988, 4, monthly newsletter.
44. "Keeping the Injured Involved," *Inc.*, September 1988, 120.
"Boosting Productivity, and Quality Too," *Inc.*, November 1988, 148.
45. "The Turnaround," Lucien Rhodes with Patricia Amend, *Inc.*, August 1986, 42–50.
46. "Crisis Management By Committee," Jack Stack, *Inc.*, May 1988, 26.
47. "The Great Rebound: Britain Is Back," Richard Kirkland, Jr., *Fortune*, May 9, 1988, 114–123.
48. "The Attack on Pay," Rosabeth Kanter, *Harvard Business Review*, March/April 1987, 60–67.
"May the Force Be with You," Bruce Posner, *Inc.*, July 1987, 70–75.
49. "The Media Company That Makes Murdock's Empire Look Small," *The Economist*, April 9, 1988, 75–76.
50. "The Attack on Pay," Rosabeth Kanter, *Harvard Business Review*, March/April 1987, 60–67.

Chapter 10. Culture Is It

1. "At Johnson and Johnson, a Mistake Can Be a Badge of Honor," *Business Week*, September 26, 1988, 126–128.
2. Terry Deal and Allan Kennedy, *Corporate Cultures* (Reading, MA: Addison-Wesley, 1982).

3. "The Downside of Downsizing," Anne Fisher, *Fortune,* May 23, 1988, 42–52.
   "For Downsizers, the Real Misery Is Yet to Come," Thomas Murphy, *Business Month,* February 1989, 71–72.
4. "The Downside of Downsizing," Anne Fisher, *Fortune,* May 23, 1988, 42–52.
5. "Shaking Sears Right Down to Its Work Boots," *Business Week,* October 17, 1988, 84–87.
6. "Fast-Cycle Capability for Competitive Power," Joseph Bower and Thomas Hunt, *Harvard Business Review,* November/December 1988, 110–118.
7. Levering, Moskowitz, and Katz, *The 100 Best Companies to Work for in America* (Reading, MA: Addison-Wesley, 1984).
8. "Corporate Antihero John Sculley," *Inc.,* October 1987, 49–59.
   "Sculley's Lessons from Inside Apple," *Fortune,* September 14, 1987, 109–120.
9. "The Downside of Downsizing," Anne Fisher, *Fortune,* May 23, 1988, 42–52.
   "What's Behind the Profit Squeeze at Salomon," *Business Week,* April 20, 1987, 72–73.
   "Wall Street Stares Hard at Revision," *Insight,* September 19, 1988, 8–17.
10. "The Downside of Downsizing," Anne Fisher, *Fortune,* May 23, 1988, 42–52.
11. "The Downside of Downsizing," Anne Fisher, *Fortune,* May 23, 1988, 42–52.

Chapter 11. Empower Individual Change Agents

1. "The Revolt Against Working Smarter," Bill Saporito, *Fortune,* July 21, 1986, 58–65.

Chapter 12. Change Happens— The Elephant Learns

1. Masaaki Imai, *Kaizen* (New York: Random House, 1986), 21.
2. Masaaki Imai, *Kaizen* (New York: Random House, 1986), 17.
3. Masaaki Imai, *Kaizen* (New York: Random House, 1986), 19–20.

Index

Index

Index

Index

Index

Index

Index

Index